Management for Professionals

For further volumes:
http://www.springer.com/series/10101

Frederik Ahlemann • Eric Stettiner
Marcus Messerschmidt • Christine Legner
Editors

Strategic Enterprise Architecture Management

Challenges, Best Practices,
and Future Developments

 Springer

Editors

Prof. Dr. Frederik Ahlemann
EBS Universität für Wirtschaft und Recht
Wiesbaden, Germany

Eric Stettiner
PricewaterhouseCoopers AG
Wirtschaftsprüfungsgesellschaft
Hamburg, Germany

Marcus Messerschmidt
PricewaterhouseCoopers AG
Wirtschaftsprüfungsgesellschaft
Düsseldorf, Germany

Prof. Dr. Christine Legner
Université de Lausanne
Lausanne, Switzerland

ISSN 2192-8096   e-ISSN 2192-810X
ISBN 978-3-642-44380-0   ISBN 978-3-642-24223-6 (eBook)
DOI 10.1007/978-3-642-24223-6
Springer Heidelberg Dordrecht London New York

Printed on acid-free paper

Springer is part of Springer Science+Business Media (www.springer.com)

Preface

Hundreds of books, white papers, and articles deal with Enterprise Architectures (EA). They address important questions and create inspiring views, some of which are referenced in this book. But they are unlikely to answer business people's or executives' questions about enterprise architecture management (EAM). The current documented body of knowledge in this domain focuses on engineering techniques such as modelling, patterns, reference architectures, tools, repositories and so on. But if we want to unleash EA's benefits, we need to better understand its management context; in other words, we need to value EAM as a top management topic.

If we therefore focus on *management*, this should appeal to all-business people. And the emphasis on *enterprise* architecture should catch the attention of the executive management, as EA describes and can help develop organisational capabilities and assets.

To test our views, we visited organisations of various sizes from different industries and countries. We wanted to see how they manage their enterprise architecture. We talked to people in business and technology departments, to C-level managers, project managers and enterprise architects. We sought out their best practices, lessons learnt, dos, and don'ts. In the process, we found that the EA challenges that businesses face have little to do with methodology or modelling. However, significant competitive advantage can be achieved:

- where the IT/IS landscape is consistent with the business strategy,
- if existing capabilities are re-used and developed in a goal-oriented way,
- when holistic thinking aligns business requirements and technology, and
- as soon as change-related management practices use a shared model to describe a future state.

This is where this book has a role to play: We describe how businesses can exploit EAM's full potential. The book deals with EAM from a non-technical, business-related perspective, and explores EAM's capacities by discussing its success components, chapter by chapter. We address the executives and decision-makers responsible for introducing or developing EAM. This book can serve as either reading matter or as a reference.

This book is the outcome of two organisations' joint efforts: PricewaterhouseCoopers (PwC) and EBS Business School. With more than 160,000 experts in 154 countries, PwC is one of the world's leading providers of assurance, tax, and business consulting services. EBS Business School is the oldest and one of most renowned business schools in Germany. Its Institute of Research on Information Systems (IRIS) conducts research on EAM, project portfolio management and IT/IS strategy. Consultants and researchers from both organisations and many countries have contributed to this book over a period of almost two years. We are grateful for the know-how, experience and research skills that they provided.

We would also like to thank the interviewees and their companies for granting us access to their views and practices and for providing feedback on our analyses, our colleagues at PwC Consulting and EBS for reviewing and commenting on the manuscripts, Ilse Evertse and her team of editors, those at Springer, and our partners for their patience and support.

We trust that you will enjoy this book and will find it inspiring. Feel free to contact us concerning EAM matters.

Frederik Ahlemann (frederik.ahlemann@ebs.edu)
Eric Stettiner (eric.stettiner@de.pwc.com)
Marcus Messerschmidt (marcus.messerschmidt@de.pwc.com)
Christine Legner (christine.legner@ebs.edu)

Table of contents

Table of figures

List of tables

List of abbreviations

ACID	atomic, consistent, isolated, and durable
ADM	architecture development method
ARB	architecture review board
ARIS	architecture of integrated information systems
aTOM	alternative target operating models
BCM	business continuity management
BDN	benefit dependency networks
BE	business excellence
BI	business intelligence
BRM	business reference model
BSCC	business solution competency centre
CCO	chief change officer
CEO	chief executive officer
CFO	chief financial officer
CIO	chief information officer
CoE	centre of excellence
COM	current operating model
CPO	chief process officer
CRM	components reference model
	customer relationship management
CxOs	c-level executives
DRM	data reference model
EA	enterprise architectures
EAC	enterprise architecture council
EAM	enterprise architecture management
FEA	federal enterprise architecture
FEAF	federal enterprise architecture framework

GRC	governance, risk and compliance
IaaS	infrastructure-as-a-service
ICC	integration competency centre
IRIS	institute of research on information systems
ITIL	IT infrastructure library
KPI	key performance indicators
LDC	less developed concept
OMB	office of management and budget
PRM	performance reference model
SaaS	software as a service
SDLC	solution development lifecycles
SDLC	software development lifecycle
SIB	standards information base
SOA	service-oriented architecture
SOM	semantic object modelling
SSC	shared service centre
TAFIM	technical architecture framework for information management
TOGAF™	the open group architecture framework
TOM	target operating model
TRM	technical reference model

Chapter 1

Introduction

Frederik Ahlemann, Christine Legner, Daniel Schäfczuk

Table of contents

Management summary

Enterprise Architecture Management (EAM) emerged as a way to deal with organisational complexity and change in an increasingly turbulent business environment. EAM's history dates back to the 1980s when information systems engineers strove to take a holistic, organisation-wide perspective on IS design. At this stage, IS engineers realised that they could only design suitable software components if they understood how the organisation works as defined by its processes, organisational structure and goals. Over time, the concept matured and has become a discipline that provides a philosophy, methodologies and tools to develop, realise and operate competitive enterprise architectures. EAM assists organisations in maintaining the flexibility, cost-efficiency and transparency of their technical infrastructure, information systems, business processes and organisational structures in line with their business goals. EAM therefore ensures that corporate change can be implemented swiftly and easily.

In this chapter, we present EAM as a management discipline that helps to systematically design and develop an organisation according to its strategic objectives and vision. For this purpose, models are used to guide EA's structured development. We identify as-is models describing the current state and to-be models describing the future EA state (target architecture). Models can cover one or several layers of the EA: the business, organisation and processes, information systems, and infrastructure. Based on this understanding, we define EAM as a management practice that establishes, maintains and uses a coherent set of guidelines, architecture principles and governance regimes that provide direction and practical help in the design and development of an enterprise's architecture to achieve its vision and strategy.

The findings and insights presented in this book are the result of comprehensive qualitative research involving a team of 13 researchers and professionals. We investigated eight case companies and identified factors and practices for a successful EAM. The research design consisted of the following five subsequent phases: preparation, data collection, data compilation, and review by the case companies and data analysis.

1.1 The need for enterprise architecture management (EAM)

Background: The turbulent and complex business environment

Companies operate in an ever-changing marketplace characterised by variable customer demand patterns, fast-paced technology innovation, the shortening of product life cycles, and increasing specialisation and competition in global value chains. While so much is in flux, one certainty stands out: The urgent necessity to adapt to the changing environment to stay ahead of the competition. Change has become the norm. Change affects all elements of an enterprise's value creation: products and services, corporate capabilities and assets, alliances, partners, suppliers, and customers. Enterprises respond to the ever-changing market environment by adapting their core competencies and strengthening their customer and supplier relationships, by redesigning their organisational structures and processes for being efficient and effective, and by leveraging information systems and information technology for digitising their business. They thereby continuously change their fundamental structure, which is the enterprise architecture. Although the changes are intended to strengthen an organisation's competitiveness, they frequently have severe and unintended side effects. If change initiatives are launched independently, with little or no coordination across the enterprise, they result in a plethora of heterogeneous, incompatible and costly changes to information technology, information systems, business processes and organisational structures. Even worse, additional investments in organisational redesign and/or information technology might not pay off because they might produce uncontrollable architectural complexity, instead of improving business performance. Investments might thereby generate risks that might even paralyse the business. The downsides of architectural complexity are manifold; these include:

Adaptation to the changing environment is a competitive factor

Poorly coordinated changes generate risks and paralyse business

Complex enterprise architecture increases costs and decreases flexibility and transparency

- **Loss of transparency.** With increasing complexity, managers might lose their organisational overview and, therefore, might lack fundamental information necessary for decision-making. They simply have to invest more effort in collecting information about the current situation in order to determine the implications of change.
- **Increased complexity costs.** A complex structure is mostly more expensive to manage than a reasonably simple, well-defined architecture. The following example illustrates that complexity is a cost driver: If different technologies are used in different parts of the organisation, IT investments will most likely be relatively high. If there is greater unity in the technology, the organisation can negotiate a better price by bundling purchasing volumes and buying one type of technology. Furthermore, it is much easier to develop the necessary skills and competencies to manage technology within the organisation when only one type of technology is used. Complexity costs may also result from using diverging business processes in different subsidiaries. If each process is run independently, using its own resources, potential synergies across subsidiaries are likely to be neglected. Unless individual processes lead to a competitive advantage, diverging business processes therefore also result in unduly costly structures.
- **Increased risks.** Highly complex enterprise architectures also increase operational risks and hamper risk management. A large number of architectural components with sprawling interfaces, media breaks, diverging business rules and procedure make it almost impossible to identify all business-critical risks and approach them accordingly.
- **Inability to consistently implement strategic directions across the organisation.** The more complex an enterprise's architecture is, the more difficult it is to restructure or redesign it, and the more problematic it is to implement strategic changes in the organisation. In its worst form, an organisation might remain in its current state because change is no longer possible.
- **Distraction from core business problems.** Complex enterprise architectures tend to tie down highly skilled and competent professionals. Instead of maintaining competitiveness, they are distracted by having to manage complexity and, ironically, end up preserving the current state, which keeps the organisation in a state of stagnation.

Many organisations lack transparency due to the number and frequency of their organisational changes and suffer from overly complex enterprise architecture. Some of the questions they cannot answer are:

- How can we successfully integrate new firms after an acquisition?
- Can we introduce new products and services, using the existing business processes and the underlying applications?
- Which business units and users will be affected by an application's migration?
- What applications and infrastructure technologies do we require to run new or redesigned business processes?

EAM as used by a global car manufacturer

We looked at a car manufacturer that makes use of EAM to manage a large, global corporation. This car manufacturer comprises a group of various brands. Each brand operates independently, and has a global market presence. The group has more than 50,000 employees and operates production plants in several countries, with a majority of these sites situated in Europe.

A sophisticated strategy is needed to manage such a large, global corporation. For example, if new production facilities are established – as is currently being done in Russia, India, and the US – it is vital to set them up in a standardised way. Therefore, the manufacturer uses a global template. This toolbox contains IT modules that implement an out-of-the-box process model. The model covers all standard business processes, including production planning, logistics, maintenance and assurance, as well as finance, accounting and HR. IT modules and processes are bundled together in a central EAM toolset, ready for decentralised introduction in new subsidiaries. When processes are improved and redesigned, which happened, for example, with the logistic processes in the US factory, these changes are approved as the current version of the standard and are then incorporated into the centrally managed toolbox. This approach enables a cost-efficient and swift set-up of up-to-date processes that can be customised to local requirements, if necessary.

At the same time, the car producer closely monitors its IT budget. The organisation spends less than 1% of its revenues on IT and claims to have the lowest IT cost per car in the industry. External contractors are responsible for many developments. With EAM, the company reduces the complexity and operating costs of its IT systems and keeps the budget under control. To realise these objectives, architects are very involved in the approval process of software architectures and the standardisation of IT components.

Obviously, the firms struggling to answer these questions have lost the information base that they need to achieve their business goals. Managers might no longer have a holistic perspective on the organisation, the business model and operating principles, the organisational structure (such as business units and regions), business processes and their distribution, applications, databases, and the underlying technical infrastructure. Only if they know how these components are interrelated, can changes be coordinated and aligned with the mid-term to long-term company objectives. Transparency is a prerequisite to reduce organisational complexity step by step and regain flexibility.

The idea of enterprise architecture management

EAM aims to maintain the flexibility, cost-efficiency and transparency of the enterprise architecture

EAM seeks to maintain the flexibility, cost-efficiency and transparency in the enterprise architecture. It emphasises the interplay between business (such as business models, organisational structures and business processes) and technology (including information systems, data and the technological infrastructure). EAM helps to systematically develop the organisation according to its strategic objectives and vision.

EAM is similar to city planning

The EAM concept is aligned with the idea that planning an enterprise's architecture is similar to planning a city. City planning includes the design of the city's development, which covers the land use, streets, utilities and waste disposal. The design is multi-faceted, complex and inter-disciplinary, since it has to fulfil several – sometimes conflicting – design objectives, as pointed out in Table 1.1. City planning must ensure that the inhabitants have access to key resources and a high quality of life, and must respect the environmental conditions, available budgets and long-term requirements, notably sustainability. If these objectives are not achieved, a number of problems may result, such as traffic jams, indirections, supply shortfalls, environmental pollution, noise, social ghettos, crime, movement of labour and emigration.

Good city planning is characterised by a number of attributes. To achieve this, the city planner must:

- anticipate future demands and requirements,
- make plans and develop the city accordingly,
- bring the different stakeholders together and discuss their interests,
- serve the city as a whole and not local interests, and
- have a holistic, multi-perspective view on the city (socially, economically and logistically).

The same is true for good EAM. Instead of buildings, streets and utilities, enterprise architecture consists of components that make up the fundamental structure of an organisation: business processes, organisational structures, information systems and technological infrastructure. Enterprise architecture management includes developing, implementing and controlling these different components.

Table 1.1: Analogy between city planning and EAM

Objective	City planning	EAM
Effectiveness	Develop the city to satisfy the requirements of its population	Develop an organisation to satisfy business goals
Efficiency	Develop the city so that logistics and supply of any kind can be realised efficiently	Develop an enterprise architecture that supports a firm's efficient operation
Economic feasibility	Develop the city within the available budgets	Develop an enterprise architecture within the available budgets
Flexibility	Be ready for future developments, such as additional suburbs and their requirements	Develop an enterprise architecture that can be quickly and inexpensively adapted to future strategic objectives
Safety and security	Enable a safe life in the city	Allow a firm's secure operation and necessary management controls; minimise operational risks
Sustainability	Develop the city in a sustainable, environmentally friendly way	Develop an enterprise architecture that is sustainable and complies with regulatory standards, or goes beyond those standards, by developing long-term solutions
Robustness / scalability	Develop the city so that it can handle peaks and growth in logistics and supply without major problems	Develop a flexible enterprise architecture that can handle business activity peaks
Quality of life	Provide a high quality life for the citizens	Develop an enterprise architecture that allows job fulfilment and motivation
Wealth	Allow the community to develop and prosper	Develop an enterprise architecture that supports profitability

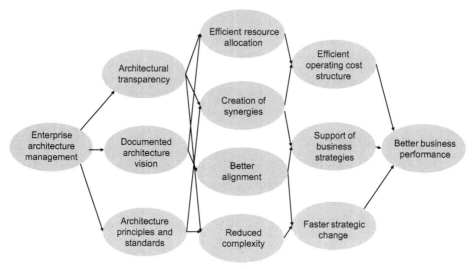

Figure 1.1: EAM effects

EAM can help to improve an enterprise's performance, as shown in Figure 1.1:

The beneficial effects of EAM result from increased transparency, documented architecture vision and clear architecture principles and guidelines

1. **Architecture transparency.** EAM establishes transparency by documenting the main enterprise architecture components and their interrelationships. The enterprise architecture model is often complemented by additional pieces of management-relevant information that relate to security, costs, benefits, compliance and risks. EAM thus creates a valuable information basis that is indispensable for actively managing an organisation: Transparency is a prerequisite for identifying synergies and allocating resources efficiently; it supports strategic decision-making, strategy implementation and operational management.

2. **Documented architecture vision**. Based on a transparent view of the enterprise architecture, management can decide on how to develop the organisation or parts of the organisation. A documented architecture vision represents multiple stakeholders' 'shared view' and enables a better alignment of the different architectural layers and components. For example, the better information systems align with business processes, the higher the business process performance will be. When alignment is weak, there is an increase in manual work, multiple systems are needed for one task, data quality is low and reporting capabilities are poor. However, alignment is not limited to information systems and business processes. The interaction between infrastructure

technology and information systems might also suffer from poor alignment if a network topology does not match an application's requirements. This mismatch would result in low network speed and application performance.

3. **Architecture principles and guidelines.** To guide the purposeful development of an organisation, management must define architecture principles and guidelines.

   Modularisation is a very powerful concept. Modules are accessible via clearly defined standardised interfaces, which increases the chance of re-use. Many advantages emerge with modularisation, such as scalability and cost reduction. Furthermore, the modularisation of an enterprise architecture increases its strategic flexibility, because enterprise architecture components may be recombined when they are needed in new business models or business processes. Moreover, modularisation allows for outsourcing or re-configuration of the value chain.

   Today, many managers adopt modularisation – or service-orientation – as an architecture paradigm to regain flexibility on all layers of an enterprise's architecture. For example, software functionality may be modularised by means of service-oriented architectures, and technological infrastructures may be modularised by cloud, grid and virtualisation techniques. Modularisation can also be applied at the organisational level. For example, an organisation can introduce shared services or modular process patterns, which might ultimately allow for the dynamic re-combination of core competencies in a virtual organisation [1].

Not all enterprises will receive all these benefits from the outset. In most cases, specific business needs and urgencies will influence the targeted benefits. It is therefore important to have a clear understanding of EAM's primary objectives. More detailed information on how EAM actually generates benefits for an enterprise can be found in Chapter 3.

1.2 What is enterprise architecture management?

History of enterprise architecture management

As a management discipline, EAM has evolved over the last 25 years. It has its roots in the 1980s and developed in three phases, as outlined in Figure 1.2.

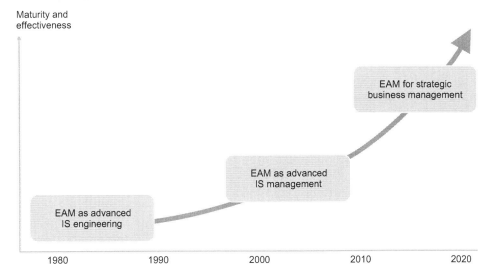

Figure 1.2: EAM development phases

Phase 1: 'Take the big picture' –
EAM for information systems engineering

EAM's formation phase was in the beginning of the 1980s, with IBM's 'business systems planning' concept [2] and the subsequent development of the Zachman framework [3]. At this time, Zachman observed that the term 'architecture' was widely used by information system professionals, but often had different meanings. Zachman's framework provided the means for a great leap forward. He introduced the conceptualisation of architectures from multiple perspectives (e.g., objectives/scope, enterprise model, system model and technical model), using different architectural descriptions (e.g.,

EAM is rooted in Zachman's framework for the holistic engineering of information system

data, function and network). The framework is described as a matrix (with 30 cells) and suggests specification documents for each cell (e.g., using entity relationship models to describe data, or using functional flow diagrams to describe processes). Although EAM has subsequently developed significantly, Zachman's ideas still inspire many EAM professionals, and almost all frameworks are based on the principles he formulated. Our contemporaries should especially acknowledge his holistic approach to viewing enterprises formally and in a highly structured way, as well as from a technology and business perspectives. Zachman's idea of a multi-perspective and multi-layered enterprise modelling approach became state-of-the-art in the beginning of the 1990s, influencing many other frameworks. Among them are FEA (Federal Enterprise Architecture) [4], ARIS (Architecture of Integrated information Systems) [5], Business Engineering [6] and SOM (Semantic Object Modelling) [7].

Phase 2: 'Adapt Your Management Processes' – EAM for IS management

Advanced EAM frameworks integrate planning, implementation and controlling processes for IT/IS landscapes

During the 1990s and 2000s, EAM professionals felt that a pure modelling approach was not enough. Owing to technological advances and the dissemination of desktop computing, local area networks and increased business process digitisation, IT/IS landscapes became increasingly complex. This also meant that more stakeholders were involved and IT/IS spending increased. In many organisations, IT/IS implementation decisions were driven by business managers. These business managers provided the funding and had little interest in slowing down the implementation through additional cross-company coordination. Consequently, there were many cases of local optimisation, isolated silo systems, shadow IT organisations, redundancies, misguided investments and IT/IS project failures. To remedy these ills, people began to focus on planning, implementing, and controlling processes to ensure transparent decision-making and to regain control of the IT/IS landscape. IT management processes and governance mechanisms became more relevant. EAM was taken to the next level by:

• defining role models,
• planning, implementing and controlling the processes for IT/IS landscapes (not only single applications), and
• defining decision rights and accountabilities.

Advanced EAM frameworks emerged. These frameworks not only provided architectural artefacts and models, but also contained guidelines for EAM planning, implementation and controlling. One of the most prominent examples is The Open Group Architecture Framework (TOGAF^{TM}) [8], which includes the Architecture Development Method (ADM), a cyclical process model. For further information on such advanced frameworks, please refer to Chapter 8.

Phase 3: 'Make it Strategic' –
EAM for strategic business management

Today, we know that architecture management can only achieve its full potential if it is closely linked to the business strategy. Consequently, EAM must align with the organisation's strategy planning and strategy implementation processes. Professionals recognise that architecture management can help organisations to remain flexible and to implement strategic change swiftly and cost-effectively. Consequently, EAM is no longer understood as just an IT department job, but as a strategic function. EAM plays an important role in organisational transformation and development, and is executed by a board member at top management level. EAM is sometimes merged with the programme management office or the business development department, which underlines the strategic importance of developing an enterprise's architecture. Why is this so? The reasons are manifold, including:

EAM becomes a strategic function attached to a board member

- **IS/IT as a means of strategic and organisational transformation.** Companies realise that their IT investments have no value unless they are used to improve organisational effectiveness and efficiency, increase employee productivity and implement new strategies. Hence, the planning of the IS landscape needs to be closely linked to the strategic and organisational directions.
- **Increased outsourcing.** Some organisations concentrate on their core competencies and outsource the other parts of the value chain. When important parts of the value chain are outsourced, thorough monitoring of the external service providers is crucial. EAM may provide the information for such monitoring activities. Furthermore, EAM can evaluate the nature and quality of the interfaces to external service providers and supervise their service provision.
- **IT/IS as a commodity.** Owing to technological trends, including standardisation, virtualisation, grid and cloud computing, as well as software as a service (SaaS), IT/IS services have become a commodity [9]. Consequently, the focus has shifted from managing technology to applying technology to support the business. This emphasises EAM's business relevance.
- **Business-IT alignment.** Many organisations have made great progress in sourcing, making and delivering IT/IS services. Service management standards – for example, the IT Infrastructure

Library (ITIL) – or the trend towards shared service organisations are indicators of this tendency. However, it is still crucial for businesses to align their IT/IS services with their business needs. EAM is a great tool for establishing this alignment.

Integrating EAM into the strategy development and strategy implementation processes results in strong synergies, improved decision-making and faster strategic change. Strategic decision-making is based on enterprise architecture information, and takes enterprise architecture-specific objectives and policies into account. Many leading organisations already follow this broader understanding of EAM and involve highly skilled EAM specialists in these processes.

A working definition of enterprise architecture

What is enterprise architecture?

Generally speaking, architecture is defined as the 'fundamental organisation of a system, embodied in its components, their relationships to each other and the environment, and the principles governing its design' [10]. Enterprise architecture (EA) is therefore understood as the fundamental organisation of an enterprise as a socio-technical system, along with the principles governing its design and development. An EA includes all relevant components for describing an enterprise, including its business and operating model, organisational structure, business processes, data, applications and technology. EA's design rules provide stipulations for the development and structuring of the components, as well as a means to ensure consistency in the use of components and in their relationships.

As in city planning, we distinguish between the actual EA (the real-world enterprise as we observe it) and an EA model (documented by means of plans or models) (Figure 1.3):

- In the course of documenting the actual EA (from here on: EA), an EA model (**as-is model or baseline**) is created. The EA model is mostly documented by means of a semi-formal modelling language. It is usually stored in a specific database (repository), but can also take the form of a drawing on paper.
- Models are developed to capture a desired target EA state (**to-be model or target EA**). The to-be model can be used to guide an EA's development. Thereby, the present architecture is transformed into the to-be-architecture.

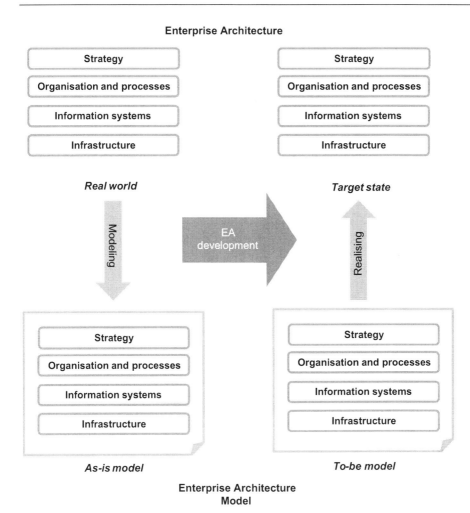

Figure 1.3: Terminology

Enterprise architecture models and their layers

In order to describe an organisation's fundamental structure, EA models often comprise a huge number of components. The EA is most inclusive of all the main components if it is presented from different perspectives at different layers of abstraction. Unfortunately, and despite the long history of EA modelling, there is no consensus on the layers or the components that should be included in the EA. In the context of this book and as depicted in Figure 1.4, we consider the following components and layers as essential:

EA models usually have layers that cover the business, processes, information systems and infrastructure

- The **strategy layer** describes the positioning of an enterprise (or its business units) at a high level of abstraction and is developed once the business strategy is defined. Typical artefacts represented on this layer are: the value networks, customers and market segments, the product, talent and service portfolio, business goals, and related KPIs. Some EA frameworks do not include this layer, while others refer to it as the firm's business or operating model. The Target Operating Model (TOM) documents the key decisions regarding how the company will operate in future, thereby representing a cornerstone of the development of an enterprise's architecture.
- The **organisation and process layer** specifies a firm's organisational structure and its process organisation. It comprises static (structural) aspects, for example, departments and other organisational units and roles, as well as dynamic (flow) aspects, for example, business processes and tasks. Some frameworks, for example, ARIS or the business engineering framework, emphasise this layer, thus focusing on IS as an enabler of organisational change and business process redesign.
- The **information systems layer** describes how information is processed and shared electronically within and across organisations. This layer can be further broken down into an application layer, a data layer, and an integration layer.
  - The **application layer** describes the main software components that implement the business logic in order to support business processes. Typical artefacts include application components and services.
  - The **data layer** describes how key business information (such as product, customer or supplier data) is represented and implemented in databases. Typical artefacts are data models and data bases.
  - The **integration layer** describes how applications share, or could share, data and functions with other applications and data-bases. This layer comprises interfaces, protocols and integration components.
- The **technology or infrastructure layer** contains the computing services that form the enterprise's technical infrastructure. The technical infrastructure is realised by computer and communication devices, as well as by system software, which is this layer's key artefacts.
- Finally, the **people and competencies** layer represents the people and competencies required to develop and operate an enterprise architecture consisting of the aforementioned layers.

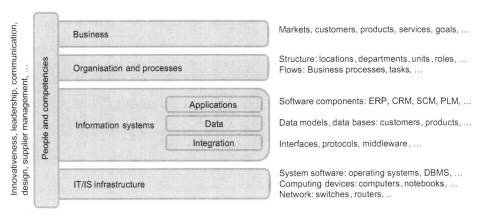

Figure 1.4: EA layers

While structuring the EA in layers helps to separate concerns, aligning them can be challenging. Alignment might be complicated due to
the different lengths of the change cycles underlying the layers. For
example, strategic changes such as the introduction of new product
lines and distribution channels are likely to occur annually, but the
redesign of an organisation to implement these strategic changes
may take up to two years. Information systems are built to last at
least 10 years, so the existing IS architecture might not be able to
deal with the organisation's constant changes in the business environment [11]. Consequently, it has become very popular for companies to investigate measures for aligning business and IT, and for
increasing its agility. However, companies are also aware that monolithic applications impose restrictions, and are concerned about
decoupling business processes and their implementation. In this
regard, service-oriented architectures are regarded as an enabler of
more flexible IS architectures, and standardisation and modularisation are recognised as architecture principles that will decrease heterogeneity.

*These layers build
up hierarchically
and relate to each
other*

Managing the enterprise architecture

While early EA initiatives focused on EA modelling and documentation, our case studies demonstrate that EAM has become a real management discipline closely linked to strategy planning and
implementation. EAM builds on the transparency provided by EA
models and documentation of the as-is and to-be situations, but

*EAM is becoming
a real management
discipline*

includes the continuous process of developing, realising and operating the EA. We define EAM as follows:

> EAM is a management practice that establishes, maintains and uses a coherent set of guidelines, architecture principles and governance regimes that provide direction for and practical help with the design and the development of an enterprise's architecture in order to achieve its vision and strategy.

To understand the characteristics of EAM as a management discipline, it is also helpful to clearly delineate what EAM is *not*:

- Most importantly, **EAM is not a tool**. Although EAM introduction is often accompanied by an extensive debate on tool support, a tool alone will not yield any impact. A tool just helps the practitioner to capture EAM documentation and store it in one place.
- **EAM is not just the modelling of the enterprise architecture**. While modelling may support EAM, our case studies have shown that modelling is one of the subordinate aspects of EAM.
- **EAM is not an IT function**, although historically it first emerged in IT departments. The successful management of IS landscapes requires more than just technical expertise in applications and infrastructure, as well as some business know-how. EAM is most effective when it is directly linked to the board or the CEO.
- **EAM is not a new management process**. EA includes a set of new management practices, but it does not produce new processes. Instead, it merely changes the way existing processes are run. Strategy planning and strategy implementation are, for instance, complemented by EAM if EAM provides them with additional information and new methods for managing complex real-world organisations.
- **EAM is not strategy development**. EAM practices are merely used in strategy development. They contribute valuable information, such as assessments of the strategic options and their feasibility, taking the firm's capabilities and resources into account, which is useful for strategy development.

To summarize, EAM *is*:

What is EAM?

- a holistic way to understand, plan, develop and control an organisation's architecture (**EAM as a management philosophy**),
- a support function to enable and improve existing strategy planning and strategy implementation processes (**EAM as an organisational function**),

- a set of management practices that helps to improve the quality of decision-making (**EAM as a methodology**), and
- an open approach to reach consensus among managers on the basis of their shared vision of establishing a global optimum for the firm, free of local and personal egoism and opportunism (**EAM as a culture**).

Chapter 2 contains more information regarding the building blocks of EAM.

1.3 Objectives of this book

This book is based on the notion that EAM serves the business *and* the IT/IS function. This means that EAM must be understood by architects, IT/IS professionals, business-side executives and decision-makers, and the firm's top management. Whereas the majority of books on EAM address the first target group, we address C-level managers and decision-makers who:

This book is targeted at IT professionals, executives and top management

- **want to learn what EAM is about.** We provide an overview of the most important EAM building blocks (Chapter 2), and discuss these building blocks in subsequent chapters (Chapters 3 to 9).
- **want to enable other people to initiate EAM.** We provide an EAM management agenda for top executives (Chapter 3) and a process model for introducing EAM (Chapter 9).
- **are responsible for introducing EAM.** We provide explicit advice on how EAM can best be introduced into organisations (Chapter 9), and explain what successful EAM looks like (Chapters 4 to 8).
- **want to improve their EAM and profit from insights on the topic.** Throughout the book we present proven best practices, which we gained from leading organisations. We also describe current and future EAM trends (Chapter 10).

To serve these different purposes, the book is:

- **management-oriented.** We avoid unnecessary methodological details and concentrate on the essence of EAM. Our focus is on those aspects that determine EAM success. Therefore, we don't discuss conceptual details in the form of document templates, frameworks, modelling techniques, or meta-models.
- **business-oriented.** We avoid a technological perspective on EAM. Instead, we discuss how EAM can help organisations to strengthen their competitiveness. Technological approaches such as service-oriented architectures may be mentioned, but they are not the crux of our discussions.
- **innovative.** The book goes beyond what the majority of organisations already do. It presents new approaches to organising, governing and practicing EAM, as well as forecasting how EAM might develop in future.

- **practice-oriented**. We only include advice and best practices that have been proven to be effective and can be implemented directly.
- **research-based**. Our insights are based on thorough case study research (see the next section) and extensive consulting experience.

1.4 Methodology

This book is based on qualitative research. We gathered our findings from 8 case studies in different industries, allowing us to thoroughly investigate and analyse the challenges and success factors of EAM.

What is qualitative research?

Most people have at least a basic understanding of quantitative survey-based research, which provides questionnaires to large samples of respondents. This type of research ultimately leads to statistical procedures for analysing the data, in order to draw general conclusions about the population. We chose a qualitative research approach because our objective was not to describe organisations by means of statistical measures. Instead, we wanted to explore the core of successful EAM in the sense of the required preconditions, success factors and outcomes. We also wanted to elaborate on crucial EAM best practices and trends. These goals could only be achieved through qualitative research, especially in the light of the limited prior knowledge.

This book is based on qualitative case-study-oriented research results

Qualitative research differs from quantitative research. It is based on small samples, consisting of cases. Qualitative research uses complex and eclectic data collection procedures, such as open interviews, documents, observations and secondary data. Statistical procedures may be applied but mostly play a minor role. Instead, researchers use the wealth of data to obtain a thorough and in-depth understanding of the cases' inherent logic, which allows them to explore the causal relationships between events. Researchers may also derive success factors and best practices; they may even seek to forecast future developments.

With qualitative research, researchers often analyse cases that are different in nature. This approach allows them to compare different approaches and practices, as well as their antecedents and outcomes. The advantage of differing data sources is that the same phenomenon can be viewed from various angles, allowing for conclusions with a higher degree of validity. Properly done, qualitative research may yield results that have a high degree of internal validity (the internal consistency and correctness of the conclusions) and a reasonable level of external validity (generalisability).

What cases were analysed?

We analysed dissimilar organisations from diverse industries that have different approaches to EAM. Table 1.2 provides an overview of the cases and their characteristics.

Table 1.2: Analysed Companies

Industry	Number of employees	Key figures	EAM characteristics
Banking	More than 50,000	balance sheet total > 700 billion EUR	Decentralised domain architecture with focus on the business side and the management of clustered application portfolios. High degree of maturity in domain-oriented landscape planning and the step-wise introduction of EAM by producing and sharing success stories.
Public administration	About 40,000 (civil servants)		The purpose is to rationalise resource use and adopt best practices for information and communication technology governance. EAM advises decentralised IS and business departments.
Tool manufacturing	About 20,000	Turnover in 2009: approx. 3 billion EUR	The strategy is to further improve IT governance by installing an architecture management. Architecture management is developed with project portfolio management as a starting point. Strong strategic orientation.
Logistics	More than 4,500	Revenue in 2009: 2,9 billion EUR	The company uses EAM for the comprehensive development of master plans, as well as the pragmatic utilisation of standardisation and commonly defined goals by incorporating these into existing governance processes. Strong strategic orientation.
Retail	More than 250,000	Sales in 2010: More than 65 billion EUR	In this group, EAM is understood as enterprise-focused management to control the business-IT alignment. Strong adaptation to the group's business model, which consists of several business lines. EAM processes apply enterprise-wide standardised tools and workflows for the development of core IT systems.

Table 1.2: *continues*

Reinsurance	More than 45,000	Turnover in 2010: Approximately 45 billion EUR	EAM as an approach to steer the organisational development by following certain principles and goals: It is guided by the strategy and has a long-term focus, is aimed at increasing profitability, and takes costs and benefits into consideration by supporting the business with information.
Food	Significant six digit number	Sales in 2010: Approximately 85 billion EUR	Worldwide standardization of the process and application landscape by means of EAM. Very high degree of maturity in terms of global governance and process management.
Automotive	Significant six digit number	One of the world's leading companies	Very complex, distributed organisational environment and several distinct but coordinated EAM initiatives on different EA layers: Long-term application landscape planning, standardisation of IT infrastructure and modularisation/service-oriented architectures. Very advanced decentralised governance structures.

The cases differ in many ways. The companies used different approaches to introduce EAM, they have different core EAM processes, different governance regimes and diverging degrees of centralisation. By investigating and comparing these cases, we could see what works and what does not. As researchers, we call these 'natural controls': We can observe what happens when a certain practice or environmental factor is observable and when it is not observable. This helps us to distinguish between important factors and less important factors, as well as between best practices and ordinary practices.

The cases analysed describe the use of EAM by leading companies in different sectors

How we did our research

Our research was a team effort by 13 researchers and consultants between the spring of 2009 and the autumn of 2010. In these two years, we passed through five phases, as outlined in Figure 1.5 and described in the subsequent sections.

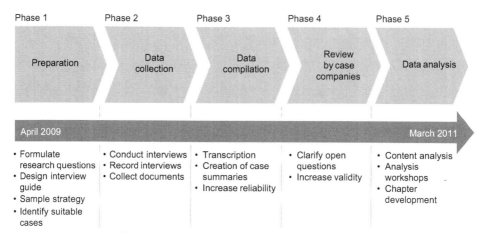

Phase 1	Phase 2	Phase 3	Phase 4	Phase 5
Preparation	Data collection	Data compilation	Review by case companies	Data analysis

April 2009   March 2011

| • Formulate research questions
• Design interview guide
• Sample strategy
• Identify suitable cases | • Conduct interviews
• Record interviews
• Collect documents | • Transcription
• Creation of case summaries
• Increase reliability | • Clarify open questions
• Increase validity | • Content analysis
• Analysis workshops
• Chapter development |

Figure 1.5: Research process

Phase 1: Preparation

Rigorous research methods were used to generate the insights that underlie this book

During Phase 1, we prepared for the research project. We collected topics and themes of interest, and formulated the research questions. We then developed an analysis framework that guided our case work. We also designed an interview guide for discussions with case representatives. One of the most crucial tasks in this phase was the specification of a sample strategy and the identification of suitable cases, which eventually led to the acquisition of the case partners.

Phase 2: Data collection

In Phase 2, we conducted interviews with EAM stakeholders from the case organisations. The interview sessions lasted between 60 and 180 minutes and were conducted by two interviewers – one consultant and one researcher. Several interviews were conducted per case in an attempt to gather data about the most important EAM roles, namely top executives, enterprise architects, portfolio managers and project managers. We recorded each interview and collected additional EAM-related documents, such as reports, EAM manuals, process maps and project plans.

Phase 3: Data compilation

After data collection, we transcribed the interviews. Thereafter we condensed the additional documents and added them to the case write-ups. Case write-ups are complete and consolidated descriptions of the cases, and contain all relevant information in respect of the themes and topics that were relevant in Phase 1. Several rounds of quality assurance improved the validity and reliability of the case write-up. During quality assurance, experienced researchers and consultants read the material, provided feedback and helped to develop the write-ups.

Phase 4: Review by case companies
Completed case write-ups were sent to the case companies for verification. The interviewees checked the correctness of our statements and conclusions, and provided feedback, where necessary. During Phase 4, we also provided more complete and clear answers to some of the questions. These corrections and additions led to the final state of the case write-ups.

Phase 5: Data analysis
During the data analysis phase, we looked for best practices, recurring patterns and success factors in the cases (within-case analysis) and across cases (cross-case analysis). The data analysis was either done in a workshop with all researchers and consultants, or by means of thorough content analysis. We obtained the findings and recommendations presented in this book and, to structure them, we developed the navigator presented in the next chapter.

Writing of the book
The writing of the book was a joint effort by the whole project team. In order to increase our work's clarity, conclusiveness, and relevance, the team participated in a number of workshops to develop and reconcile the chapter contents.

1.5 How you can read the book

What is in the book?

This book has a simple, easy-to-understand structure. In the next chapter, we introduce a conceptual model that outlines the most important EAM building blocks, and serves as a navigator throughout the book. We then present an EAM agenda for top executives. In the subsequent chapters (Chapters 3 to 9), we discuss the important building blocks and outline successful EAM. In Chapter 10, we forecast how EAM might develop over the next decade.

How can you read it?

We made it as simple as possible for you to access and apply the contents of this book. To allow for an easy orientation, we added a number of concepts and graphical elements that allow you to find contents quickly, grasp the bottom line of what is being said, and find more detailed and related information, when required. The concepts we use for this purpose are:

- **Navigator.** The structure of the book follows an easy-to-understand framework that is called 'navigator' (see Chapter 2). Once you understand the navigator, you can access the book contents without reference to the table of contents.
- **Separate chapters.** Each chapter of the book can be read independently. You don't have to read previous chapters, and you don't need prior knowledge. Every chapter is self-contained and includes cross-references, where required.
- **Chapter abstracts.** The contents of each chapter are summarised in the form of a management summary right at the beginning. If you are in a hurry, or want to know if a specific chapter is relevant to you, just use this summary.
- **Tables and figures.** Instead of writing lengthy texts, we use tables and figures whenever possible. The tables and figures are self-explanatory, but are also referenced and explained in the text.
- **Margin notes.** We use margin notes to summarise sections and paragraphs. In addition to headings and sub-headings, these notes help you to orient yourself and find contents quickly.

- **Case examples.** Case examples are clearly identifiable as such; they are in grey-shaded boxes. Case examples have a twofold purpose: Firstly, they illustrate abstract ideas and concepts; secondly, they may inspire you to improve your EAM.

References

[1] R. Wigand, A. Picot, and R. Reichwald, *Information, Organization and Management: Expanding Markets and Corporate Boundaries*, Berlin: Springer, 2008.

[2] J.A. Zachman, "Business systems planning and business Information control study: a comparison," *IBM Systems Journal*, vol. 21, 1982, pp. 31–53.

[3] J.A. Zachman, "A framework for information systems architecture," *IBM Systems Journal*, vol. 26, Sep. 1987, pp. 276–292.

[4] "FEAC™ Institute - Federated Enterprise Architecture Certification Institute.", http://www.feacinstitute.org/ [accessed on 19.06.2011]

[5] A.W. Scheer, *Wirtschaftsinformatik: Referenzmodelle für industrielle Geschäftsprozesse*, Berlin: Springer, 1997.

[6] H. Österle, *Business Engineering. Prozess-und Systementwicklung*, Berlin: Springer, 1995.

[7] O.K. Ferstl and E.J. Sinz, *Grundlagen der Wirtschaftsinformatik*, München: Oldenbourg Wissenschaftsverlag, 2006.

[8] The Open Group, *TOGAF™ Version 9*. USA: The Open Group, 2009.

[9] N.G. Carr, "IT Doesn't Matter," *Harvard Business Review*, vol. 81, 2003, pp. 41-49.

[10] IEEE, "IEEE Recommended Practice for Architectural Description of Software Intensive Systems (IEEE Std 14712000)", 2000.

[11] R. Winter, R., „Architektur braucht Management", *Wirtschaftsinformatik*, vol. 46, no. 4, pp. 317-319, 2004

[12] B. Mueller, G. Viering, C. Legner, G. Riempp, "Understanding the Economic Potential of Service-Oriented Architectures", *Journal of Management Information Systems*, vol. 26, no. 4, pp. 147-182, 2010.

An EAM navigator

Frederik Ahlemann, Fedi El Arbi

Table of contents

Management summary

Enterprise Architecture Management (EAM) is a comprehensive, interdisciplinary management approach that builds on techniques and practices from computer science, organisational engineering and change management, as well as business process management and other fields. Owing to its complexity, focussing on just one aspect of EAM – such as modelling or tools – will not yield results. Our research revealed seven important building blocks of successful EAM initiatives:

- *Top management awareness and support (a CxO agenda).*
- *EAM governance and organisation.*
- *Embedding EAM into strategic planning.*
- *Embedding EAM into the project life cycle.*
- *Embedding EAM into operations and monitoring.*
- *EA frameworks, modelling and tools.*
- *People, adoption and EAM introduction.*

We consider each of these building blocks as crucial to any EAM initiative and will explain why you should consider them. Our empirical work shows that companies that (a) have a thorough understanding of these building blocks and (b) include these building blocks in their EAM initiative are more likely to succeed than others. We have compiled these building blocks in the form of a navigator that will guide you through the book. The navigator will also help you to identify the content relevant to you.

2.1 Introduction and motivation

Enterprise Architecture Management (EAM) is an instrument to address a multi-dimensional fields of action and decision. A pure modelling approach, a followed by many organisations with limited EAM maturity, is inappropriate. Equally, focussing exclusively on EA implementation processes or governance will not yield sustainable results. The opposite is true: Our field experience and case analysis clearly indicate that many different facets, including EAM integration in existing processes, organisational structures and governance regimes as well as specific cultural aspects determine EAM's success. This is not surprising. After all, EAM is not an end in itself. It is a means to ensure realistic strategic decision-making, to set clear and focussed project scopes and monitor the firm's development. EAM is a social phenomenon, it needs to be integrated into existing processes and affects numerous elements of an organisation. For example:

EAM as a multi-dimensional decision domain

- EAM requires a proper institutionalisation with people who have the power to make decisions and enforce their implementation. ⇨ **EAM is an organisation and governance issue**.
- EAM requires integration into existing processes, such as strategy development, project prioritisation, budgeting and project implementation, because these are influenced by EAM practices. ⇨ **EAM is a process issue**.
- EAM introduces specific management methods for the modelling, analysis and design of the enterprise architecture. ⇨ **EAM is a methodological issue**.
- EAM requires executives to rethink the (architectural) consequences of their decisions and to create a shared vision. It affects the way people perceive their enterprise and perform joint decision-making. ⇨ **EAM is a cultural issue**.

Although one would think that this expansive notion of EAM is the norm, many organisations focus on modelling or planning activities but lack the power, skills, or enthusiasm to face the real-world problems of developing and optimising their enterprise architecture. Our case research shows that many organisations also don't get it right the first time: Several attempts are needed to establish EAM before it becomes a living management practice.

One-sided EAM initiatives are likely to fail

In an attempt to tackle challenges of deploying EAM in your organisation, this chapter has a twofold objective: Firstly, we want to help you to understand what is important when you implement EAM. Secondly, we want to give you an overview of the structure of this book. We do so by:

Objectives of this chapter: Present the success factors and offer a guide through the book

- presenting important building blocks of successful EAM,
- relating the building blocks to one another in the form of a navigator, and
- explaining how the navigator guides you through the book.

In the next section, we will introduce the navigator, then discuss its building blocks. In Section 3, we will elaborate on how the navigator may be used to design an EAM initiative, as well as to describe how to assess this initiative for viability and completeness.

2.2 Building blocks of successful EAM

During our case research, top executives and enterprise architects repeatedly raised certain issues regarding successful EAM. We found that there is a uniform set of challenges that must be addressed when an organisation decides to implement EAM. From our cases, we also learned that ignoring these issues will significantly decrease the likelihood of EAM success and will ultimately lead to EAM project failure or to EAM having a low impact on an enterprise's performance.

As these practical success factors are very relevant, we collected them, transformed them into separate fields of action and compiled them into a compact and easy-to-understand frame of reference for successful EAM. To avoid confusion, we refrain from using the term 'framework', since there are many EA frameworks available, each with a different purpose (see Chapter 8). Instead, we decided to use the term 'navigator' for this frame of reference, because it has been designed to guide you through this book as well as to guide your EAM initiative.

The navigator as an aggregation of EAM success factors

Despite its orientation towards success, the navigator (see its building blocks in Figure 2.1) does not describe an ideal EAM scenario. We believe that EAM implementations depend on situational factors, and there is no 'one size fits all' solution. Nevertheless, the navigator may draw your attention to those constituents of EAM that make a difference.

The navigator consists of seven building blocks. Properly implemented, these building blocks strongly influence EAM success. In the following section, we will describe the navigator's building blocks by (1) explaining what they are, (2) motivating their importance, and (3) outlining their relationships and interdependencies. Additional information can be found in the rest of the book: Each building block is described in a separate chapter.

Seven building blocks that influence EAM success

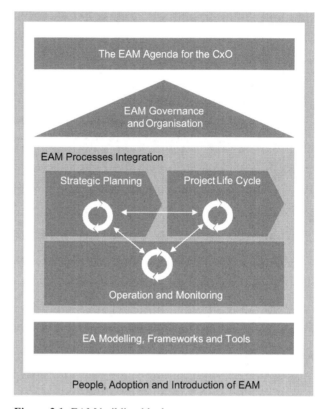

Figure 2.1: EAM building blocks

The EAM agenda for the chief executive officer

What is this?

EAM objectives are always enterprise-specific

If organisations are not convinced that EAM will yield benefits, they certainly will not invest money in it. Firms need to believe that EAM can help them to stay competitive in an ever-changing global market space. But even if there are typical EAM-related benefits, for example, better alignment or increased flexibility, most companies need an 'urgent pain': A business case and a project sponsor to start an EAM initiative or extend an existing one. Top-level executives (CxOs) must invest time, money and resources in EAM. They therefore need to understand what EAM is and how it helps to improve enterprise performance. Based on this understanding, CxOs can define clear EAM-related objectives and create an environment in which EAM can achieve its full potential. Such objectives and the environment necessary to reach them are always enterprise-specific and depend on the EAM context.

Why is this important?

For successful EAM, top management needs to be involved; it needs to define the EAM objectives and create a corresponding environment with the help of a management agenda. Only senior management can provide the budget and resources necessary to make EAM successful. Furthermore, senior management members need to be available when problems require escalation, because their power can help to overcome conflicts and resistance that may emerge when people have to change their behaviour or – in some cases – lose some of their power.

Senior executives are crucial

There is some truth in the statement 'what gets measured gets done'. It is hard to plan and control an initiative without clear objectives. Both the project sponsor and the EAM team need objectives, because they help to set priorities when it is simply impossible to achieve everything at once. Because EAM is a broad field of action, staggered achievements and benefits can be expected. Objectives also help to direct staff, measure success and define corrective actions, when necessary. Furthermore, clear objectives may allow the stakeholders to better grasp the concept and logic of EAM and to identify with EAM.

What gets measured gets done

How is it related to other building blocks?

We consider a clear top management agenda for EAM an important precondition for an effective EAM. Furthermore, EAM initiatives are best driven by top management. For these reasons, we place this building block at the top of our navigator. The best way to initiate EAM is top-down. Besides defining high-level objectives, one of the first things top executives should think about is how to empower the EAM team. For this reason, this building block is closely linked to the next one: EAM governance and organisation. Top management must ensure that the organisational setting and the governance mechanisms in place really enable and serve the EAM team.

Think about organisation and governance first

More information on EAM objectives and the CxO agenda can be found in Chapter 3.

EAM governance and organisation

What is it?

EAM governance and organisation deal with the manner in which EAM is institutionalised in an organisation. In this context, manage-

Decision rights are crucial

ment must define the organisational components, roles, and commit-tees to perform EAM-related tasks. Therefore, these organisational elements, as well as their tasks, responsibilities and decision rights must be specified. Especially the latter are important, since there is a close relationship between staff members' EAM decision rights and an EAM initiative's effectiveness. In decentralised and distributed organisations, the institutionalisation of EAM is a particular chal-lenge, since management must choose an appropriate EAM organi-sation and governance model that balances local autonomy and global coordination.

Why is it important?

EAM is about decision-making in the interest of the organisation as a whole. One must ensure that the right people are empowered to make EA-relevant decisions, and that the implementation of these deci-sions is not hindered by an adverse organisational structure. A clear accountability framework along with transparent escalation proc-esses and well-documented decisions can significantly leverage EAM's effectiveness. These factors are of particular relevance for larger organisations, which frequently struggle to align local inter-ests and global strategic objectives.

How is it related to other building blocks?

Organisation and processes are two sides of the same coin

An effective organisation and governance structure is a necessary precondition for functioning strategic planning and strategy imple-mentation processes. In fact, they are closely linked to each other, since the organisation and governance structure defines who carries out what tasks during a process, whereas the process defines how all these different tasks are carried out in a logical and temporal sequence to achieve the desired outcome. These processes are described in Chapters 5 and 6.

More information on EAM organisation and governance can be found in Chapter 4.

Embedding EAM into strategic planning

What is this?

Strategic initiatives almost always affect the EA

The development of an enterprise's architecture is mostly a long-term and incremental activity. It requires investments in technology and reorganisation projects. Conversely, most projects carried out in an organisation either directly alter, or are at least affected by, the enterprise architecture. Consequently, EAM is closely linked to the following strategic planning activities (Figure 2.2):

- situation analysis,
- elaborate strategic options,
- develop an architecture vision,
- roadmapping and migration planning,
- project portfolio planning, and
- evaluating the architecture evolution.

These planning activities link to EAM in two ways: Firstly, strategic planning can bring about dedicated architecture initiatives for the EA's structured development. Secondly, all other strategic initiatives must be documented in the EA model and analysed in terms of their impact on the EA. As a result, the EA team may initiate EA-related objectives and investments, and may also review and assess all the other objectives and investments with regard to their EA impact. The existing strategic planning processes therefore need to be complemented by EAM practices, such as EA analysis or EA documentation, so that a long-term EA development can be ensured (see Figure 2.2).

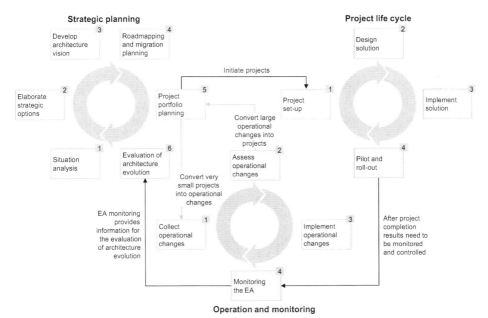

Figure 2.2: EAM process integration

Why is this important?

*Strategic EA
planning prevents a
chaotic and
arbitrary EA
development*

First of all, EAM is a powerful management approach that improves strategic decision-making and the organisation's structured development. It not only assists in mastering real-world complexity by analysing the existing capabilities, but also in defining smart and feasible strategies and migration paths. Secondly, if strategic initiatives that guide an organisation's future development do not align with the architecture vision and principles, they jeopardise long-term strategic EA objectives by creating facts. In such cases, EAM will barely have an impact, because the development of the architecture will remain arbitrary and chaotic. Thirdly, by creating a shared understanding of complex, multi-dimensional dependencies, EAM can also become a communication tool to spread strategic visions and goals in the organisation.

How is this building block related to other building blocks?

Strategic planning naturally precedes the project life cycle, as outlined in the navigator (Figure 2.2). EA operation and monitoring result in secondary relationships when the strategic objectives not implemented in the form of projects are realised as small(er) operational changes, or are simply translated into targets for the organisation (departmental targets).

More information on the embedding of EAM into strategic planning can be found in Chapter 5.

Embedding EAM into the project life cycle

What is this?

*Projects are the
instrument for
implementing EA
change*

Strategic objectives are mostly realised in the form of projects and project programmes. Organisations normally choose to implement architectural change in project form because projects are temporary endeavours with a clear target and dedicated resources. Therefore, they allow for an efficient development of architectural components, such as infrastructure, information systems and business processes. From an EAM perspective, the project life cycle may be subdivided into the following subsequent phases (as outlined in Figure 2.2):

• project set-up,
• design solution,
• implement solution, and
• piloting and roll-out.

Why is this important?

In most cases, projects do not go as planned. Environmental changes can never be anticipated fully and a project's course can never be predicted precisely. Furthermore, the project team often only has a rough understanding of the project results, which makes it even harder to plan every project execution detail. Requirements volatility is another major challenge for contemporary projects: During project execution, project sponsors sometimes change their minds about project objectives. If a project's scope changes, its impact on the EA will probably also change. If there is no constant monitoring of projects and EA-relevant decision-making during project execution, the project's outcome might not align with the intended target architecture.

Projects almost always influence the EA in unintended ways

How is this building block related to other building blocks?

Strategic planning initiates the above-mentioned projects. Beyond this, sub-processes of EA operation and monitoring (see next section) may support project execution by providing relevant data about the EA components of interest, such as service requests and key performance indicators (KPIs).

More information on embedding EAM into the project life cycle can be found in Chapter 6.

Embedding EAM into operations and monitoring

What is this?

Sometimes, projects are the vehicle for large EA changes, but most changes are small. Owing to their minor impact, these operational changes do not require large projects for their implementation. Organisations often have several dozen projects in their portfolio, but several thousand potential change requests in their incident or change request management system. These changes are handled during routine EA operation. There is always the risk that small changes might affect the functionality of applications, the topology of the network infrastructure, or the control flow of a business process. Although mostly useful, these changes might be implemented in ways that conflict with EA guidelines or cause unforeseen side effects. Furthermore, they may not be documented properly, and future decision-making might therefore not be based upon complete information. Operations and monitoring need to establish pragmatic procedures for the efficient handling of smaller changes in the EA in order to counter these risks (as outlined in Figure 2.2):

Small changes have risks too

- collect demands and changes,
- assess changes,
- implement changes, and
- monitor the EA.

KPIs are required
to systematically
control the EA's
development

The structured development of an EA consisting of hundreds or even thousands of components, including infrastructure components, applications and business processes, is impossible with only EA models. Organisations can use metrics and KPIs to measure certain EA characteristics, for example, cost efficiency, service quality, alignment and risk. Optimally, such measurement is a continuous monitoring process.

Why is this important?

Uncontrolled
changes may
jeopardise your EA

Without proper operation and monitoring processes, an organisation will soon lose control over its EA. Uncontrolled modifications of EA components have the potential to derail any EA plans. Furthermore, an EA's structured development requires an up-to-date information base and the timely provision of information to relevant stakeholders. EA operation processes ensure that those changes which impact the EA are systematically tracked and that EA information is up to date. Monitoring processes also provide a good and concise overview of the EA as a basis for early warning and escalation processes.

How is this building block related to other building blocks?

As noted, the processes of EA operation and monitoring deliver valuable information for strategic EA planning and implementation. Metrics and KPIs provide the means to assess the EA and derive strategic objectives; they can also be used to measure whether or not targets are being reached.

More information on embedding EAM into operations and monitoring can be found in Chapter 7.

EA frameworks, modelling and tools

What is this?

A large body of EA frameworks, modelling techniques, and tools is available today (e.g., Zachman's framework). These are useful for defining and developing the detailed description of the architecture, the principles governing its development and the standards applied during the architecture's development. Frameworks comprise guidelines, procedural models and methodologies for the EA's structured development. Software tools have the potential to lift these activities to a new productivity level.

Why is this important?

The underlying idea of developing all these frameworks, modelling techniques and tools is simple: Organisations can adopt best practices to accelerate EAM implementation, reduce the risk of EAM failure and make EAM more efficient and effective. However, every approach has strengths and weaknesses. Practitioners must be aware of these to make informed decisions when choosing the frameworks, modelling techniques and tools to fit their organisation.

At best, you can accelerate your project and reduce the risk of failure

How is this building block related to other building blocks?

Frameworks, modelling techniques and tools play an important role in all EA-related processes. They serve as a toolbox from which architects can choose in order to do their EAM work. Therefore, there is a close relationship between the strategic planning, the project life cycle, operations and monitoring.

More information on EA frameworks, modelling and tools can be found in Chapter 8.

People, adoption and introduction of EAM

What is this?

EA publications are dominated by 'hard methodologies' based on EA frameworks, tools and modelling techniques. These components undoubtedly influence EAM success. Despite the undeniable relevance of such 'hard methodologies', many practitioners feel that EAM's impact is also heavily influenced by 'soft factors' resulting from the social sphere in which EAM is applied. Individual resistance, incentives and supportive stakeholders therefore all play an important role.

Do not underestimate the EAM social dimension

Why is this important?

EAM requires many stakeholders to change their behaviour. Firstly, it is simply not enough to make a strong business case for EAM only at the enterprise level. Stakeholders will maximise their individual benefits, although they probably won't admit doing so. Secondly, EAM leads to a high degree of transparency about EA-related decision-making and work practices. This results in fear that past management mistakes might come to light and that managers will be criticised for inefficient behaviour and work patterns. Thirdly, people tend to have habits they do not want to change. The introduc-

Enemies of EAM: Individual interests, fear of transparency and habits

tion of EAM can therefore be a challenging endeavour and might result in resistance. Proactive management of the social dimension can significantly reduce the risk of failure and increase all involved parties' satisfaction.

How is this building block related to other building blocks?
Social factors play an important role with regard to all the navigator's building blocks. For this reason, this building block surrounds all the other components.

More information on people, adoption and EAM introduction can be found in Chapter 9.

2.3 Using the navigator to check your EAM initiative

How can the navigator help me to develop EAM?

The navigator presented in the previous section can be used to check EAM initiatives for viability and completeness. At best, an EAM strategy should include concepts that relate to each of the navigator's building blocks. Nevertheless, see if you can answer the following seven key questions:

1. **What are EAM's overall objectives and do we have management support?** (⇨Chapter 3)
   Do you have clear EAM objectives and top management support? Does the EAM team have enough resources to do its job?
2. **Do we have effective EAM governance and organisation?** (⇨Chapter 4)
   This question refers to whether an organisational and governance model has clearly defined EAM-related tasks, responsibilities and decision rights that fit the organisation.
3. **Do our strategic planning processes leverage EAM?** (⇨Chapter 5)
   This question is about the integration of EAM practices and classical strategic planning processes, such as strategy definition, budgeting and project portfolio planning. If decision-making considers the EA perspective, organisations will gradually develop in line with the enterprise architecture vision and targets.
4. **Do we have project execution processes in place that are in line with EAM?** (⇨Chapter 6)
   This question refers to the way one enforces EA-compliant project execution. EAM must ensure that projects are always in line with EA-specific rules, principles and objectives, thus avoiding a chaotic and unintended modification of the EA.
5. **Do we have working processes for enterprise architecture operation and monitoring?** (⇨Chapter 7)
   Furthermore, a continuous monitoring of the EA by means of metrics and KPIs helps to identify weaknesses and optimisation potentials. EAM must identify and keep track of operational changes that cause critical modifications in the enterprise architecture

6. **What are our frameworks, modelling approaches and tools? (⇨Chapter 8)**

This question refers to a reasonable, pragmatic and decision-oriented approach to modelling the EA with suitable tools and applying suitable frameworks. EAM must be based on a results-oriented approach to modelling in which modelling is not an end in itself.

7. **How do we address EAM's social sphere and introduce EAM in the organisation? (⇨Chapter 9)**

The introduction of EAM is a complex change process that has a methodological, an organisational and a social dimension. It is necessary to have a clear strategy for introducing EAM that will take diverse stakeholder interests into account.

Do I need to have all of this right at the outset?

Don't try to achieve everything right at the start, but be aware of what is needed

Although it would be nice to have all these building blocks already addressed right at the start of your EAM journey, we realise that it is neither reasonable nor feasible to expect this. As a management concept, EAM is too complex to be implemented in a single step. But even if you cannot implement everything right at the outset, we recommend that you make a conscious decision about the order of the activities based on a thorough analysis of your organisation's maturity, capability, the nature of your management support and your vision. You should also develop an EAM roadmap that fits your overall EAM objectives. When developing your EAM roadmap, you should be able to answer the following questions:

• Who are our relevant stakeholders and sponsors?
• When will I address the different EAM aspects?
• In what order will I address them?
• Have I considered the dependencies?
• Have I thought about quick wins?

To give you a taste of how an organisation may approach EAM, we provide an example.

How a bank introduces EAM and sets priorities

A large European bank's latest effort to introduce EAM has been a success. Powerful key stakeholders from the IT organisation consider EAM crucial to the bank's long-term transformation. These stakeholders support the EAM initiatives by providing both resources and decision rights. From past experience, the team driving the EAM initiative is also aware that EAM requires a shift in culture, which can only be realised one step at a time. Consequently, a relatively small but empowered team of very experienced enterprise architects with a solid business background generates 'success stories' by following a very pragmatic approach to EAM. Architects are linked to the business departments and are involved in the early strategic planning phases, thus shaping the future domain architectures. They also accompany selected projects that leverage the development of the overall architecture. The architectural projects' measurable and sustainable outcomes, which include reduced costs, increased flexibility and shortened delivery times, are specifically emphasised through the development of a service-oriented architecture. The team does not engage in areas in which EAM awareness is limited and where quick wins would be unlikely. By providing hands-on help and demonstrating obvious impact in areas in which change and success can easily be reached, the team convinces the rest of the organisation step by step.

More information on the topic can be found in Chapter 9. You will also find more examples in the various chapters.

Chapter 3

The EAM agenda for the CxO

Eric Stettiner, Marcus Messerschmidt

Table of contents

Management summary

In this chapter, we introduce enterprise architecture management (EAM) as a management philosophy that embraces holistic and sustainable corporate change. In a constantly changing business world, executives are likely to require a significantly improved knowledge base of current and future corporate assets and capabilities. They will seek to introduce pragmatic change governance and processes, which support the successful and consistent implementation of strategic decisions and reduce, or even prevent, unwanted variations.

This is where EAM enters the picture, as it provides an opportunity to position strategic and business-imposed change needs to drive change initiatives, while considering existing and required future business capabilities and assets.

We promote the idea that EAM should be seen as an endeavour that senior management sponsor and direct. Executives should provide the objectives, resources and leadership that guide the layout and the benefits of architecture management in their organisation. We suggest key issues that should interest top managers (CxOs) to maintain and improve their business' capabilities in order to effectively manage change. Finally, we describe, from an executive perspective, the primary aspects that should be considered during the implementation and operation of a solid enterprise architecture (EA) function.

3.1 EAM motivations and objectives

A prudent observer will discern two fundamentally different directions regarding how companies currently manage their capabilities and assets. On the one hand, organisations are progressively delegating the business of serving their customers, inventing and making their products, and managing their technology and resources. Using call centres, low-wage countries or the Cloud, they start orchestrating on-demand services, suppliers and infrastructure components, and rely increasingly on different types of external providers. On the other hand, we have seen corporations repatriating and insourcing business and technology capabilities to the extent that they have already altered their business model and started offering new services to new business partners.

The common carrier is the global internet-enabled platform that links providers and users, sources and sinks of knowledge, information, automation capabilities, technology and work. Both trends are building complex dependency networks that require increased management attention.

In our view, these trends are here to stay, and we know that they entail significant opportunities and key risks, especially for businesses that buy and outsource services and knowledge. Opportunities take account of access to a global customer base, value-adding partnering and cost reductions. The risks include increased reliance on external infrastructure, key business partners and their capabilities, the potential loss of central visibility and control and an inability to act strategically with regard to future shifts. Given the increasing frequency and impact of externally induced change that affect our ways of working, these risks appear at inconvenient times.

To mitigate these risks and to improve their decision quality when considering new opportunities, business executives will soon want a much better knowledge base of existing and required enterprise capabilities and assets. They will establish an approach to consistently manage intended change. This is where enterprise architecture management (EAM) enters the picture, as a well-operating EAM function can provide both these needs.

Integration and alignment

'John, what are you currently working on?' It was Mike, our CEO, asking this question in the elevator. I could hear myself mumble, 'I am working on enterprise architecture matters'. 'Oh, I didn't know we were planning to make changes to our buildings', was Mike's response. I smiled awkwardly and assessed the time I needed to explain the significance of my work for the company's future when we reached the fifth floor and I had to leave. Through the closing doors, I could hear Mike asking his assistant to set up a meeting with Jack, our head of infrastructure, to discuss a cost-cutting opportunity.

While many things had gone wrong in this elevator speech, what should John's message have been? 'I am aligning business and IT' might have left Mike thinking about the recent mobile device roll-out that had failed due to an insufficient server sizing. Perhaps 'I am helping to operationalise your business strategy by means of EAM' could have drawn some interest, possibly even an invitation to take the elevator to the top floor? However, even in this case, John would have had plenty of opportunities to fail. Technology subjects often carry negative equity when 'real' business people are confronted with them. So, why should Mike care?

EAM is a holistic management philosophy concerned with corporate change

- Firstly, enterprise architecture (EA) should not be equated with technology. While some of the first architecture concepts were indeed invented in a dark corner of a data centre when engineers sought to explain to one another how all the boxes, cables and disks had to be set up in order to work, architecture has moved on, embracing applications, data, business structures and processes. It has gradually broadened its scope, increasingly taking an enterprise-wide perspective. Today, EAM comprises a management philosophy that approaches enterprise-related changes in a holistic, unambiguous and consistent way, with the goal of aligning all an organisation's assets and capabilities with its strategy.
- Secondly, enterprise architecture inherited, understood and promoted the idea that different people have different perspectives and interests when they look at something. Consider the following: 'Real' architects use a different set of graphs and words when they explore and discuss building requirements with a project developer than when they explain planned installations to a plumber. The object of interest might be the same (e.g. a shower), but the way in which the information is presented differs. By adopting this idea, EA becomes a powerful approach, as it allows all stakeholders to contribute, using their own words and perspectives, while maintaining consistency in the underlying concept. EA uses dedicated

architecture models to bridge islands of understanding, drawing together silos of shared views and language – at headquarters, on the fifth or top floor, in a corner in the data centre, or somewhere abroad. EAM provides the structure with which we manage all relevant activities in order to conceptualise, implement and execute enterprise strategies.

So, why should you care? Because EAM allows us to vertically integrate strategic directions with tactical concepts, design decisions, and operations; because it allows us to horizontally align business change with technology and vice versa (see Figure 3.1). We call this Reason #1.

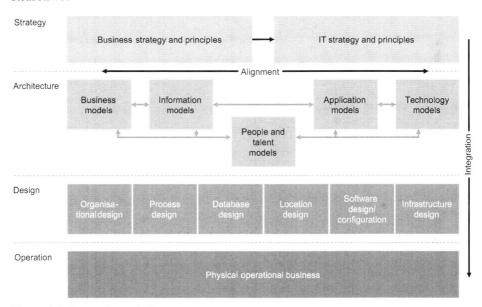

Figure 3.1: Integration and alignment

In the performance driver seat

If we consider EAM a sensible approach that adds value due to its ability to support an enterprise-wide vertical integration, as well as horizontal alignment on a conceptual/logical level, it should become a top management topic: The CxO's job description includes – as one of the most important duties – the setting of the organisation's strategy and vision. This should provide a clear view of how top management will ensure long-term organisational performance. In short, the key areas of concern include market positioning, market servicing, resources use and development, the ability to develop or adopt trends, the relationship with external regulators and attention to the less controllable factors that we summarise as 'luck' (see Figure 3.2).

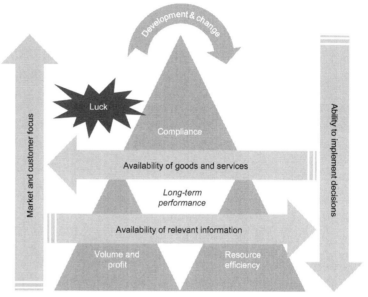

Figure 3.2: Key factors impacting long-term organisational performance

While the influence of a specific performance-driving factor may vary according to the industry, market and over time, we find that many top-level executives currently improve company performance by addressing at least one of the following business concerns:

- Revenue growth – driving improved turnover, margins and customer satisfaction.
- Convergence – moving towards bundled customer service offerings and multifunctional products.
- Deal value – maximising opportunities before and after a merger & acquisition.
- People and change – handling business, organisational and people change programmes.
- Global sourcing – understanding and applying mixed sourcing models, including multi-sourcing and outsourcing.
- Technology integration – aligning the use of available technologies with the business vision and strategy.
- Enterprise performance management – obtaining more accurate and accelerated financial and operational data and applying these to improve business performance.

- Risk and regulation – understanding and complying with regulatory requirements, as well as dealing with security and operational risks.
- Crisis management – dealing with unexpected events or disputes.

For each of the above strategic business matters, we encounter various barriers to improvement, which can be found in different parts of the organisation, and which bear the risk of allowing a great idea fail. We believe that this risk can be mitigated if strategic decisions are subject to confirmation and refinement. The strategic direction should therefore be translated into a holistic and consistent model, which will help management to understand the tactical interpretation and operational implementation options. Such an architecture vision or target operating model (TOM) could define management information requirements, the process framework, the organisational structure, talent requirements, and the supporting applications needed to execute the strategy. It can be used to refine or tailor strategy, making it more effective and efficient. *'Selecting an operation model is a commitment to a way of doing business. That can be a daunting choice.' [1]*

A TOM can reflect the implications of strategic decisions

How a media company refined its strategic decision after the initial implementation option was presented

The senior management of a global media company decided to move all its European HR functions into one shared service centre (SSC). During the feasibility study, all necessary activities and projects related to the organisation's process, structure, people, and technology dimensions were identified. The technology team suggested that a common European HR system should be a prerequisite. The team felt that this platform would drive common standards, thereby enabling the central group to provide an efficient service. However, the senior management team disagreed. They concluded that such an enabling project would redirect the business and IT focus for approximately the next year to discussions on process and data standardisation, allowing the initial SSC efficiency goals to be ignored.

Executives re-enforced the strategic decision, and the project team changed some of its initial concepts. The refined operating model, which was then accepted and implemented, included two support locations for the new SSC, a simplified customer/country-driven team organisation scheduled for review in favour of a more process-driven structure after two years of operations, moderate process and data harmonisation goals to be implemented in two different enterprise applications, one common set of KPIs, and one new 'umbrella' content management system for SSC staff and its new clients.

Why should EAM attract senior management's attention? In our view, this approach can provide greater transparency on how your management team has interpreted and conceptually translated your strategic directives. In turn, this will enable you to refine your decisions and challenge the derived concepts in a timely manner. This could save huge sums of money, as well as years of time. We call it Reason #2.

Volatility ahead!

We understand intuitively that if such a consistent, transparent and agreed-upon architecture vision or TOM were available, the actual realisation of the intended benefits would be easier to prioritise, plan, implement and control. All the known and largely established change governance models and processes – including strategic planning, portfolio management, change implementation, and operational controls – could relate their decisions to a shared reference point. This 'missing' content can build the basis for a better and consistent resource deployment plan. A TOM contains the information that allows deeper insight into an intended change's implications, and supports improved senior stakeholder alignment and expectation management. Over time, this aligned vision can be developed into a more detailed to-be architecture, covering the layers impacted by a project or programme, an entire business domain, or even the complete enterprise.

EAM may become a crucial element of future management practice

We think it is likely that such an integrated to-be model will become an enabling element of your future management practice. It will represent the knowledge base that enables you to shift gears in order to act on strategic opportunities in a timely manner. We want you to consider two interacting and growing forces that will drive this need:

• Velocity of business. Time to market is decreasing and life cycle management from strategy to execution is becoming more intertwined. These changes are a reaction to customer sophistication, the incremental innovation of existing technology, globalisation, competitive pressures and regulatory requirements. Measured in relative or absolute numbers, time, or percentage of market penetration, business seems to be moving towards a state of constant flux [2]. The lead-time for action, reaction, or adaptation is shrinking from years to months, days or even minutes, making the timely implementation of strategic initiatives more important than ever.

• Volatility in the markets. The constant flux of change in contemporary business life is superimposed by an increasing number of major discontinuities [3] that result from a variety of factors, including capital and human resources' volume and mobility, a lack of global controls in a globalising marketplace, emerging disruptive new technologies and products, political and religious disputes, natural disasters and the excessive use of our natural resources. These events, which are hard to plan for, are establishing a new key differentiator between organisations: Their ability to perceive and understand a fundamentally changed marketplace and to adapt accordingly.

We call this Reason #3: Our business life is changing. We need to manage a flow of constant change interrupted by major unforeseen events. EA – as a philosophy, as a framework, or as a process – will enhance your organisation's ability to sense, analyse and respond effectively to change, be it new business practices, technology, or the next financial crisis. EA allows businesses to more easily identify and reuse existing assets and capabilities when pursuing novel strategic initiatives.

3.2 The architecture impact

Some organisations have started to apply an EA philosophy in pursuit of improved corporate change capabilities. They generally do so by following one of two alternative routes:

- Bottom-up. Architecture skills were initially developed in IT, and the established EA structures and processes are reaching out beyond the technology turf. IT leaders need more and better business direction and involvement to maintain and increase their function's positive value contribution. These initiatives often lack 'real' business sponsorship and tend to remain IT-heavy. However, a significant value contribution may be realised through improved management of the IT assets.
- Top-down. EAM is adopted as a result of a strategic initiative to improve business control of IT. A business architecture function is set up that reviews and refines ways of working with IT architects and IT delivery organisations. These new teams are generally empowered and enjoy senior business management sponsorship. However, they often establish a challenging communication structure between the business and the technology delivery organisation.

Besides the starting position and the terminology used, a major step is achieved once we unite the organisation's business and technology 'think tanks' to work jointly on solutions. Although it is rarely measured, we generally perceive an added value resulting from both the integrated concepts and holistic governance that approves, rejects and oversees business and technology projects.

But how can we ensure that this added value can be sustained? We suggest three themes with which top-level executives should concern themselves: achieving a balance between standards and versatility, embedding the strategic and business imperatives and using improved insight.

Balancing standards and versatility

Not all tasks in an end-to-end process can or should be standardised

Process standardisation remains a focus area for many organisations. The definition of standards has resulted in significant business value where transaction-driven tasks were the subject of analysis. Today's enterprise applications support or automate a set of linked transactional tasks required to execute end-to-end processes in different industries. Strict standardisation fails, however, when dealing with the integration and monitoring of creative and inventive tasks or human interactions, which frequently denote a valuable difference between competitors. It is often difficult to start defining standards for such versatile tasks, and where we do, the results can be unconvincing. Since standardisation tries to reduce variances and increase the automation level, it appears to be the natural opponent of creativity and variability, which are essential qualities for defining strategies and plans, for successfully accomplishing R&D work and for conducting good partnership management [4].

When the technical architecture is examined, we find an univocal statement that, contrary to the above, standards enable flexibility. Only by using standards can we define and operate the specific portfolio of applications and technology components that best support the business direction. A similar statement can be expected from any business intelligence or enterprise performance team that either makes use of common data and structure definitions, or spends a significant amount of time and effort converting data from different sources into a comparable and meaningful set of information by implementing transformation logic into the integration layer between transactional and reporting systems.

Businesses need to define the level of standardi-sation which best supports their strategy

If we put people with business, data and technology backgrounds in a room, we expect them to argue their points on the basis of their backgrounds. *Data* and *technology* people will tend to push for a higher level of standardisation, while *process* people will repeatedly find good reasons for variances and differences. If the standardisation level varies per layer or domain, this requires management attention. Businesses need to define the standardisation level that best fits their strategy:

• in the continuum between centralisation and local responsibility,
• regarding the level of automation and the integration of variable human-driven tasks and transactional activities,
• regarding the degree of common information and data structure definitions, and
• regarding the scale and dominance of the talent, functional, application and technology policies and standards.

EAM can be used to derive, set, and change the principles that describe how companies want to operate their business and how their resources should interact or be deployed. These principles translate the strategy into more tangible guidelines for the construction of a business and technology architecture up to the physical implementation. These principles are signposts needed to consistently drive future change.

Embedding the strategic and business imperatives

Enterprises adapt. They can re-organise themselves, gain experience and change. The constant flow of adjustments in a complex environment is a challenge to any long-term and strategic planning. If we want to establish a model driven by strategy and business in order to define, develop, and maintain enterprise capabilities and assets, we need to know what the business is going to do differently tomorrow and then steer change accordingly. But how can an organisation develop this skill?

As a start, it is very important that a senior executive assumes the EAM sponsorship and makes integration and alignment one of the new function's key objectives. We have seen a variety of reporting options: While the most common sponsor is the CIO, companies have started to make the CEO, CFO, or COO responsible for EA functions (for more details see Chapter 4). The sponsor should suggest and agree with his or her peers on the appointment of a chief enterprise architect, who will establish and lead 'the office of the architect'. If comparable capabilities are at hand, we recommend that the EAM sponsor is from a business function, and the chief architect from IT.

Senior sponsorship is a critical success factor for a successful EAM

The EAM initiative should kick off its work by reviewing the business and technology strategy, and establishing the foundation that will further guide the architectural work:

1. The strategy must be translated into architecture principles.
2. The relevant architecture services must be defined and prioritised.
3. The established corporate change governance structure and project delivery approaches must be refined to integrate EAM at strategic points.
4. The baseline architecture must be documented.
5. The TOM or architecture vision must be defined and agreed upon.
6. Opportunities, gaps, and solutions must be identified.
7. Migration planning and roadmap development must be completed and communicated.

Consider
timeboxing the
basic EAM
activities

Clearly, this will not happen overnight. However, we believe that this should not take longer than 12 months. Depending on the size and complexity of your business, we recommend that you implement basic EAM within a time frame of 6 to 12 months. If the basic activities take longer, you run the risk of building an ivory tower, or damaging the reputation of the new EAM function in your organisation. To maintain positive momentum, we recommend that you define communicable and measurable units of work that produce tangible deliverables every 2 to 3 months. The above thoughts, applied to the basic EAM, should result in a draft plan in which the activities in Points 1 to 3 are defined within 6 to 8 weeks after the initial launch, while the activities in Points 4, 5 and 6 take between 2 to 4 months each.

You might wonder whether we believe that a complex, global company or division can realistically define its baseline architecture and TOM within 6 to 12 months. Yes, we do! And we can quote examples of the Fortune Global 500 that have reworked and adjusted their businesses during the recent economic crisis. Therefore, if some of these companies could fundamentally change their operating model within that time, are the barriers that your organisation faces really that insurmountable?

Perhaps the level of analysis is too low. Many teams and tools struggle to draw the line that divides the architects' conceptual and logical thinking from actual design and implementation work. This could lead to the development and maintenance effort for your architecture deliverables or artefacts growing exponentially, while you find it difficult to involve the right people in your organisation in the process of guiding and reviewing these deliverables or artefacts. The incremental value of more detailed information may decrease or even turn negative. Pushing for a pragmatic and phased adoption approach while putting a time limit on the EAM set-up is therefore a good way to avoid unnecessary details and keep the involved people focused and on their toes.

Using improved insight

EAM significantly improves the knowledge of what drives business change, offering alternative solutions and routes to address requirements, as well as their possible implications for process, structures, people, applications and technology. We hold that senior executives can use this knowledge to advance certain aspects of their agenda; for example:

- improved control over business and IT change initiatives in order to manage complexity,
- implementation of sustainable solutions,
- use of change-related or benefit-related KPIs and a total cost of ownership analysis, and
- removal of barriers and limitations resulting from the current operating model.

Once the to-be state is described, the gap between the current and future assets and capabilities becomes apparent. To close it, we can define actions, solutions and projects, but identifying those efforts that best support the strategic business agenda will make a valuable difference. Benefit dependency networks and portfolio management techniques can be employed to organise the solution continuum into an actionable roadmap and plan. Top-level input is required for this critical step to ensure that significant attention is paid to the strategic objectives and expected measurable benefits, allowing them to remain the axis of the solution prioritisation, selection and implementation design. Where successful, such involvement will accomplish a major EAM benefit: The efficient, goal-directed allocation of time, people and money.

How to manage the gap between the current and future assets and capabilities

How improved insight helped establish a continuous improvement cycle

Using a global programme, a large packaged goods company defined and implemented enterprise-wide standards and concepts. When this step had been completed for major parts of the organisation, the next task was to identify and implement best practices to further leverage the advantages of the enterprise-wide solutions. To remain at the forefront of innovation, global business champions were identified by means of KPIs and benchmarks.

For example, the responsible business architect began to analyse the monthly closing process's time and effort in the different countries' accounting departments. The architect opened a discussion with the top-performing accounting departments. He investigated local work practices to find what could be of value for the wider community. He then made this knowledge available to the relevant managers worldwide.

Since processes will continue to evolve and technology will continue to improve, the initial implementation optimisation initiative is now an ongoing programme. Every year, another country or manager might emerge as the global champion, providing useful and relevant insights for their peers. This effort is assisted by the central support team, which plans to increase its R&D focus, ensuring that all parts of the solution remain up to date.

Through the implementation and continuous improvement of standards, the company has created a competitive gap between it and its competitors. Certain benefits that have resulted from this initiative:

- The post-merger integration effort was reduced to 25%,
- the consistency of cross-country reporting and compliance controls was improved by means of global data and process standards, and
- the number of data centres was reduced by 97%.

An interesting side effect has been the employees' increased participation in cross-functional collaboration. The hits on the relevant intranet sites have increased tenfold.

3.3 How do you get there?

Every business is based on EA, whether it is deliberately managed or not. If you use EAM, you are aiming for a consistent approach that defines sustainable solutions, supports strategic decisions and delivers better information about the availability and use of enterprise assets and capabilities. EAM allows you to establish a superior view of how to deal with external and internal events, which either open opportunities for your current business model, or impact or even threaten your ways of working.

While EAM is not easy to explain, it seems even harder to digest. As it has a broad, cross-functional scope, it at times encounters corporate resistance. We often find elements or building blocks of EAM already implemented, sometimes using different acronyms or referring to specific but diverse management disciplines, including portfolio management, business process management, IT governance and IT service management (e.g., the configuration management database). These disciplines are all of critical importance for the organisation's change capabilities and can provide real value for the business. If you ask the people in your organisation to see these disciplines as part of a holistic management approach and to regard them as an integral EAM element, this may lead to negative reactions from the function's sponsors and owners. Nobody likes the new kid on the block if he immediately demands the quarterback position.

EAM will refine functions and processes established to manage change

When do you start?

Is there a good time to initiate EAM in your organisation? If we understand EAM as a management philosophy that refines and frames management practices to holistically address change, it can be introduced at any point in time. But we know that there are specific situations that create a positive environment and therefore support EAM introduction:

- **Changing business models.** Enterprises deal with increasing challenges resulting from new business models, globalisation and compliance requirements. Every major business decision, such as merging with another enterprise, carving out special business units and moving into emerging markets, will leave a footprint in your

EA. If you are an active member of the M&A community, or are working in a highly regulated industry, establishing EAM is helpful to conceptualise and operationalise change. An integrated view on how an initiative could impact the different architecture layers will help you to identify key activities and prioritise efforts accordingly.

- **Preparing for cost reduction.** During an economic crisis, almost every enterprise runs a cost reduction programme. In many cases, such programmes focus on taking out a given percentage of the department or asset costs without any further specification. When this happens, companies with established EAM principles have an advantage, as they can identify the best opportunities for cost saving by analysing the impact of a potential cost reduction in business and technology across the enterprise or domain. Consequently, they may decide to reduce related service levels to decrease the operating costs, they may alter the procedures and business process support consistently, or they might refine the combined business and IT projects portfolio to meet the budget.

- **Effectiveness of standardisation programmes.** In the past 20 years, many enterprises have experienced significant technology-enabled change. In the 1990s, almost every company implemented an enterprise resource planning (ERP) package to integrate and standardise business processes and data structures, and sought to reduce process variances and costs. Many companies defined enterprise standards and ran global rollout projects while enhancing the solution to support local statutory and critical business requirements. But how successful were these projects? A number of issues challenged these global solutions:
  1. Key local requirements were often not known or not recognised, and the global solution had to be adjusted during the roll-out.
  2. The governance and budget process frequently remained unchanged. This became the root cause of a growing number of local and regional extensions and exceptions.
  3. Software vendors used dedicated, interfaced systems to enable new functionality, such as customer relationship management (CRM), business intelligence, supply chain management (SCM), as well as governance, risk and compliance (GRC). The interdependencies between functions and the heterogeneity of the deployed applications and technologies increased development and test efforts, while negatively affecting solution flexibility and the delivery organisation's agility.

4. Governments around the world defined an ever-growing number of different and complex compliance and reporting regulations.

As a result, many companies ended up with a fragmented, complex, expensive and inflexible enterprise application environment that often did not achieve the initial goals [5].

Business leaders and architects have started to re-think this 'one size fits all' approach and are using EAM principles, models and patterns to develop the new version of the enterprise standardisation map, which – per layer – renders different standardisation clusters, from the distinct local to enterprise-wide solutions. The standardisation clusters allow for more consistent standards definition, communication and control, as well as the identification of gaps and optimisation potentials.

- **Data quality.** In a vastly simplified view of the past, data management did not present a problem. You bought the data structures with the selected software package and if the field definitions did not adequately support the information need, you would use some of the spare fields. The 'good old days' are gone and today we often look at data and information with some concern. Time and again we have found ourselves maintaining duplicate data in different applications, or spending half of the development budget on interfacing them. These time-consuming and expensive solutions pose a significant risk for good business decisions, which should be founded on 'single truth' information. Therefore, data management initiatives have emerged that promote the idea of regarding data as a valuable enterprise asset. Successful initiatives define data ownership and a unique maintenance procedure, while the supporting technology solutions ensure consistency and transparently transform the data into meaningful, rich information that supports business decisions and processes. EA models help to build such a holistic view across business, organisation, process, information systems, technology- and talent layers, as well as the interoperability between applications or even enterprises. Well-established EAM practices will always include a thorough investigation of a change initiative's implications on business information needs.

What does it take?

We have said that enterprises are adaptive, since they learn and react. However, we find that their capacity and talent to identify and promote the necessary change, to define the specific change need, as well as plan, implement and operate change in a way that realises the intended benefits vary significantly. While EAM can advance your ambition in this field, it is not a tool that can be deployed for instant use. It is a management philosophy on how to approach, define, analyse, consider, decide, communicate and implement corporate change. EAM will:

- influence the way strategies are developed,
- affect the way change demands are captured and decisions are made,
- change the way projects and initiatives are prioritised and managed as a programme, and
- alter the way root cause and impact analyses are done and documented.

Table 3.1: Main characteristics of EAM implementations

Characteristics	Past practice	Good practice	Leading practice
EAM adoption	Driven by tool and model	IT driven, but with a holistic approach	As a strategic business initiative
Alignment focus	Application and technology	Business and IT	Strategy and operations
Approach	Tool-driven and IT-focused	Defined use of a set of frameworks and methods	EAM integrated into existing management practices, optimised use of different frameworks supported by tools and established standards
Change drivers	Technology enabling business change	Business demanding technology change	Strategic and business imperatives guiding technology change
Reporting and sponsorship	IT governance board	CIO	CEO, COO, CFO
Scope	Variable	Project, business domain	Enterprise detailed by domain and service
Staff commitment	IT-heavy	Separate but communicating teams focusing on business or technology layer architectures	Think tanks from business and IT working together on domain solution architectures
Value tracking	Initial business case, no follow-up action	Benefits tracking based on KPIs	Benefits management supported by event-driven analysis and KPI-based operations monitoring

Furthermore, EAM will evolve to become the key content provider when management and staff need to examine the enterprise's DNA. To help you make EAM scope and approach decisions that suit your organisation, we have classified typical characteristics into past, good, and leading practices (Table 3.1).

EAM will document the enterprise's DNA

Good and leading practices cannot be implemented within weeks or months, but will evolve over years, requiring continuous senior management support, direction and monitoring. Businesses will benefit from EAM if the involved stakeholders refine their behaviour when they discuss strategies, or direct new business processes or technologies. They should follow the established guidelines and principles of the common framework while considering change holistically. Behavioural change requires time, and establishing EAM means dealing with the organisation's think tanks – people who are seldom easily convinced.

We suggest that the core team establishes a change management and communication plan for the start-up and initial EAM operations, involving top-level executives. You can help clarify EAM objectives, demonstrate sponsorship and support, and deal with people's fears and their resistance to change. The model in Figure 3.3 is based on the approach we describe in Chapter 9, but focuses on those aspects we believe should be addressed with senior management's visible support in order to win the hearts and minds of people involved in managing corporate change.

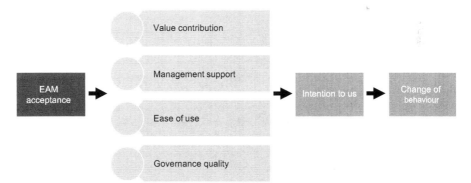

Figure 3.3: Key factors driving EAM perception that executives should promote

Senior management can improve EAM acceptance by attending to:

- Perceived value contribution. The stakeholders understand the EAM concept and support the value proposition.
- Perceived management support. The stakeholders see that senior management drives EAM and uses EAM practices in corporate management.
- Perceived ease of use. The stakeholders accept the changed ways of working as balanced and pragmatic. Relevant, high-quality work products result from the changed approach.
- Perceived governance quality. Those in charge of strategy definition, change governance and delivery organisation (i.e. the right people) are involved.

Before you launch your EAM initiative, you should undertake an effort estimate of the basic activities and the ongoing EAM operations. The following indicators could assist you to verify the work level that you require:

- As noted, we recommend the establishment of the EAM function within a time frame of 6 to 12 months.
- The number of people involved will vary in line with the size of the organisation, the scope of the initial services and the selected implementation approach. The core team usually consists of 3 to 20 people.
- During the set-up period, you can expect the team to grow from only the key architect position to a full team.
- Depending on the starting position, a significant amount of effort might be required from the business and IT organisation(s) to determine the baseline architecture.
- This involvement will continue at a reduced level when the architecture vision (TOM) and the transformation roadmap are developed and approved. However, you must ensure that your key players and top management are involved in this activity.
- With regard to ongoing operations, start with an honest estimate of the total effort currently spent on initiating, conceptualising and governing change in your organisation. As a starting point for EAM operations efforts, you can add the working hours of any newly hired staff in your architecture function to the afore-mentioned number of hours. In other words, don't expect the change process to be efficient right from the outset; expect it to be more effective. If you set store by Boehm's exponential cost of a change model [6], the additional effort in the early days of a change initiative is time well spent.

The CxO's agenda for enterprise architecture management

If it is your goal to embed EAM as a new philosophy to manage change in your company, we recommend that top-level management should sponsor and drive its adoption. EAM will require the refinement of many aspects of your established change and delivery organisation, even after the first benefits become visible. It may take years before all the set objectives can be met. Summarising the content of this chapter, we recommend that senior management engages in EAM initiatives and work to the following agenda:

1. Establish a top-level EAM sponsor.
2. Identify and agree on the appointment of a chief architect with your peers.
3. Put together the think-tanks from business and technology and empower them.
4. Explain the drivers and objectives of the business and IT strategy to the EAM team and key players. Contribute to and sign off the architecture principles and vision (TOM).
5. Put a time frame on the EAM set-up and consider a phased implementation.
6. Ensure that the strategic and business imperatives are being institutionalised.
7. Strike a balance between standards and versatility.
8. Define your involvement in the architectural work. This should include reviews of the architecture concepts of major change initiatives to refine or reconfirm your strategy, involvement in the prioritisation of initiatives and change programme definition.
9. Ensure that additional information is used: Challenge silo views, demand holistic perspectives and KPI-driven benefits management.

The bit at the end

Recently, when I left for lunch, I met Mike in the elevator. He introduced me to his visitor: 'This is John, our chief enterprise architect. He will join our meeting to discuss the implications of our new product partnership programme.'

References

[1] J. W. Ross, P. Weill and D. Robertson, *Enterprise Architecture as Strategy: Creating a Foundation for Business Execution.* Bosten, Massachusetts: Harvard Business School Press, 2006.

[2] H.-D. Evers, S. Gerke and T. Menkhoff, *Wissen und Entwicklung – Strategien für den Aufbau einer Wissensgesellschaft.* ZEF Policy Brief, Volume 6, 2006.

[3] N. N. Taleb, *The Black Swan: The Impact of the Highly Improbable,* 2. ed., New York: Random House, 2010.

[4] V. Baya and B. Parker, *PwC Technology Forecast Q2/2010: Managing the end-to-end process.* Delaware: PricewaterhouseCoopers LLP, 2010.

[5] M. Messerschmidt, J. Stüben and E. Stettiner, *Did your investment in ERP processes and applications pay off?* Frankfurt: PwC Whitepaper, 2008.

[6] B. W. Boehm, *Software Engineering Economics.* Englewood Cliffs, NJ: 1981.

Chapter 4

EAM governance and organisation

Glen Hobbs

Table of contents

Management summary

An effective model for enterprise architecture management (EAM) governance and organisation is vital. EA governance provides project teams with a structure to guide their decision-making, especially with regard to solutions design and technology choices that optimise the value of architecture components across the enterprise. EA organisation design establishes the effective division of roles, responsibilities and reporting relationships. We propose that the architecture resources be organised into one or more architecture bodies, depending on the level of architecture maturity and corporate structure. The architecture bodies we propose are the enterprise architecture council (EAC), the architecture review board (ARB) and the architecture forum. We discuss different organisational structures and present different decision and escalation processes and practices between which you can choose.

When you apply EA governance, you have to find the right balance. You cannot have too little control, but you also cannot be dictatorial. Too much control would impose onerous and unnecessary constraints on the organisation. The challenge is therefore to pragmatically structure the organisational components dedicated to EAM, balancing between the extremes. Once you've established the best level of control, you can define the roles, responsibilities, and the scope of the activities to maximise the business value. In general, we can distinguish four types of EAM organisation models. Centralised EAM organisations are appropriate for very centralised organisations in which most of the IT services are performed from a central unit or location. The decentralised model is appropriate for organisations that operate largely autonomous divisions, business units or territories. The centre of excellence (CoE) model, also known as the competency centre model, is gaining popularity. In this model, resources are grouped together in areas of specialisation, offered as a shared service to other organisational entities. The fourth model we discuss is the hybrid or federated model, which is a combination of the decentralised model and the centres of excellence (CoE) model.

The frame of reference that you apply when making architecture decisions is another factor that will influence your EAM governance and organisation structure. Our research has identified four distinct frames of reference or architecture archetypes. These are: the

(1) model-driven, (2) strategic applications and vendors, (3) architecture paradigm and (4) governance frames. A dependency exists between the specific architecture archetype adopted by a company and the governance and organisation structures put into place. Certain archetypes are more suitable for certain organisations in terms of size and model. The governance model should therefore support the archetype that is adopted.

There is no 'one size fits all' approach. Every organisation is unique, and while there are generalised governance and organisation models that can provide a useful starting point, they must be tailored to every company's specific needs.

4.1 Introduction and motivation

In the preceding chapter, we discussed enterprise architecture management's (EAM's) strategic value and the need for it to be addressed at the top management (CxO) level. We also stated that uncoordinated individual contributions need to evolve into dedicated efforts by a well-organised architecture practitioner team and team efforts should align with the company's organisational structure to maximise business value.

You need to avoid two unhelpful extremes when you establish EAM practices in your firm: The first is implementing minimal EAM; in other words, dabbling in EAM without a real commitment. This approach will at best produce sporadic and inconsistent results. At the other extreme, EAM organisations can become self-serving, become enamoured with their own brilliance and lose sight of their true purpose, namely to deliver business value. In this case, EAM organisations become useless ivory towers. An organisation that shall remain nameless established a large, award-winning architecture, which it documented in minute detail (the architecture diagrams alone covered four walls of a conference room from floor to ceiling!), and appeared to cover every conceivable eventuality. There was just one problem: It was so involved and complicated that no one attempting to use it had any idea where to start. The teams that did attempt to use the elaborate architecture ended up significantly over-engineering the solution, which led to major scope, time and cost overruns. This EA team was out of touch with reality. The architecture organisation was not structured to serve and support its business constituents, and no effective decision-making structures were in place. After several well-publicised project failures, with multimillion dollar consequences, the organisation eventually reorganised its EA efforts and put new leadership into place. They discarded the elaborate target architecture in favour of a much simpler and more pragmatic approach.

Studies have shown the challenge and the importance of governance in EAM:

Two unhelpful extremes

> 'One of the greatest hurdles to achieving an effective architecture discipline is designing a governance model that is both systematic and aligned with established decision-making styles. A recent Enterprise Architecture Executive Council diagnostic sur-

vey highlights the EA function's struggle with key governance activities such as EA project engagement, roadmapping and planning, and standard setting and governance.' [1]

The right governance will ensure that good decisions are made at the right time and in the right way, ensuring that EAM value is delivered and sustained over time.

Similarly, the right organisation structure is key to effective EAM execution. Having the right people, with the right skills, in the right roles doing the right things in a correctly empowered way is necessary for EAM benefits realisation.

Together, governance and organisation are the keys to maximising and sustaining EAM's value.

Therefore, the questions we will address in this chapter include the following:

- What are the roles and responsibilities that you need to define for your EAM organisation?
- Why do you need EAM governance?
- What is the right level of EAM governance for your organisation?
- Where in the organisation should the EA group be situated, and who should they report to?
- How should your EAM organisation be structured?

These questions centre around a key truth: There is no one solution that fits all firms. Each organisation is different, with different cultures, decision styles and objectives. An effective EAM governance and organisation structure must therefore be tailored to every company's unique needs.

4.2 Challenges to EAM structuring

First, we consider some of the various challenges that organisations face and must balance as they develop their EAM capabilities; these include:

- being overly controlling of activities versus rubber-stamping them,
- a centralised versus a decentralised structure,
- the common good versus project needs,
- reactive decisions versus proactive decisions, and
- a strategic view versus a tactical view.

The first challenge is the balance between **overly controlling impact and ineffectual impact** (rubber-stamping). While this challenge can occur at any EAM maturity level, a common mistake is applying too much control too early in the EAM implementation process. Another mistake is to indiscriminately apply the same governance controls to all processes within the company. For example, the controls that need to be in place for innovation and the early stages of product development may be very different to those that support operational IT environments. The objective is to implement 'just enough' governance based on the current EAM maturity level, and develop the EA governance model in line with the increasing EAM maturity level.

Implement 'just enough' governance

Deciding between **centralised and decentralised** EAM structures (or anything in between) is another consideration. This decision will largely be influenced by whether the company as a whole is centralised or decentralised, although other factors such as the specific EAM goals and objectives and the current EAM maturity level will also influence the decision. Unhelpful dynamics such as corporate politics may further complicate this decision and challenge optimal EAM structuring.

How a leading cargo carrier was challenged to balance between centralised and decentralised EAM

A leading cargo carrier in the international air traffic industry historically had a decentralised structure, with several local business units having their own IT departments. This made the business units very innovative. However, over the years, it caused an almost unmanageable complexity. The local IT units' uncoordinated developments of a central host system, for example, led to an escalation in operating costs and a growing applications landscape complexity. In order to overcome these problems, the company decided to centralise its IT developments and to modernise the application landscape. An EAM department was formed as part of this centralisation. The challenge faced by the CIO was finding a trade-off between a central and a decentralised EAM orientation, avoiding overly centralising and becoming an 'ivory tower', or decentralising the EAM to the project level and risking it becoming a 'paper tiger' driven by the project's needs.

The challenge of balancing between **the common good and project-specific objectives** is similar to the challenge of deciding how centralised or decentralised the EAM organisation should be. This is one of the more difficult challenges, because there are very real cost and time implications regarding developing solutions for the common good versus more directed project solutions. These competing priorities can also produce organisational conflict if the right EAM decision processes are not in place. The clearer the guidance and standards are for determining when a project should serve the common good, the smaller the chance of opposing motivations and politics playing a role. This matter highlights the importance of establishing effective governance and EAM decision processes.

Most EAM organisations' goal is to cover the full spectrum from **reactive** activities (for example, having architecture reviews) **to proactive** activities (for example, developing target architecture and formulating standards). The challenge, however, is to establish a good balance between these activities, based on the priorities and available resources, recognising that it is important to be pragmatic and not to overload the EAM organisation.

Over time, EAM organisations evolve towards more strategic activities

When determining a balance between **strategic and tactical** objectives, it is important to consider how far into the future the EAM organisation's planning activities are projected. EAM organisations generally start with tactical activities such as standard setting, putting guiding principles in place and having architecture reviews, and then evolve towards more strategic activities such as target state architecture blueprints and roadmap development.

4.3 Current state assessment of existing EAM activities and assets

EAM governance and organisation design are usually not conducted in a greenfield way. In other words, you probably have some form of architecture activity being performed at various levels of maturity and in different parts of the organisation. It is therefore important to conduct a current state assessment to identify these activities and assets, as they may influence your EAM governance and organisation planning activities. Your assessment should include investigating the level of formality, as the activities may be very formal or completely informal. Likewise, consider that stakeholders are already involved in the firm and that this must be factored in as part of the as-is assessment.

Similarly, before you determine the appropriate EA organisation and governance, you should gain an understanding of the proposed EAM target state, and should define the process whereby the firm will evolve towards this target as EA capabilities mature.

In summary, the current state assessment should include:

Current state assessment of EA governance and organisation

- identifying existing architecture stakeholders and architecture activities,
- assessing the current EAM maturity,
- identifying any pre-existing EAM structure and culture,
- assessing existing EA skills across the organisation,
- determining the existing corporate and IT governance models, and
- capturing any pre-existing or new target state scope of architecture.

Remember that the organisation structure and governance model are interlinked and affect each other. While we write about them sequentially, in practice they should be considered in an integrated way. Please refer to Chapter 9 for more information on how to introduce EAM in your organisation.

4.4 The EA governance model

We have stated that an effective governance model is vital for delivering on EAM's promise. EA governance provides project teams with a framework to guide their decisions, solutions design and technology choices that will optimise IT's value across the enterprise. Effective governance:

- ensures a business mandate and involvement, with the EA development driving real business value,
- fosters ongoing business-IT strategic alignment, and
- drives the adoption of standards and strategy, which lowers the total cost of ownership.

EA governance covers:

- the definition and operation of governance bodies, including the roles, responsibilities and decision rights to ensure effective EA evolution and operations,
- the establishment of guidelines, standards and references to ensure that the right things are done at the right time, and
- integration within project life cycles and other organisational processes and entities to ensure timely and effective decision-making (we discuss this in Chapters 5 to 7).

We will consider each of these in turn.

Governance bodies, roles, responsibilities and decision rights

Many different types of architecture governance bodies have been proposed and described in the literature. Every organisation has specific unique requirements, but most governance structures generally include entities that set direction and standards (setting), and entities that ensure adherence to these standards and direction (vetting). Both the setting and vetting entities could be further segmented, based on the enterprise structure (centralised versus decentralised), geographic locations or architecture domains (particular architecture focus areas).

Figure 4.1 shows typical architecture governance bodies and their relationships to IT, business units and project teams, as well as participation and escalation paths.

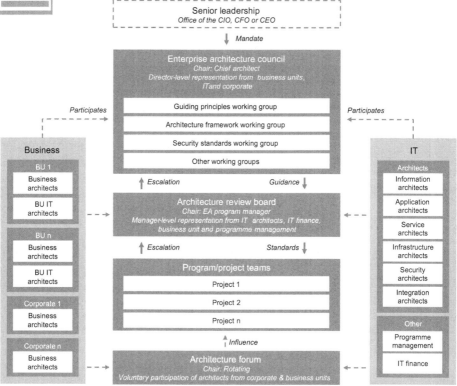

Figure 4.1: Architecture governance model

The principle architecture bodies

In this generalised architecture governance model, the key architecture bodies are the *enterprise architecture council* (EAC), the *architecture review board* (ARB) and, possibly, the *architecture forum*. The intent is *not* that all these entities are required in every situation. The specific EAM goals and objectives, the EAM maturity level and the organisational structure (centralised or decentralised) will determine which architecture body or combination of bodies will be most appropriate at a given point in time.

The ARB provides the point of contact for project teams to ensure compliance with architecture standards and direction. The EAC is responsible for setting best practices, guiding principles, standards, reference architectures and other architecture guardrails, and may utilise working groups in the development and maintenance of these. The architecture forum provides an option for a less formal structure that can facilitate collaboration between interested parties where more formal structures are not practical or desirable.

The EAC and ARB consist of representatives from business and IT. The EAC is usually overseen by the chief information officer (CIO), although chief financial officer (CFO) or chief executive officer (CEO) oversight is found in some more mature organisations.

Figure 4.1 represents a typically centralised organisation. In a decentralised organisation, the above may be replicated by a division, territory, or business unit. In a hybrid or federated model, some elements can be centralised (such as a single EAC) and other elements can be distributed (such as multiple ARBs). Note that at the early EAM stages, it is possible to combine the ARB and EAC into one organisation, or to simply begin with an architecture forum. We next present more detailed descriptions.

Enterprise architecture council (EAC)

The EAC, which is sometimes called the *enterprise architecture steering committee*, typically serves as the principal oversight body for enterprise architecture. The EAC therefore busies itself with the implementation and governance of EAM within the enterprise. Furthermore, the EAC ensures coordination and collaboration of architecture initiatives in the organisation.

Responsibilities

Typical EAC responsibilities are to:

- set and manage expectations regarding EAM's business value for the organisation,
- establish the overall EAM scope within the organisation,
- be accountable for the EA programme's overall effectiveness,
- define and evolve the EAM organisational and governance structures,
- ensure business alignment,
- coordinate with other entities in the organisation,
- participate actively in business strategy sessions and planning,
- establish, monitor and report on EA metrics,
- oversee the ARB,
- manage escalations from and provide guidance to the ARB,
- set strategic technology direction for the organisation,
- establish the architecture guiding principles, policies and standards,

- establish working groups, if necessary, and
- approve or deny major project exception requests, and issue waivers for legitimate exceptions.

Participants

EAC members include empowered business and technology stakeholders. The EAC's chair is the organisation's chief architect, who is usually connected to the CIO's office. The following applies to EAC participants:

- The EAC usually has 5 to 10 participants (depending on the enterprise size and heterogeneity of the business).
- The EAC includes director-level participants from business and IT.
- The participants should represent the EA layers of the strategy, process, and information system (including the application data and integration unit(s)), as well as the technology/infrastructure layers (see Chapter 1).

Architecture review board (ARB)

The ARB ensures and extends IT's business value by assessing compliance with architecture standards, guiding principles, reference architectures and blueprints. The board resolves non-compliance issues to reduce deployment risk and to ensure constant evolution towards the intended target state.

Responsibilities

Typical ARB responsibilities are to:

- enforce standards,
- provide architecture guidance to project teams,
- review and approve or reject project teams' architecture recommendations,
- identify gaps and dependencies,
- review project scope change requests that have architecture implications,
- adjudicate architecture-related conflicts, if necessary,
- issue waivers when warranted, and
- forward any irresolvable issues related to the enterprise architecture process to the enterprise architecture council for adjudication.

Participants

The following applies to ARB participants:

- The ARB usually has 5 to 12 permanent members, with additional invitees on an ad hoc basis.
- The ARB includes architects and manager-level resources from IT and business.
- The ARB usually includes representatives from:
  - line-of-business,
  - process architecture,
  - information architecture,
  - application or service architecture,
  - infrastructure architecture,
  - IT operations,
  - IT finance, and
  - programme management.

Architecture forum

Sometimes, collaboration is needed between independent organisations, each of which has dedicated architecture resources but no formal reporting lines to a central architecture organisation. In this case, an architecture forum is a useful option. An architecture forum is constituted when the different architecture organisations within business units or territories voluntarily unite and collaborate on topics of mutual interest, such as architecture standards or technology standardisation. An architecture forum helps to drive collaboration. The forum can perform many of the EAC's functions, but is based on voluntary commitment rather than formal responsibility and accountability. An additional benefit is the opportunity for knowledge sharing between groups. The chair of the architecture forum rotates periodically (usually annually) between the participating business units. As with the EAC, various working groups may be constituted to focus on specific topics of mutual interest.

A second scenario where the architecture forum may be appropriate is in companies at an early stage of architecture maturity. As mentioned earlier, it is important to be pragmatic and not apply an architecture enforcement level that exceeds the current EAM maturity level. An architecture forum may therefore be appropriate when the company is just starting out with EAM.

Finally, an architecture forum may be the right structure where EAM is applied to a part of the organisation that is primarily innovation focused. In this case, the emphasis should be more on collaboration and the cross-pollination of ideas, and less on constraining decisions. The architecture forum is well suited to this.

The importance of
exception handling

Decision processes and rights

Clearly articulating decision rights is vital to EAM effectiveness. Many different architecture models can exist, but unless decision rights are expressly and unambiguously defined and clearly communicated, EAM is unlikely to deliver the intended value. The effectiveness of decision rights is largely determined by the handling of exception cases – those situations in which different viewpoints, conflicting motivations, and budget or resource constraints exist. Therefore, in considering decision rights, it is vital to establish the exception, waiver and escalation processes. Furthermore, senior leadership must empower and support the decision processes and rights, and leaders must never abuse their authority by overriding decisions outside the established processes.

Decision protocols

Decision protocols must provide a framework for representation and voting rights, participation, decision thresholds, the appeal process and escalation frequency. While many decision protocol permutations can exist, we present two options and highlight their benefits.

Majority decision
If the decision protocol is a majority decision, the following applies:

- Group decisions can be reached if a quorum (such as 65%) of voting members is present.
- Decisions will be binding, irrespective of attendance (assuming a quorum).
- Representatives of business units must be empowered to vote. Delegation of attendance is discouraged; nevertheless, delegated representatives must have the authority to vote.
- A majority decision carries.
- Close decisions (40% to 60%) can be appealed to a higher authority (e.g., the EAC).
- A ranking process should be followed for decisions that relate to the ranking of multiple options (such as project portfolio prioritisation).
- All decisions should be documented and communicated to the core and extended stakeholders.
- For meeting management protocols, see *Robert's Rules of Order* [2].

Variations regarding the quorum number, decision threshold and appeal range can be adjusted to suit the organisation's needs. This option is the most democratic and is suitable when there is a large number of voting members (10 to 15).

Consensus decision

If the decision protocol is consensus decision, the following applies:

- Voting members can abstain (if they have no strong point of view, or if the outcome is immaterial to them). However, every voting member must agree with the decision before it can be approved. If a member does not agree, the decision will not be taken; every member essentially has a veto right.
- The delegation of voting responsibility is not permitted, but voting members can vote ahead of time if they are unable to attend in person.
- Decisions can be appealed to the next higher authority (e.g., the EAC) if a working group is unable to resolve the issue.
- A ranking process should be followed for decisions that relate to the ranking of multiple options (such as project portfolio prioritisation).
- All decisions should be documented and communicated to the core and extended stakeholders.
- For meeting management protocols, see *Robert's Rules of Order* [2].

This option suits a smaller group of voting members (4 to 6). It can easily generate escalations, which are usually cumbersome, but in certain organisations this may actually be desirable, as escalations provide senior leadership with insights into the more significant and contentious EAM decisions.

Exception or escalation process

An exception mechanism supports a business unit's need for responsiveness without threatening the governance process's integrity.

Exceptions may be required in the following circumstances:

- when a swift response is needed to an urgent business opportunity,
- when invalid or obsolete policies, processes, or standards are identified,
- when local project needs are unique, and
- when there are legitimate cost factors.

Exceptions should also be leveraged as an opportunity to formalise organisational learning, including:

- identifying business unit pain-points, and
- identifying existing policies, processes and standards that have become obsolete.

Exceptions, especially for cost reasons, should be strongly discouraged. An exception of this nature usually signals a lack of financial planning for, and commitment to, the target architecture and EAM in general. The organisation should expect an initial cost premium to align with the target architecture. This expectation should be communicated and planned for at the outset.

Exceptions may originate at any of the checkpoints (sometimes called stage gates; see Chapter 6 for more details). Exceptions may also result from situations that require standard processes, policies, or procedures to be circumvented. Exceptions need to be dealt with promptly; failure to do so will result in pent-up frustration and therefore might facilitate maverick activity. To avoid frivolous exception requests, exceptions need to be well motivated. A motivation should include the business impact of not following the prescribed policies and procedures. In the case of an exception, the governance team decisions should be documented. If necessary, the matter should be escalated on the basis of the decision protocols.

If an exception occurs, the organisation should review its policies or procedures to eliminate future occurrences of this exception. However, the organisation should ensure that the additional policies and procedures don't burden the process without adding significant value. If an exception only occurs once and is unlikely to occur again in the near future, a new policy should not be created.

With regard to the governance model (illustrated in Figure 4.1), some organisations deliberately fine-tune their decision protocols so that a certain percentage of decisions are escalated. For example, they might expect 20% of first-level (i.e. ARB) decisions to be escalated to the second level (i.e. EAC), and 5% of second-level decisions to be escalated to the third level (senior leadership). This escalation ensures a desirable level of senior leadership engagement and visibility. If the percentage of escalations is too high, it implies insufficient empowerment, while too low a level may suggest senior leadership abdication, which would have negative long-term implications for EAM. Therefore, firms should track and number the escalations by establishing and tracking an exception metric.

Guidelines, standards and reference architectures

Guidelines, standards and reference architectures act as guardrails that provide project teams with parameters within which to operate. The teams need to know how much flexibility they have and where the limits are. One key to effective governance is balancing flexibility with control, because too much constraint will lead to excessive red tape. On the one hand, if there already is a lot of red tape, firms might consider EAM a bottleneck and project teams might try to find ways to work around the system to get the job done. On the other hand, if there is too little direction and constraint, the potential EAM benefits will not be realised. Therefore, the right balance between flexibility and control must be established. Desired objectives can be achieved by putting pragmatic limits in place, providing some guidance and applying just the right level of constraint.

Guidelines, guiding principles and best practices *influence* project teams and, depending on the context, are usually subject to interpretation and applicability. Standards are generally more universal. Standards are normally enforced, thus providing *control*. A recommended approach is not to create a new standard for every issue that arises, but to identify the top 3 to 5 issues at any one time through periodic assessments and run-time metrics, and to focus on these. For example, if it is evident that data quality is the cause of most of the production problems, the EAM organisation should focus its energies on resolving this issue through new data standards and data quality guidelines before tackling the next biggest challenge. By focusing on the most important issues only, the guardrails can slowly be constrained over time (see Chapter 6). The architecture review board has the authority to issue a waiver with regard to a particular standard. When this occurs, it is important to track the consequences of such non-compliance over time.

Reference architectures are *generalised* models. They encapsulate corporate, vendor, or industry best practices in a model that can act as a starting point. The model can then be copied and adapted to suit the firm's specific needs. A target state architecture draws from these reference architectures, standards and guiding principles. The target state architecture produces a *specific* representation of the desired end state for a particular organisation. These target state architectures can be produced at various levels of abstraction, and are very powerful decision-making tools (see Chapters 5 and 8).

4.5 EAM organisation models

The initial EA objectives will influence the EAM organisation model, as well as the corresponding lines of reporting. As most EAM organisations started with IT architecture rather than business architecture activities, it is most common to find EAM groups established within the CIO organisation. Even for those more mature EAM groups that are organised and driven from a business architecture perspective, 88% still report to the CIO, and only 12% to the CEO [5]. However, those EAM organisations that do report to the CEO have demonstrated significantly higher levels of business alignment, maturity and organisational acceptance.

Alternative EAM reporting lines

How a global reinsurer improved business alignment and organisational acceptance of EAM

A globally operating reinsurer had a turnover of 45 billion EUR in 2010. The company implemented EAM successfully as an IT-led initiative. The value delivered warranted making EAM an organisation-wide initiative. In early 2008, the company founded the Global Business Architecture department. The department's primary objective was to achieve business-IT alignment. Today, the Global Business Architecture (GBA) department is a main driver and decision-maker in the project portfolio and project management process. Together with the global process owners, it is responsible for developing global standards. The GBA department reports to the CEO. A business architect notes:

'We have a major advantage when it comes to business-IT alignment compared to other companies, since we are organisationally not attached to IT or to the CIO. We belong to the CEO and have a mandate from the Strategy Committee [the highest organisational board at holding level], which means a group mandate ... This implies that we have access to the business and to the strategy, and this gives us an extraordinary position.'

Corporate structures can be autonomous business units, very centralised organisations, or anything in between. The existence and location of architecture roles in the corporate structure depends on several factors, including:

- the current EAM state and scope,
- EAM maturity,
- the governance model, and
- the size of the organisation.

If the organisation is small and the EAM is less mature, some of the responsibilities may be consolidated in one role. For example, one individual might be responsible for both the business and domain architecture. It is advisable to outline the path from the as-is state to the target state. This can be done by describing the target model, taking into account all the architecture services and resources identified (the target state), and then describing a scaled-back version that includes the milestones on the path towards the target state.

Centralised organisation model

The diagram in Figure 4.2 provides an example of a largely centralised architecture organisation.

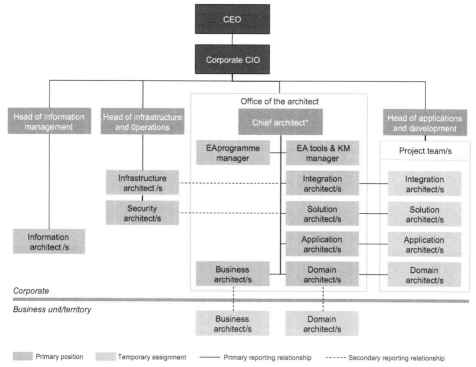

Figure 4.2: Centralised EAM organisation model

This model is appropriate for very centralised organisations in which most IT services are performed from a central location. In this model, an 'office of the architect' is established. This office performs the majority of the architecture services, providing strategy, planning, blueprinting, standards, governance and development support. The majority of the architecture resources have a direct reporting relationship to a chief architect. Certain architecture roles, such as infrastructure, security and information, may play a more fixed organisational role, while business, application and solution architects might have a more temporary project role.

Decentralised organisation model

The decentralised model is appropriate for organisations that operate largely autonomous divisions, business units, or territories. The diagram in Figure 4.3 is an example of architecture resources in a decentralised model.

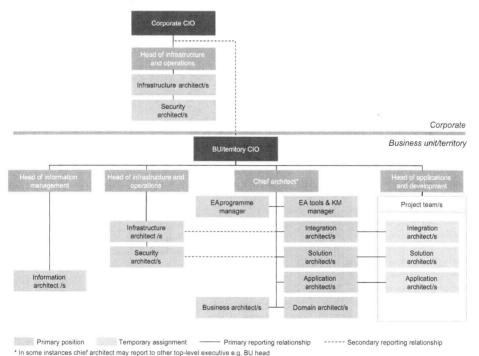

Figure 4.3: Decentralised EAM organisation model

In the decentralised model, the majority of the architecture resources exist within the various organisational entities (divisions, business units, or territories). Each entity operates largely autonomously, and maintains separate architecture resources. The extent and maturity of the entities' architecture capabilities may vary significantly. For example, a large division may have almost all of the architecture resources depicted in Figure 4.3, while a smaller division may just have a few solution and application architects.

In this model, a limited set of architects could still exist at the corporate or global level for a small sub-set of common capabilities, most notably security, email, some infrastructure services and offer support to central units like corporate finance, tax, legal and reporting. In this case, there might be some duplication of roles.

Centres of excellence model

Some firms establish *centres of excellence* (CoEs), also known as competency centres. This approach is gaining popularity. In this model, resources are grouped together in are as of specialisation, which is offered to other organisational entities as a shared service. The diagram in Figure 4.4 represents such a model.

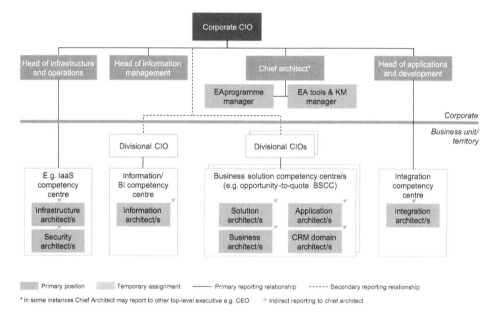

Figure 4.4: Centres of excellence (CoE) model

Common competency centres include:

- **Business intelligence (BI) competency centres.** Responsible for providing common services in business intelligence, reporting and analytics.
- **Infrastructure competency centres.** Multiple competency centres may exist that cover computing hardware, storage, networking and email. An example could be an *infrastructure-as-a-service* (IaaS) *competency centre*, possibly at the corporate level, as depicted in Figure 4.4.
- **Business solution competency centres (BSCCs).** BSCCs are responsible for the end-to-end functional business process design and business process implementation. A BSCC typically focuses on one or more business domains. The BSCC enables the development of the related end-to-end business process vision, skills, mindset and shared knowledge [3]. An example is an *opportunity-to-quote competency centre* that a business unit has developed and matured, and that provides guidance and services to other business units.
- **Integration competency centres (ICC).** An ICC provides a shared service to address one or more integration 'realms', including meta-data, as well as data-information, applications-services, process and portal-user interface integration.

Responsibilities for different competency centres may be distributed between divisions, territories, or business units. When business units specialise in certain areas and offer that expertise to other units, this has the potential to mature the organisation more efficiently and quickly. Consequently, the architecture responsibilities are divided among the various competency centres, thus allowing greater focus, depth and maturity. Each division is responsible for driving architecture standards and guidance, as well as offering services in its specialty area to other units. Each competency centre may have its own ARB, although a single centralised EAC chaired by the chief architect is recommended. Similarly, architects have their primary reporting relationship to the division or unit hosting the competency centre, with an indirect reporting relationship to the chief architect.

If it is probable that the corporate strategy may entail divestments, the CoE model may not be a good structure to adopt, as key architecture capabilities may be lacking in the business unit to be divested or, conversely, key architecture capabilities required by other parts of the business may be contained within the business unit to be divested.

Hybrid or federated model

Hybrid or federated models are a combination of decentralised models and centres of excellence models. Some functions are centralised or shared by organisational units, and some architecture functions exist exclusively for the benefit of specific units. In fact, it is common for top-performing global organisations to have governance models that deliberately blend centralised and decentralised IT decision-making in order to benefit from the best features of each. According to Weill and Ross, *'Top performing firms balancing multiple performance goals had governance models that blended centralised and decentralised decision making. All top performers' governance had one aspect in common. Their governance made transparent the tensions around IT decisions such as standardisation versus innovation.'* [4]

4.6 Architecture archetypes

As we conclude this chapter, there is one more consideration to address that may influence the selection and implementation of your EAM organisation and governance models. From our interviews, we have identified four distinct frames of reference that shape the architecture decisions made by businesses. We have termed these the EAM archetypes. Table 4.1 below shows the characteristics of each of these archetypes. We assume that businesses use an EA archetype that naturally aligns with the business and EA context, rather than making a conscious decision. However, the set-up has significant implications for achievable benefits and EA operations.

There is a correlation between the architecture archetype that an organisation adopts and the governance and organisation structures that it puts in place. Certain archetypes are suitable for certain organisation sizes and models, and the governance model must support the adopted archetype. *EAM organisation and archetype*

- The **model-driven** archetype is most conducive to smaller organisational units (smaller centralised companies, or decentralised business units or CoEs) in which the size and complexity of the EA models are manageable. As the organisation becomes larger (or, more specifically, the architecture's complexity increases), the effort to maintain a central EA model will require increasingly more resources, and a point of diminishing returns may be reached. A key to maintaining the model-driven archetype is to include governance steps that formalise and enforce a model update as changes are made. An organisation might demand that the update takes place before EA signoff at the final project stage and when operational changes are made (see Chapters 6 and 7).
- The **strategic applications and vendors** archetype can apply to any organisation model or size that is largely dependent on a specific strategic application and vendor (e.g., a major ERP system). However, this would be more typical of smaller centralised organisations, as larger or decentralised organisations would be more likely to operate a multitude of interconnected systems. Furthermore, industry trends towards more compartmentalised approaches and the rise of software-as-a-service (SaaS) is decreasing the prevalence of this archetype. For organisations that plan to move away from the strategic applications and vendors archetype, a recom-

Table 4.1: EAM archetypes

EAM archetype	Model-driven	Strategic applications and vendors	Architecture paradigm	Governance
EA development approach	Model the as-is state and target architectures, followed by solution selection and implementation	Mostly determined by the architecture of the chosen focal information system	Concentrate on an architecture paradigm	Establish a clear governance structure and an enterprise portfolio of target patterns
Example	Use an EA modelling tool to create a complete model of the as-is state and target architectures. Use these models for EA communication, planning, and development	Support the majority of business processes with SAP and allow the use of other applications only by exception	Decide to follow the SOA paradigm and transform the EA into an SOA; whenever change is requested and accepted, implement it using SOA pattern	Local decision-makers follow centrally defined governance rules and architecture patterns; objectives and borders are common, but implementation decisions are made locally
EAM is facilitated by	Models and frameworks	Single IS vendor / single product strategy	The architecture paradigm	Governance rules and processes, and a well-defined enterprise continuum
Architecture characteristics	Low or medium EA complexity, variety of IS and business processes	Low or medium EA complexity, a central IS that covers most of the core business processes and dominates the IS landscape	Medium or high EA complexity, large number of systems with numerous interfaces, often legacy applications	High or very high EA complexity, complex and decentralised organisational structure, complex political situation
Advantages	Supports logical derivation of strategic investment roadmap	Reduced or outsourced complexity	Makes 'best fit' functionality available	Supports decentralised management style and highest architecture complexity
Disadvantages	Requires significant in-house architecture skills and efforts	High dependency on one IS vendor and its strategy	Complex integration layer development and operations	Managed, but still complex overall EA

mended approach is to begin to incrementally decouple the strategic system by using service-oriented and middleware technologies, to the point where the strategic system is a collection of services orchestrated in a best-of-breed fashion with other systems (see the following description of the architecture paradigm archetype). Governance mechanisms that support the strategic applications and vendors archetype may include the publication of reference architectures and the more formalised involvement of key vendors or subject matter specialists supporting the application.

- The **architecture paradigm** archetype can apply to any organisation model or size, but it is particularly useful for larger organisations with a large number of interconnected systems. For example, *service-oriented architecture* (SOA) and *cloud computing* are two architecture paradigms that are gaining popularity in large and small organisations. From a governance perspective, the chosen architecture paradigm would typically be codified in the form of guiding principles, standards, or reference architectures. Conformance is vetted by the instituted governance bodies such as the architecture review board.
- The **governance** archetype is usually adopted by large organisations with many architecture stakeholders. In this type of organisation, a structured approach is necessary to produce alignment, ensure conformance and deliver the intended business value. While these organisations may embrace aspects of other archetypes, such as architecture paradigms, the dominant contributor of business value is a robust and mature architecture governance process.

In conclusion, there is no 'one-size-fits-all' governance and organisational model. Every organisation is unique, and while there are generalised governance, organisation, and architecture archetypes and models that can provide useful starting points, these must be tailored to a company's specific needs.

References

[1] Enterprise Architecture Executive Council, *"EA Governance Models: Guiding IT Investment and Project Decisions for Business Impact,"* Corporate Executive Board, 2008.

[2] H. Robert, *Robert's rules of order, newly revised, in brief,* 1st ed. Cambridge Mass: Da Capo Press, 2004.

[3] TIBCO Software Inc, *"TIBCO Service-Oriented IT Organizational Structure Best Practices: An Introduction,"* http://www.tibco.com/multimedia/wp-tibco-service-oriented-it-organizational-structure-best-practices-an-introduction_tcm8-2424.pdf, [Accessed on 19.06.2011]

[4] P. Weill, *IT governance: "how top performers manage IT decision rights for superior results,"* Boston: Harvard Business School Press, 2004.

[5] Enterprise Architecture Executive Council, *"State of the EA Function – EA Priorities, Activities, Metrics, and Organizational Models,"* Corporate Executive Board, 2005.

Chapter 5

Embedding EAM
into strategic planning

Frank Radeke, Christine Legner

Table of contents

Management summary

Aligning enterprise architecture management (EAM) with the existing management practices guiding a company's strategic and organisational development is a key challenge. Our study reveals that organisations struggle to realise EA's defined objectives and principles if EAM is a stand-alone activity and not linked to existing strategy processes.

In this chapter, we discuss how EAM practices enhance strategy formulation, planning, and evaluation: As a starting point, the documented as-is architecture provides input for discussing different stakeholders' viewpoints and analysing the organisation's existing capabilities. During strategy formulation, EAM techniques assist managers with explicating and refining strategic directions in the form of target architectures. Finally, the documented as-is and target architectures help managers to identify migration plans and resolve interdependencies, which are often overseen without EAM. EAM practices thus ensure that, given the firm's capabilities and limitations, the chosen strategies are feasible.

We conclude that EAM has two important roles in the strategy cycle: Firstly, it supports planning, formulating and coordinating strategic initiatives by means of EA documentation and EAM methods. Secondly, EAM initiates dedicated architecture initiatives that improve the architecture's overall quality and prepare it to support existing and future business requirements.

5.1 Approaching EAM from a strategic perspective

EAM's role in guiding organisational development

Changes in the business environment force organisations to continuously reposition themselves in the market. Repositioning is accompanied by the reorganisation of internal structures, which are often complex and difficult to change. These shifts require the firm to improve its ability to plan and implement change. As a management philosophy, EAM enhances an organisation's ability to sense, analyse and respond more effectively to change by:

- *Aligning the organisation with the strategic goals.* EAM can help management to assess whether business and IT programmes, as well as other initiatives, fit in with the strategic goals. It thus focuses investments and resources on those initiatives that generate significant business performance improvements, instead of wasting them on projects that might have questionable, or even contrary, effects on the strategic goals.
- *Coordinating the interdependencies and different change cycles in business and IT.* EAM assists with synchronising business and IT strategies. Entering a new market, for example, might require redesigning CRM processes to closely interact with the sales agents and customers. This might ultimately generate the need for an additional online sales platform. Although time-to-market is a key goal in this situation, different change cycles might not be compatible. While the market entry strategy will be developed and rolled out to the sales organisation over several months, it might take one or two years to migrate to a new sales platform. EAM can help management to coordinate the implementation of the business and IT changes by outlining a migration roadmap.
- *Preparing the organisation for agility.* Silo applications, redundant and inconsistent data repositories, as well as heterogeneous technical infrastructure components hinder companies from responding to change effectively. EAM allows companies to regain their fundamental structure's transparency; this is a prerequisite to launch dedicated architecture initiatives to overcome overly complex and rigid structures. The architecture's standardi-

sation and modularisation enable swift responses to changing business environments.

EAM's holistic perspective enables organisations to strengthen their strategic competence: Firstly, as-is architecture's documentation and analysis provide firms with a clearer picture of their current state and their corporate assets. Secondly, EAM teases out the desired target state's formulation by explicitly specifying and documenting the target architecture. Finally, EAM guides the purposeful transition to this target state, which involves formulating roadmaps and implementing *strategic business, IT,* and *architecture initiatives*, as well as aligning the *emergent initiatives and operational demands* with the strategic directions (see Figure 5.1).

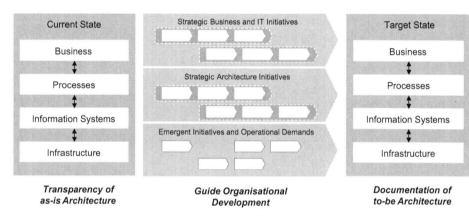

Figure 5.1: EAM's role in guiding organisational development

Strategic initiatives implement far-reaching changes and are a cornerstone of organisational development. They are '[...] collections of finite-duration discretionary projects and programs, outside the organisation's day-to-day operational activities that are designed to help the organisation achieve its targeted performance' ([1], p. 103), Since they shape the firm's development, EA considerations should complement business or IT units' evaluation of strategic initiatives. Owing to the differing objectives, scope, and EAM's role in their initiation, we distinguish between two types of strategic initiatives:

EA practices should support evaluating, planning and implementing strategic business and IT initiatives

Business and IT initiatives are launched as a result of corporate, functional, or regional strategy processes. Business initiatives comprise changes to the business model and product portfolio, customer relationships, channels, operational processes and organisational structures. IT initiatives imply implementing information systems and infrastructure, their migration and operations. For example, a firm might implement a new ERP system and decide to outsource major parts of the IT function. Since senior managers at corporate, functional, or regional level primarily drive business and IT initiatives, EAM mainly has a supportive role: Firstly, EAM practices, such as EA documentation and additional analysis techniques, can improve the set-up of the initiative and its implementation. Secondly, EAM provides the transparency required to coordinate and actively manage the changes induced by parallel strategic initiatives.

The EAM function can also launch dedicated *architecture initiatives* (e.g., process harmonisation and architecture modularisation). These initiatives are specifically promoted by the enterprise architecture council or EAC (see Chapter 4), which oversees the organisation's EA activities, to create synergies and prepare the architecture for the future. Architecture initiatives are also needed if fundamental problems hinder the business and IT initiatives' effective implementation, and if these problems cannot be solved within their scope. For example, a monolithic legacy systems running on an outdated technology platform might evolve into a hindering factor when new business requirements, such as the increased use of electronic channels, are implemented. In this case, an architecture initiative can address the stepwise migration from wrapping the existing functionality as services to more modular applications that are more responsive to change. While the EAM function acts as the main driver of these initiatives, it works closely with those responsible on the business and IT sides (including the functional management, as well as the business process and application owners).

Dedicated architecture initiatives address EA|s structural problems and prepare the organisation for the future

Besides these two types of strategically planned initiatives, companies are confronted with a large number of short-term operational requirements and unforeseen incidents. As outlined in Chapter 7, these emerge bottom-up, and induce urgent and mostly unanticipated EA changes. EAM is only successful in guiding the transition to the target architecture if it establishes pragmatic guidelines for managing *emergent initiatives and operational requirements* with the defined architecture principles and the target EA. Table 5.1 summarises each of these initiatives' characteristics and EAM's role.

Table 5.1: EAM's role in different types of initiatives

	Strategic business and IT initiatives	Strategic architecture initiatives	Emergent initiatives driven by operational demands
Goal	Implement corporate, functional, or regional strategies	Improve the overall EA quality and maturity	Implement short-term change requirements and operational demands
Initiator	Senior management	EAM function	Operational units
EAM's role	Supportive: contribute to strategic EA development	Active: drive strategic EA development	Reactive: ensure EA compliance
EAM's tasks	• Support formulation and planning of the strategic initiative by means of target architectures and roadmaps • Coordinate and actively manage the changes induced by the different strategic initiatives	• Kick-start the initiative • Formulate, plan, implement and evaluate the initiative	• Ensure that short-term changes and demands comply with the architecture principles and support their alignment with the strategic directions (see Chapter 7)

Anchoring EAM in the strategy cycle

To realise EA objectives and principles, EAM practices need to be embedded in existing strategy processes

If EAM is a stand-alone activity without any links to existing strategy processes, the organisation will struggle to realise EAM's defined objectives and principles. This implies that EAM practices need to be carefully embedded in the strategy processes, instead of launching parallel activities. We build on the idea that strategic management is an ongoing process comprising four phases: strategy formulation, strategy planning, strategy implementation, and strategy evaluation [2-4]. EAM practices and techniques add to the strategy cycle's different phases. Figure 5.2 depicts the EAM-enhanced strategy process (upper left cycle) and its interrelationships with the project life cycle (Chapter 6), as well as operations and monitoring (Chapter 7).

During *strategy formulation*, companies elaborate and evaluate different strategic alternatives. They usually start by analysing the as-is state and assessing the firm's internal strength and weaknesses, as well as external threats and opportunities. EAM helps the firm to perform the following strategy formulation tasks:

(1) Analysing the situation. EA documentation and analysis help to capture and assess an organisation's current situation. On the basis of a structured and comprehensive EA model, EAM complements traditional strategy tools by adding multiple perspectives of the organisation's existing capabilities.

(2) Elaborating on strategic options

    (2a) Accessing strategic business and IT options. EAM helps to assess the firm's strategic options on the basis of their potential implications for the processes, structures, people, applications and technology. EAM thereby supports the selection of initiatives that are aligned with the organisation's capabilities and potentials.

    (2b) Formulation of strategic architecture initiatives. In addition, EAM can develop strategic options to address structural architecture issues, such as complexity, and to prepare the organisation for future requirements.

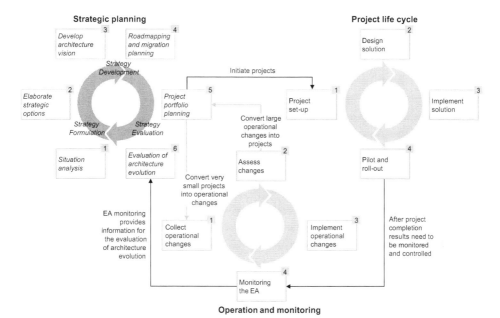

Figure 5.2: EAM process cycles

Strategy planning translates the chosen strategic option into tactical plans by deriving and aligning corresponding strategic initiatives. EAM supports this phase by:

(3) Developing an architecture vision. By developing and documenting target architectures, EAM provides a much clearer and more detailed picture of strategic initiatives' implications and consequences. This explication of the architecture visions eases communication and the further refinement of strategy plans in the subsequent planning steps.

(4) Roadmapping and planning migration. While the target architecture is valuable, roadmaps translate the architecture vision into feasible tactical plans. EAM ensures that roadmaps reflect the relevant constraints and interdependencies at different architecture layers. Roadmaps are an important input for future project teams working on different aspects and highly dependent on one another.

(5) Assessing and prioritising the project portfolio. Strategic initiatives are implemented in projects and programmes. EAM helps the firm to structure its project portfolio by resolving conflicts, promoting the projects that have the highest strategic contribution and revealing the synergy potentials between projects.

Strategy implementation covers the realisation of associated project programmes and projects. We discuss EAM's assistance during the implementation of programmes and projects in detail in Chapter 6 of this book.

Strategy evaluation comprises the monitoring and evaluation of strategic goal achievement. EAM assists in this phase by:

(6) Evaluating the architecture evolution. EAM supports the evaluation of whether the enterprise architecture is developing in line with the architecture vision and the architecture roadmaps. In Chapter 7, we cover additional aspects related to EA monitoring by means of KPIs.

In the following section, we illustrate the strategy formulation and planning phases in detail and highlight the changes that EAM brings about in the different phases. Case examples illustrate EAM's successful integration into the strategy cycle.

5.2 Leveraging EAM for strategic planning

(1) Analysing the situation: Achieving transparency concerning the as-is state

Strategy processes depend on a reliable information basis. Especially in strategy formulation's early phases, managers are mostly concerned with situation analysis, i.e. 'identifying the position of the firm in respect of the business environment it operates in and how its resources and capabilities meet the demands of that business environment. Such analysis forms part of the background to which strategic decisions are made and provides insight into the difficulties of implementing strategic change' ([5], p. 19). A well-documented as-is architecture, or baseline architecture, allows a quick overview of a firm's strategy, processes, organisation, information systems and technology infrastructure. It assists with the situation analysis phase by offering insight into cross-domain architecture relationships, generally through projections and intersections of underlying models, but also by means of analytical techniques.

EA documentation complements the traditional information basis for strategic decision-making

The challenge for enterprise architects is to create EA documentation and reports that can swiftly provide decision-makers with crucial information. Successful EA modelling and documentation require stakeholders and experts' intense involvement, not only to define the relevant architecture models, but to choose the appropriate analytical techniques and easy-to-understand depictions. For example, landscape maps are a practical way to generate overview tables for managers, as well as process and system owners. By interviewing stakeholders about their EA concerns and views, enterprise architects are more likely to determine the right scope, define an appropriate purpose that a view must serve, and the content it should display.

Documenting the EA is not an end in itself. Since documentation requires many resources, one should avoid getting lost in a never-ending effort. The case analysis reveals that architects choose a sequential approach when creating the initial EA documentation. Depending on the sponsors' concerns, architects often start by documenting selected architecture layers, such as the application landscape or the business processes. Starting with this documentation, they add related components from associated layers to demonstrate the interdependencies, such as the business processes supported by the documented applications, or the technical infrastructure underly-

EA documentation should be created step by step

Involve stakeholders and experts in creating EA documentation

ing the application landscape. The level of detail is initially kept to a minimum, with a focus on the understanding of key EA components and their relationships, as well as on defining weak spots. The level of detail increases as an EA initiative matures.

Since EA know-how is distributed across the organisation, the as-is documentation is obtained from workshops or interviews that involve architects, decision-makers and the persons responsible for the EA components. The latter could include functional managers, process managers, application owners, or those responsible for the technology infrastructure. To keep documentation and maintenance efforts at a reasonable level, one should reuse as much of the information already captured for the key EA components as possible. Over the past decade, companies have created comprehensive process or application documentation, and they can therefore start by linking this documentation to or integrating it into the EA repository. However, one should ensure that the overall EA documentation is well-structured and that EA components are linked intelligently to the adjacent EA components. This endeavour requires a well-defined meta-model as a foundation for the EA repository.

Once the main aspects of the as-is state have been captured, organisations must ensure that this documentation remains up to date. The presentation of EA documentation and analysis in planning and operational meetings is a key instrument to ensure their periodic update. Other instruments that are suitable for this task are dedicated EA documentation reviews, as well as the project closure, which compels projects to maintain EA documentation (see Chapter 6).

EA documentation at a leading cargo carrier

An international cargo carrier swiftly achieved a comprehensive picture of its current EA by focussing on the most important EA components for defining the future IT strategy right from the outset. The documentation of the application landscape comprised the 60 to 70 core applications that are the carrier's responsibility. The architects subsequently added descriptions of the application interfaces and services. The applications were then assigned to seven primary domains and 25 sub-domains derived from the carrier's core business processes. Regarding the business processes, the architects could rely on the business units' business process documentations and reuse them. Governance mechanisms ensure that project members, in cooperation with architects, incorporate all the changes made while projects are underway into the EA documentation.

A business architect assesses the central overview gained through the EA documentation:

'EAM provides overall knowledge of the organisation's business regarding how the business really functions and how everything interrelates. This knowledge is rarely found in the business units or in the projects, but resides within the EA, and constantly increases.'

Management recommendations

As a basis for a company's situation analysis, gaining EA transparency requires:

- Carefully setting the architecture documentation *scope* in order to address the main stakeholders' concerns and to keep the documentation and maintenance efforts reasonable. Successful firms have chosen sequential approaches, starting at a specific EA layer and focussing on the core architecture components at the outset.
- A strong *functional management involvement* increases awareness and acceptance of modelling activities. This involvement ensures not only that EA documentation addresses the stakeholders' concerns and views, but also that it closely reflects the current situation.
- Management must *mandate the preparation and maintenance of architectural descriptions* as part of project management guidelines in order to ensure that changes are incorporated into the architecture documentation.

(2) Elaborating on strategic options through EAM

Scanning the environment may reveal major changes to which organisations must adapt. The internal analysis already exposes new or adjusted ways of doing business. Matching the results of internal and external analyses leads to a number of potential strategic options, which are evaluated to determine the organisation's future agenda. EAM's role is to help assess and evaluate these options and to address strategic architecture concerns by initiating dedicated architecture-driven initiatives.

(2a) Strategic business and IT options

Strategic changes determine a company's investments and development for the next years. When evaluating strategic options, managers should not only take opportunities into account, but also the organisation's capabilities, potentials and limitations. For example, given the existing skills, business processes and applications, entering a new market may be risky if the planned go-to-market approach differs completely different from that used in the existing markets. Overlooking such implications may hinder successful strategy implementation, or require costly strategy modifications at a later

EA analyses illustrate how strategic options affect the different parts and resources of the organisation

stage. The EAM function produces knowledge of the interplay between strategic directions, organisational design and the underlying IS landscape, which is very difficult to find in any other organisational unit. It is sensible to use this precious architectural knowledge to assess strategic options in order to more consciously formulate, and select an alternative.

Using EA analysis techniques increases the likelihood that the strategic alternatives under consideration fit the organisation's capabilities and long-term strategic goals. Decisions can be taken more consciously because:

- *The impact of strategic options, notably the required changes in business and IT, becomes explicit.* On the basis of sound EA documentation, architects can better analyse how a specific strategic option, such as an extended product portfolio or the acquisition of a new firm, will affect the processes, structure, people, information systems and infrastructure. The architect can also spot alternatives that have a greater chance of successful implementation, which he or she can then promote.
- *The scope of the initiatives is set more appropriately.* The architect's cross-domain knowledge enables him or her to identify overlaps between different initiatives and to detect unforeseen side-effects. In doing so, interdependencies, or even conflicts with other strategies, are detected earlier.
- *Business-IT communication is enhanced.* With a multi-dimensional EA approach and models, architects help to translate strategic business initiatives to the IT domain. In the same way, architects may explain how strategic IT initiatives provide the technical basis needed to achieve strategic business goals. Furthermore, they recognise strategic IT initiatives that enable new business opportunities.

Ensure architects' participation in strategy processes

However, an important precondition is the enterprise architects' participation in the strategy processes. The chief enterprise architect should participate in strategy and board meetings. The architecture team can contribute by compiling architecture documentation, evaluating different options and thereby prepare the information basis for strategic decision-making.

The architecture team's involvement in strategy formulation at a global insurance corporation

This insurer's architecture team participates in the executive board's strategy proposal evaluation. The architects review the business case, identify the affected processes and evaluate the proposal's effectiveness and hidden effects on the architecture. If the architects have architectural concerns regarding a proposal, they provide a counter-proposal and reconcile it with the submitter. Generally, no strategic proposal is made without an architectural assessment of its overall implications and usefulness.

The architects also attend strategy meetings to record the planned changes and to identify their impacts on the target operating models and target architectures. The architects evaluate and discuss the effects of strategy changes with the various process owners. Their involvement thus helps to explicate the effects on existing processes and process standards.

The insurer emphasizes that the architectural transparency gains facilitate the identification of changes caused by new business models or targets. By assigning the insurer's architecture management to the CEO, architectural implications are considered early on in the strategy process. The architects seek to further strengthen this involvement in future; a business architect describes this as follows:

'Our vision and understanding are that the management board talks to three parties when it wants to introduce a new business model: the head of strategy, the business architect, and human resources.'

Management recommendations

- Management must mandate the evaluation of strategy proposals with regard to their impact on the EA.
- Management must ensure that the EAM team is placed so that it is actively involved in strategy formulation. The chief enterprise architect should also participate in strategy and boards meetings.

(2b) Strategic architecture initiatives

EAM has a supporting role in business and IT strategy planning, but it is also a driver of strategic architecture initiatives. Such initiatives comprise all architectural levels by addressing:

An EAM is the driver of strategic architecture initiatives

- *Standardisation and harmonisation*, with the goal of reducing the heterogeneity and complexity of business processes, applications, data and infrastructure technologies.
- S*ervice orientation and modularisation*, with the goal of creating reusable services and modules, and thereby removing redundancies and leveraging enterprise-wide synergies.

Architecture initiatives prepare the organisation to better cope with future requirements

- *The implementation of reference models and industry norms*, with the goal of adopting best practices.

These initiatives' general purpose is to improve the EA's overall quality by eliminating obvious deficits that hinder its adaptation to a changing business environment and thereby improving cost efficiency [6]. Architecture initiatives, such as standardisation and modularisation programmes, help to prepare the organisation for the future and to address changing business environments. Data standards and state-of-the-art technology components that follow industry norms, for example, facilitate realizing company-wide integrated business processes and engaging in new partnerships with distributors and retailers. Process templates allow the firm to rapidly establish sales and production units in new markets, whereas modular components enable flexibility concerning local consumer needs. Furthermore, software services enable quicker responses to business process changes than rigid silo applications.

Dedicated architecture initiatives ensure that structural problems are systematically addressed

   Such initiatives are not new to organisations. However, a dedicated EAM function and architects' close participation in strategy planning ensure that architecture issues are openly discussed and systematically addressed. This is particularly important, since other business and IT projects often do not have the means or the incentives to solve underlying architecture problems. EAM also provides analysis techniques [7] that, for example, assess an architecture's homogeneity level or identify redundancies and gaps in IT's support of the business.

Management recommendations

- The EAM team should be encouraged to suggest dedicated EA-related objectives and evaluate business cases for strategic architecture initiatives.
- Management must promote architecture initiatives to tackle enterprise architecture deficits. Such initiatives reduce the burden for business and IT projects, which are often beset by architecture issues, but do not have the means to solve them within their project scope.
- Management must assign sufficient resources (e.g., a dedicated budget), since it is difficult to create short-term business cases for architecture initiatives; if not, the initiatives' effectiveness may be harmed by architectural constraints, local politics and resource battles.

Strategic architecture initiatives

(1) Global process standardisation at an international insurance provider

Initiative synopsis	An international insurance provider has assigned several important core processes the status 'global process'. Associated global process owners are in charge of optimising these processes and defining process standards.
Strategic goals	The initiative seeks to harmonise and standardise the core processes in the group and thus establish global best practices across the entire organisation.
EAM's role in the initiative	Global process owners and enterprise architects cooperate closely in the initiative. The EAM team ensures that the global processes fit into the overall architecture. The team also identifies strategic changes' impact on the existing global process standards. Thereafter, based on the EA's current analysis, the architects assess the current level of process harmonisation and standardisation. They report on KPIs that inform the management board of the initiatives' progress.

(2) Modernisation of the application landscape at an international cargo carrier

Initiative synopsis	In the past, a central host system's uncoordinated developments led to an operating cost escalation, as well as high complexity in the cargo carrier's application landscape. An IT master plan addresses modernising the application landscape, replacing the central legacy system and centralising the services and data. The IT master plan comprises a budget of about 50 million EUR and about 50 projects.
Strategic goals	The IT master plan seeks to modernise the cargo carrier's application landscape. It intends to reduce complexity and decrease operating and development costs. Furthermore, it aims to increase the data reliability, especially operation-critical data, such as shipment details.
EAM's role in the initiative	EAM ensures transparency in all the modernisation program's implications, especially as the legacy system impacts all business domains. Based on the EA documentation, the EAM team arranges and aligns the initiatives within the IT master plan. The EAM team also regularly identifies how business changes affect the IT master plan.

(3) Service orientation at a global bank

Initiative synopsis	The bank created a 'SOA Centre of Excellence' in order to set up a repository of reusable service modules and develop governance mechanisms that enforce service orientation in projects. A pilot project proved the SOA concept's feasibility. Subsequent projects made use of the existing services and developed other services.
Strategic goals	The SOA initiative seeks to master the transformation from fixed and rigid applications to modular services. It thus intends to increase reuse and interoperability and to reduce the efforts required to adapt IS/IT structures to changes in the business processes.
EAM's role in the initiative	The enterprise architects were deeply involved in the 'SOA Centre of Excellence'. They identified service candidates and developed blueprints for the future deployment of services. Furthermore, EAM oversaw the identification and deployment of services in projects and monitored reuse of the services provided in the repository.

The architecture vision refines and explicates the strategic directions

(3) Developing the architecture vision

The EAM's core undertaking is to develop an architecture vision explicating the strategic directions. By developing a high-level architecture model, such as a target operating model (TOM), companies describe the primary aspects of the company's future operations, before further refining and detailing the strategic intentions in the form of an architecture model. A TOM determines the cornerstones regarding how an organization operates across process, organization and technology domains in order to deliver value. In respect of the strategic goal of launching a new product, for example, the TOM helps the firm to clarify key aspects, such as:

(1) Which customers and regions will the new product address?
(2) Will the firm keep its revenue model and build on the existing distribution channels?
(3) How should the firm change the existing sales processes and applications to launch the new product?

Based on answers to these questions, the target architecture operationalises the desired strategic goals and specifies a coherent vision of the firm's designated future state. The various EA models, such as process maps, as well as application and data models, provide answers to questions such as:

(1) Can the existing online shop and the order management application handle the new product or does the firm need to implement new information systems?
(2) What does this mean for the underlying technical infrastructure?

The target architecture provides a collaborative view that many managers and architects create in a joint effort

The development of an explicit architecture vision facilitates communication related to strategies, as it provides the necessary level of detail to refine the different functional areas. It is also an essential first step to the migration and development of the strategic initiatives' tactical and operational plans. Overall, the firm thus paves the way for a more purposeful development to the elaborated target state. While senior managers must specify the TOM, the target architecture development task is a collaborative process involving business unit managers, process owners, experts and architects. The resulting target architecture represents a collaborative view created by many contributors and taking their different views into account. Ideally, the target architecture integrates the anticipated strategic initiatives' changes, comprising, on the one hand, strategic business and IT initiatives and, on the other hand, strategic architecture initiatives. Instead of one global target architecture, organisations often employ complementary target architectures that focus on selected layers, or document specific strategic initiatives. However, architects and strategy planners should ensure consistency between these architectures.

The architecture vision at an international car manufacturer

This car manufacturer's architecture management team set up a master construction plan to document the architecture vision for the global application landscape. In workshops with global representatives, the managers agreed on a shared vision of the required IT support for the main business processes, with the aim of standardising business applications across locations and plants, of which there were more than 600. An EA tool documents the architecture vision in terms of a target application portfolio. Defining the master construction plan is part of the corporate-level planning cycle and provides the basis for the subsequent local planning rounds. By creating a frame of reference for the entire group, the master construction plan improves the use of budgets and complements the project-driven culture with long-term objectives for application standardisation.

Management recommendations

- Senior management should specify the target operating model that describes, at a high level, how the firm will operate in the process, organisational and technology domains in future.
- Strategic initiatives' desired effects should be documented by means of the target architecture. This target architecture comprises EA models specifying the organisation's designated future state and keeps projects focussed.
- The architects should cooperate closely with the relevant stakeholders, such as the functional managers, process owners and IT experts in order to reflect their concerns and views in the target architecture and to attain stakeholder identification with the planning results.

(4) Roadmapping: Migrating from the current to the target architecture

Once strategic options have been evaluated and selected, the architecture vision must be transformed into a migration plan or roadmap. The target architecture – as discussed in the previous section – explicitly describes the alterations brought about by strategic directions. By comparing the as-is state architecture and the target archi-

Roadmaps specify the migration paths from the current to the target architecture

tecture, management can derive roadmaps (see Figure 5.3). Architecture roadmaps – as defined in TOGAF [8] – that list the individual change increments and place them on a timeline to show the progression from the current to the target architecture, are a valuable tool in this endeavour.

The development of roadmaps is an incremental process. Strategy teams can leverage up-to-date architecture documentations that provide transparency regarding the as-is state and the desired strategic state architectures to identify intermediate states. EAM also supports the discussion of roadmap alternatives, as well as the roadmap decisions by revealing interdependencies in different EA components' migration paths. Roadmap alternatives describe the paths along which the firm can travel to reach the target state. These alternatives should be discussed with decision-makers to evaluate their feasibility with regard to time and budget constraints. Discussions should lead to the selection of a viable roadmap supported by business and IT stakeholders. A global roadmap may be refined into sub-roadmaps with a specific scope, such as a selected EA layer or different planning levels. The roadmap steps suggest the first project ideas to implement the desired changes. Finally, these proposals are translated into the project portfolio for further assessment and prioritisation.

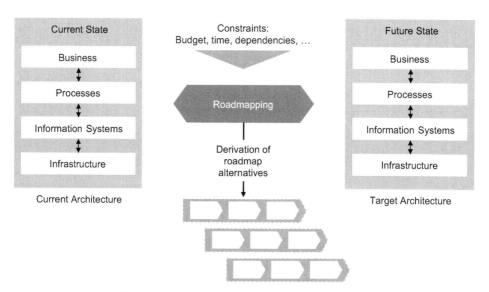

Figure 5.3: Roadmaps as migration paths from the as-is state architecture to the target architecture

Roadmapping at an international insurance company

This insurer defined its architecture vision in terms of target operating models. These models were used to derive roadmap scenarios that describe migration alternatives and lead to the targeted state. Each scenario was evaluated by means of a rough cost-benefit analysis and the intended implementation timeline. An IT architect highlighted the benefits of a target architecture in this context:

> 'The advantage of the target architecture is that one has a long-term perspective and does not decide on an ad hoc basis. [...] One has an overview of the planned investments and the main targets, and can budget more precisely with the available money.'

Evaluating the scenarios resulted in a choice of the most advantageous scenario, from which projects were derived. The insurer thus increased the number of projects that developed directly from strategic directions codified in the target architectures. The insurer consequently addressed strategic changes more proactively. A business architect described the more planned organisational development as follows:

> 'We do not want projects to occur randomly, but each has to be a step towards the desired target state defined by target operating models.'

Management recommendations

In terms of roadmapping, managers should:

• Motivate the relevant stakeholders to participate in the roadmap planning process in order to achieve alignment between their requirements and constraints in the resulting roadmap alternative.
• Define intermediate states in order to create a shared understanding of and commitment on how the target state can be reached.

(5) Assessing and prioritising the project portfolio through EAM

In the introduction to this chapter, we stated that an organisation's strategic development from an as-is to a target state takes place by means of two types of initiatives: *strategic initiatives* as well as *emergent and operational initiatives*. Both types of initiatives generate project demands. These project demands must be aligned in the project portfolio (see Figure 5.4). As discussed in the previous paragraphs, in an EAM-supported process, *strategic project demands* evolve from strategic business and IT initiatives, as well as from strategic architecture initiatives. These initiatives ultimately generate strategic project demands. A project portfolio further comprises additional *emergent and operational project demands*. These are

demands that develop bottom-up from operational needs in the business and IT areas. Chapter 7 further elaborates on the management of
this type of change and provides a checklist to identify the architectural relevance of operational and tactical changes.

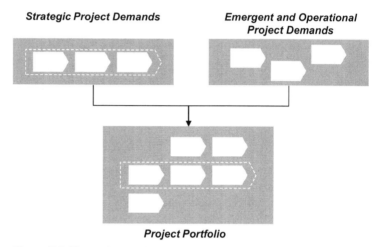

Figure 5.4: The project portfolio comprises strategic and operational project
demands

*EAM complements
traditional project
portfolio techniques*

Most organisations do not have the resources to simultaneously
implement all the suggested project demands in the project portfolio.
Therefore, they need to identify the most critical projects and the
most promising projects. Assessing a project's strategic contribution,
and identifying implementation interdependencies and potentials for
shared developments are not new in organisations with advanced
project portfolio management. However, EA documentations and
analyses techniques enhance these practices and increase their effectiveness. EAM supports the assessment and prioritisation of projects
in the project portfolio by:

- *Assessing the projects' strategic contribution and conformance
  with the target architecture.* EAM can help a firm to objectify the
  assessment of a project's contribution to strategic goals and to
  evaluate how well it aligns with the architecture vision. It therefore
  complements existing assessment tools, which are often experi-
  enced-based and qualitative. This is especially important in the
  case of *operational* project requests (see Figure 5.4), which are
  likely to focus on short-term requirements and sometimes conflict
  with the defined architecture principles. For example, a project
  may seek to implement changes in a self-developed application

that will be phased out and replaced by a software package, or it may use technologies that do not conform to the defined architecture standards. EAM helps to ensure that projects align with the architecture vision and that resources are assigned in a way that moves the organisation towards the desired target state.

EAM to organise the project portfolio

Cargo carrier   This cargo carrier updates its project portfolio twice per year. Two to three months beforehand, the business and IT organisations start collecting project ideas in a portfolio tool. Besides business-driven projects, the IT organisation and the architects also recommend IT-driven and architecture-driven projects. The ultimate projects are suggested by development teams or are derived from a strategic IT master plan or from the IT strategy.

A central overview of all the project demands allows the project management unit and the architects to analyse the projects in terms of redundancies and dependencies. This is done on the basis of project schedules, a strategic IT master plan and information provided by the architecture documentation. Criteria for project prioritisation include profitability, costs, required resources, business criticality and the projects' correspondence with the IT goals.

Government   This European government agency has a federated
agency   structure that consists of a variety of local agencies responsible for policy implementation in defined areas. This structure results in a multiplicity of projects across the organisation. The agency's architects record all these developments and create an overview by annually collecting documents from all local agencies on their ongoing and planned projects.

The central EAM team uses this information to pinpoint the local agencies' common development potential. On the basis of this information, the architects establish contact between agencies that plan similar projects. They also comment on the planned developments' architectural aspects and use the data to advocate shared development efforts in the way they distribute budgets.

These processes have enabled the agency to achieve greater collaboration between all the local agencies. Furthermore, these agencies have coordinated their progress in alignment with the global strategic targets.

- *Identifying and resolving interdependencies and implementation conflicts in project portfolios.* For example, architects can identify critical enterprise architecture components that have been changed by several projects and rethink the portfolio. On this basis, the firm can organise projects to create synergies and avoid conflicts between them.
- *Identifying potentials for shared developments.* EAM reveals redundant activities. Thereby, the firm can identify potentials for the shared development of components or services across projects. For example, the EAM team can identify IT projects that implement similar business process functionalities or comparable technological components. If the team could create synergies between these projects, resource savings could result, thus avoiding redundant developments.

Management recommendations

In terms of assessing and prioritising the project portfolio, we recommend that managers:

- Motivate enterprise architects to participate in the project portfolio management processes in order to apply EA methods and analysis techniques effectively, and to ensure conformance with the defined roadmaps.
- Oversee all strategic and operational project demands that have a critical size or significant impact on the EA.

(6) Evaluating architecture development: Steering strategy implementation

During the *project realisation* phase, the target EA will be implemented in the form of projects. The project life cycle is discussed in detail in Chapter 6. The strategy cycle is concluded with a strategy evaluation phase that monitors and evaluates the strategic goal achievement. EAM supports strategy evaluation by:

EAM regularly monitors and reviews the current EA status

- *Measuring and reviewing EA status and evolution.* EA analysis techniques and reports allow managers to regularly track and discuss the EA status with their peers. For example, a heterogeneity analysis can be applied to assess conformance with defined technology and application platforms. Other checks might reveal consistency issues in the as-is state architecture.

- *Monitoring the progress of strategic initiatives along the agreed roadmaps.* The strategic initiative implementation progress should correspond to the roadmap defining the sequential transition from the as-is towards the target architecture. Managers can steer strategic initiatives more effectively by comparing how the current implementation status, as captured in the up-to-date EA model, corresponds with the implementation status foreseen by the roadmap. EA models can help to trace and resolve the causes of discrepancies.

EAM evaluates the progress of strategic initiatives

- *Linking business performance indicators to EA models.* Integrating existing KPIs into EA models allows more advanced analyses than either system could offer. Organisations use, for example, cost information from accounting systems and assign these to EA components such as applications or processes. This could be especially relevant when, for example, monitoring an architecture initiative's achieved operating cost reduction.

EAM can readily support further strategic information needs

As before, the effective application of EAM in this phase depends on up-to-date information in the EA model repositories and the stakeholders' deep involvement. As the EA is constantly developing, keeping the information relevant requires managers in all the ongoing projects to regularly update the architecture changes in the EA models.

Strategy evaluation

European government agency	This government agency's architects regularly review the strategic e-government programme that implements the agency's most important IT strategy objectives for a period of five years. Since the EAM team has an overview of all the projects, it can assess the progress in the various local agencies and can, accordingly, set priorities for the next planning period.
Cargo carrier	Business architects in the cargo carrier's EAM team assume responsibility for controlling the IT strategy implementation. The EAM team also monitors the progress made in realising the IT master plan – a strategic programme that aims to modernise the systems, reduce complexity, displace systems and centralise common data and services distributed among the domains. The architects also analyse how the overall operating costs develop during the master plan implementation.

EAM allows managers to track and evaluate strategy implementation in detail. The main instruments are the agreed roadmaps. The application of EAM analysis techniques provides data about the effectiveness of the architecture improvement and allows firms to identify architectural deficits or inconsistencies early on.

Management recommendations

In terms of evaluating the architecture evolution, we recommend that managers:

- Understand that achieving and maintaining up-to-date EA documentation are essential for strategy evaluation through EAM.
- Mandate the use of measures and performance indicators. The EAM cockpit in Chapter 7 describes a suitable structure and the KPIs.
- Understand that incorporating additional data in the EA models may support further usage scenarios and thereby increase EAM awareness and acceptance.

5.3 Management implications

Organisations that do not integrate EAM practices in their existing strategy planning and implementation processes reap only limited benefits from their EAM efforts. Such EAM endeavours are often referred to as 'ivory towers' that lack awareness and acceptance in the organisation. This chapter illustrated how EAM practices enhance strategy formulation, planning and evaluation. However, the benefits of EAM practices can only be gained when the firm acts in line with certain success factors:

- *EAM practices complement and enhance existing management practices, rather than replacing them.* During strategy planning, one can use the documentation of the as-is state (or baseline) architecture to discuss different stakeholders' viewpoints and analyse the organisation's existing capabilities. The EAM practices thus ensure that given the firm's capabilities and limitations one chooses feasible strategic options. During strategy formulation, one should use EAM techniques to explicate and refine strategic directions in the form of target architectures and migration plans. In project portfolio planning, the documented as-is and target architectures assist one with identifying and resolving project interdependencies, which are often overlooked without EAM.

  Careful integration enables EAM's full strategic effectiveness

- *EA documentation provides a collaborative view that can be shared by managers, architects and employees:* The effective employment of EAM as the basis for strategy planning largely depends on the EA documentation's ability to create a shared understanding of the organisation's current and target states. Instead of striving for completeness, one should concentrate on those EA components and views of most interest for key stakeholders. Furthermore, bear in mind that EA documentation provides the required information basis in an explicit EA model form. In order to enhance situation analysis and decision-making, one needs to add suitable reports and analyses to the EA models. The development of the target EA cannot be undertaken by a small team of architects; it needs to be a collaborative effort by management, subject matter experts and architects. Governance mechanisms must ensure that EA documentation is regularly updated, for example, by mandating timely updates of EA models during project execution (see Chapter 6 for more details).

  EAM's strategic use relies on a sound EA documentation

Top management mandates the use of EAM practices in strategy processes

- *Strategic initiatives are the means to migrate towards the target architecture:* As the development of an EA is a long-term and incremental activity, one should leverage EAM to guide strategic initiatives and, if necessary, launch dedicated architecture initiatives.
- *Top management must be committed:* Since EAM is a management philosophy, top management's wholehearted commitment is required to change established working procedures. This comprises mandating the use of EAM techniques and methods in the strategy process, an appropriate organisational assignment of the EAM function and the architects' participation in strategy-relevant boards and committees.

Table 5.2 provides a checklist summarising EAM's application in the strategy process.

Table 5.2: Checklist of strategic EAM integration

Checklist of strategic EAM integration	
	Reference point
EAM has documented the current state of the organisation in an as-is architecture and has created appropriate EA reports for situation analysis.	➜ *(1)*
EAM contributes to the assessment of strategic business and IT options by identifying and evaluating changes to the different enterprise architecture components.	➜ *(2a)*
Based on regular EA assessments, EAM formulates dedicated EA goals and launches strategic architecture initiatives to improve the architecture quality.	➜ *(2b)*
EAM develops an architecture vision that explicates changes brought about by the strategic initiatives.	➜ *(3)*
EAM supports the development of roadmaps, which describe the transition from the current architecture to the target architecture. EAM supports the selection of the most feasible roadmap.	➜ *(4)*
EAM information is used during project portfolio planning to identify the projects' impacts, their interdependencies and potentials for collaborative developments.	➜ *(5)*
EAM data are used to monitor the architecture's development and its progress in migrating towards the target architecture. EAM is used to evaluate the strategic roadmaps' implementation status.	➜ *(6)*

References

[1] R. S. Kaplan and D. P. Norton, *The Execution Premium – Linking Strategy to Operations for Competitive Advantage*, vol. 1. Boston, MA, USA: Harvard Business School Publishing, 2008.

[2] B. De Wit and R. Meyer, *Strategy: Process, Content, Context - An International Perspective*. Cincinnati, Ohio, USA: South Western Educ Pub, 2004.

[3] A. C. Hax and N. S. Majluf, *The Strategy Concept and Process: A Pragmatic Approach*. Upper Saddle River, New Jersey, USA: Prentice-Hall, Inc., 1996.

[4] H. Mintzberg, *The strategy process: concepts, contexts, cases*. Upper Saddle River NJ: Prentice Hall, 2003.

[5] P. Dobson, K. Starkey, and J. Richards, *Strategic management: issues and cases*. Hoboken, New Jersey, USA: Wiley-Blackwell, 2004.

[6] J. W. Ross, P. Weill, and D. C. Robertson, *Enterprise Architecture as Strategy. Creating a Foundation for Business Execution*. Boston, MA, USA: Harvard Business School Press, 2006.

[7] K. D. Niemann, *Von der Unternehmensarchitektur zur IT-Governance*, vol. 1. Vieweg, 2005.

[8] Opengroup, *TOGAF Version 9*. Zaltbommel, Netherlands: Van Haren Publishing, 2009.

Chapter 6

Embedding EAM into the project life cycle

Johannes Lux, Frederik Ahlemann

Table of contents

Management summary

Developing a target enterprise architecture (EA) is necessary for the purposeful development of the organisation according to its strategic objectives and vision, but not of itself sufficient to ensure success. Realising a planned EA by means of a set of architecture-aware projects creates new challenges, such as having to translate strategic, long-term EA objectives into operational, short-term targets; additional, numerous stakeholders; the diverging objectives of the 'planner' and the 'implementer'; the day-to-day management of scarce enterprise architecture management (EAM) resources; and the management of hundreds of 'micro-decisions' that all determine the future EA. A holistic EAM should therefore include a set of practices that structures, controls and monitors the projects that shape your EA.

EAM plays an important role throughout the project lifecycle. This chapter presents practices that help execute projects in an EAM-compliant way. During the project set-up phase, approval gates need to be defined, EA information must be made available to the project team, and architects need to be assigned to the project organisation. During the solution design and implementation phases, it is important to ensure that the project team develops a solution that aligns with the target architecture, as well as the architecture principles and standards. For this, project reviews can be conducted at certain points along the project life cycle. It is also useful to put escalation processes in place. They may come into play if enterprise architects and the project team have diverging ideas of what the solution architecture should look like. It is also worth considering how to enrich the existing project status reports with EA-related information. In the piloting and roll-out phase of a project, EAM may aid the search for a suitable piloting environment and help to organise a solution's smooth roll-out. The chapter closes with management recommendations for increased architecture awareness in project practices. Because we acknowledge that each organisation operates in a different environment, we discuss three different modes of EA realisation in the project lifecycle: (1) advising, (2) participating and (3) managing.

6.1 The relevance of embedding EAM in the project life cycle

Bridging the gap between the right strategies and better results

If you have done your homework during the strategic planning process (as described in Chapter 5), you will now have a target state for your EA, a roadmap of how to get there and a resulting project portfolio. This should all be neatly documented in the form of conceptual blueprints, and might even take the form of models big enough to wallpaper your office. Now what? How can you ensure that your organisation realises the strategy? Blueprints alone will not make this happen.

The sound planning of strategic objectives should be followed by such objectives' implementation. A strategy is more likely to succeed if the corresponding project portfolio is properly organised, controlled and monitored. Theory and practice teach us that what gets measured gets done. This simple truth is also valid for enterprise architecture management (EAM). Therefore, this chapter deals with EAM practices that support the target architecture's realisation by controlling and monitoring project progress, and by escalating project problems.

As with any other management practice, EAM requires controlling and monitoring procedures

Interestingly, firms often experience severe problems when implementing their EA-related strategic objectives. A closer look at the project processes reveals that organisations face several typical difficulties:

Realising a target EA is a challenging endeavour

- **Translating abstract long-term objectives into specific short-term objectives**. Strategic planning brings about objectives that are long-term, abstract and limited in number. They frequently refer to more than one EA layer or EA domain and affect larger organisational units and executives. However, projects require short-term, operational targets that can be used to steer project teams and individuals.
- **Numerous stakeholders**. Project execution involves significantly more stakeholders than strategic planning does. Whereas the latter already requires specialists from various functions, such as architecture, finance, marketing, or operations, the teams tend to be relatively small. The opposite is true during project execution when

teams tend to be larger, and competency sets (e.g., including pro-gramming, quality management and service management) tend to be more specific.

- **Diverging objectives**. The people required to execute a project may follow personal agendas that do not align with overall strate-gic objectives. Conflicts of interest, politics and opportunistic behaviour may jeopardise strategy implementation.
- **Complex resource management**. Compared to the preceding planning phase, resource allocation in implementation projects is usually more complex due to the need for more detailed planning schedules, higher resource availability, volatility as a result of unforeseen events (e.g., illness and project problems) and difficult effort estimations. This is especially true for scarce resources such as enterprise architects.

EAM alters strategy realisation processes

In this chapter, we discuss how organisations can address these chal-lenges and implement a project process that oversees all architectural objectives and principles. To this end, we will focus on altering and extending the project life cycle with EAM practices. Project manage-ment plays an important role, as larger EA changes are usually car-ried out by means of projects (and larger project programmes). In this regard, there is no need to re-invent the wheel. The project man-agement discipline has much to offer regarding governing transfor-mation initiatives. Software Development Life Cycles (SDLC), project management standards and project management tools are just a few examples of what can be used. Yet, these techniques reveal little about how to make projects 'architecture-aware'. In this chap-ter, we therefore concentrate on the question of how EAM can be embedded into the project life cycle. We take for granted the use of concurrent standard project management routines like a SDLC (pos-sibly documented in the form of a project management handbook); we therefore do not provide explicit instructions regarding general project management. Please refer to existing project management standards for more information on how to steer projects [1-3].

Some projects are more relevant than others for realising the target EA; therefore, we distinguish two project types (see also Chapter 5.1):

Projects may be designed to develop the EA; if not, they must at least be EA compliant

- **Strategic architecture projects** (or initiatives) are initiated for architectural reasons and are designed to implement the target EA. Examples are large change initiatives, such as business process reengineering, consolidating the application landscape and harmo-nising IT infrastructure technologies. What do all these initiatives have in common? They affect a larger number of architectural components, usually on several EA layers.

• Projects may also be derived from **strategic business initiatives**, or they may be **driven by operational demands**. These are initiated without the intention to further develop the overall architecture. Instead, they are set up to solve one or more specific business problem(s). Such a solution usually consists of or affects one or various EA components, which is why this type is EA-relevant and needs to comply with the architecture principles and the overall architectural objectives. An example is the introduction of a new business application, or a new business process as a result of new products or services.

How the project life cycle fits into the overall planning and control cycle

The project life cycle is one of three major planning and controlling cycles influenced by EAM (see Figure 6.1). Whereas the other two cycles are concerned with strategic planning (see Chapter 5), and EA operations and monitoring (see Chapter 7), this chapter includes all the process steps from the project set-up to the piloting and roll-out of solutions developed throughout the project:

1. **Project set-up**. The project set-up usually starts after a project portfolio has been defined and approved. It deals with the required resources' allocation, the project scope definition, goal communication, project risk analysis, cost planning and scheduling.
2. **Design solution**. The solution design phase comprises all detailed design activities prior to the actual implementation. This includes the definition of the architectural components, the selection of technologies, the specification of interfaces, and changes in processes and organisational structures. This happens after the project proposal has been approved in the strategic planning cycle, which includes defining the business requirements and the technical requirements.
3. **Implement solution**. Implementation includes all activities necessary to implement the solution designed in the previous step.
4. **Piloting and roll-out**: Solution roll-out can be a challenging task, particularly for large, multinational companies. For introduction in more than one location or organisational unit, project managers usually use pilot tests that prove the working concept and help develop a solution package that is easy to implement in other parts

of the organisation. After the successful completion of this process step, the solution is handed over to operations and monitoring.

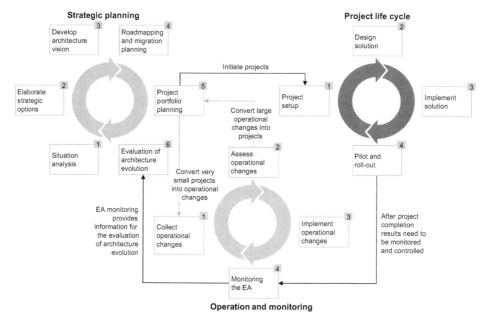

Figure 6.1: EAM process cycles

We structure the remainder of this chapter as follows: The next three sections address the practices that help execute projects in an EAM-compliant way. They follow the aforementioned project life cycle steps. We conclude the chapter by making some managerial recommendations, and provide a model of three modes for incorporating EA into project practices.

6.2 Project set-up: Preparing EA-compliant project execution

During the project set-up phase, the enterprise architects and the project team need to ensure that three important preconditions for an EAM-compliant project execution are met:

1. **Approval gates must be defined**. The project plan must have clearly defined approval gates for checking the project's architectural compliance.
2. **EA-relevant information must be available**. The project team needs architectural information to develop an EA-compliant solution design.
3. **EAM-specific resources must be assigned**. Scarce architectural resources must be managed in a way that maximises their impact.

We'll now discuss these preconditions in detail.

Definition of approval gates

During a project, several detailed design decisions are made that refine the agreed high-level solution design. Enterprise architects need to ensure that such decisions conform to the target EA and EA principles. Milestones with approval gates are a sound platform for such an evaluation, and architects should therefore ensure that the project is well structured and has sufficient approval gates. They usually do so by adding such gates to the general project process model (or SDLC), which is then used as a template for individual project planning. A detailed list of potential EAM approval gates can be found in Table 6.1 on page 156.

Ensure the use of appropriate approval gates

Provision of EA-relevant information

Project teams will need architectural information to design architecture-compliant solutions. This information will help them understand how their solution fits into the overall architecture, and will help them follow the architecture principles and standards, as well as the strategic architectural objectives. It is therefore necessary to:

The project team needs architecture-relevant information

- grant the project team access to global **architecture management repositories** that contain detailed information about the present architecture and target architecture, and
- provide the project team with **documents from the project initiation process** that describe the project's architectural direction; this specifically includes the project proposal (project charter) and preliminary architectural blueprints for the planned solution.

Information taken from these documents can be used to complete templates required during project execution, for example, the requirements or specification documents. It will also help the project team to develop the solution-specific architecture and document it by means of EA models, if necessary.

The project team should generally have a solid understanding of the following three aspects:

- **Project role**. How does the project fit into the overall strategy? How does it contribute to the target architecture's realisation?
- **EA integration**. What EA layers are affected by the project? What are the adjacent architectural components? What interfaces are needed to these components?
- **Relevant principles and standards**. What architecture principles and standards are relevant for the project?

This knowledge will not only allow for the development of a sound and compliant solution architecture, it will also help the team understand its role in the strategy realisation process. This may contribute to team motivation and alignment.

EA-specific project staffing

In any firm, the EA experts' capacity is generally very limited. The challenge is to assign architects to those projects that they will impact most. The following criteria may play a role in assigning enterprise architects to projects:

There are several reasons for assigning architects to projects

- **Project type.** Strategic architecture projects will always require participation of architects in the project team, whereas projects which are carried out to solve one or more specified business problem(s) may not always need participation of an architect.
- **Architectural complexity**. Some projects are architecturally particularly complex, because they involve numerous layers, require many interfaces to adjacent EA components, or involve new design patterns or EA principles. In such cases, experienced archi-

tects can mitigate the risk of project failure and ensure compliance with the target architecture.

- **Limited competencies**. In some cases, the project team might have limited architectural competencies. Furthermore, the team members might lack the knowledge and experience to apply architecture principles and guidelines. In such cases, an enterprise architect can complement a team's skills portfolio.
- **Quick wins and architectural impact**. Sometimes, a project can be an extraordinary architectural success with very little effort. An enterprise architect may prove very useful to achieve such quick wins.
- **Strategic relevance**. Projects with a significant strategic impact might be preferred when it comes to architectural support, because an organisation may want to reduce the risk of failure due to architectural challenges. In such cases, assigning architectural resources might be the result of the project portfolio planning process.

In many organisations, the chief architect and the project sponsor are in charge of assigning enterprise architects to projects. There are two types of assignments: *full membership* in the project team and a weaker, *on-demand consulting* affiliation. Figure 6.2 provides an example of how scarce enterprise architecture resources are allocated to projects.

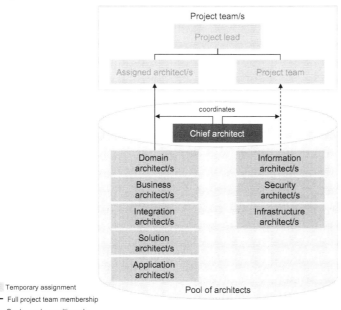

Figure 6.2: Assignment of architectural roles to project teams

How a large car manufacturer coordinates the assignments of specialised architects to projects:

For each of their business process domains, this firm employs one master architect who oversees software projects. In the early phase of a project, 'he is the single point of contact for the business departments and project managers'. He plans the involvement of the technical competence centres that mostly implement the software and hardware modules. Before he withdraws from a project, he assigns a project architect who focuses on the project's consistence with internal standards, and a technical project leader who coordinates the technical competence centre's involvement. This set-up facilitates the early project phase and allows the master architects to put their project landscape overview to optimal use.

How a European bank manages its portfolio with limited architectural capacity through project prioritisation

This bank has a large portfolio of around 2,000 projects. The EAM team currently comprises eight internal domain architects who each oversees and optimises about 30 applications. Consequently, managing the available architects' capacity is crucial. Architects with particular knowledge of the required domain design high-level architecture for high-priority projects. They also put together the appropriate implementation teams and decide how to use architecture-conformant technologies. On the other hand, domain architects do not strongly influence low-priority projects.

6.3 Solution design and implementation: Keeping the car on the road

A typical problem in the solution design and implementation phases is that projects face obstacles; these require actions that might take the project off the initial course. Common obstacles in EA realisation projects include sudden changes in the requirements, unplanned budget adjustments, time constraints and problems with the solution's realisation. In software development, for example, developers usually identify many ways to solve a single problem, such as using different technologies, programming languages, paradigms, algorithms, and so on. Although this might be an advantage, it also means that these projects can easily veer off the track. Therefore, organisations need a 'guard rail', which EAM practices can provide:

Sudden course corrections can be dangerous

- **EA reviews** help with gaining an understanding of where the project stands in terms of the architecture. Architecture teams carry out reviews every few weeks or months.
- **Escalation processes** allow for controlled deviation from architectural standards and principles.
- **Progress reporting** allows control of the target architecture realisation status. The project manager prepares progress reports every few weeks and makes these available to the enterprise architects and the project steering committee.
- **Tools** help streamline these activities.

Before we discuss these four EAM practices, you need to understand the nature of the architectural work in projects.

The nature of architectural work in projects

During the solution design and implementation, you will deal with architecture projects and projects that address specific business requirement(s). While the former derive from the EA strategy and should thus require less attention concerning their general fit, business-driven projects must often first prove their architectural fit. This means that the project team should elaborate a particular solution architecture that:

A solution requires an architectural fit

- fits into the overall present architecture and target architecture,
- is composed of standard EA components (as far as possible), and
- adheres to the organisation's architecture principles.

Project teams should assess these criteria with regard to each EA layer.

We will now describe how the EA strategy is aligned with the projects in the course of the solution design and implementation process (see Figure 6.3): (1) Depending on their type, projects are derived from the EA strategy and the target EA (architecture projects), or they simply result from a business requirement (business-driven projects). (2) In both cases, the enterprise architects should check whether or not the project and the resulting solution comply with EA standards and principles. (3) Beyond this, they need to evaluate whether or not the solution can be integrated and operated once it has been deployed. For these purposes, enterprise architects assess architectural documents, such as functional or technical specifications. (4) During the implementation phase, architects should also ensure that the solution developed is in line with the original project objectives, the detailed specifications and the anticipated solution benefits. (5) Finally, the solution is created and the present EA is further developed in line with the target architecture.

How the EA strategy finds its way into the projects

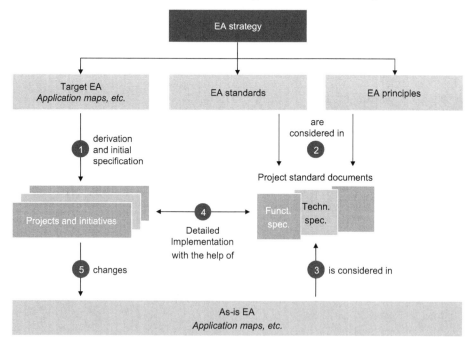

Figure 6.3: How the EAM specifications influence projects

How a professional service firm detects architectural problems resulting from solution designs

The extension of a corporate web portal at a professional service firm included the development and implementation of a travel expense accounting module. On the application layer, this project showed no integration problems, as the data exchange with other databases and the required technical interfaces were straightforward. However, on the business process level, an evaluation showed that the new web portal implicitly created a business process with 24/7 availability, while the accounting module had limited availability requirements. The project thus had to deal with the misalignment of the business processes, as well as with accountability issues.

EA reviews

EA reviews are a means to regularly assess the solution's architectural quality and EA compliance during project execution. The reviews are usually carried out when project milestones are reached or particular project phases are completed, and the project team has finalised the (intermediate) project results, such as specifications, architectural designs and prototypes. During an EA review, a team of architecture experts (in most cases, internal enterprise architects, but sometimes also external service providers) assesses the solution's architecture with regard to its compliance with standards and principles, as well as its compatibility with the present EA and the target EA. Table 6.1 presents typical EA reviews along a project's life cycle.

Reviews along the project life cycle

Some EA reviews may already be undertaken during the strategic planning phase, while others are subject to operation and monitoring processes after the project execution. As a result of reviews, architecture governance activities are more proactive – from their concept through to the design –, with the EA team providing planned architectures, standards, guidelines and consulting input to shape and guide the solutions being developed. During the solution implementation stage, EA involvement becomes more reactive to changes. It evaluates potential changes' architecture impacts, as well as ensures that there are no deviations from the approved architecture direction. For this reason, it is necessary to ensure that there is an architectural 'hook' in the change control process, such as a project steering committee to approve important decisions and review the achievement of milestones. Figure 6.4 presents a process model of how projects are steered from an EAM perspective, illustrating how the EA-relevant reviews fit into a project life cycle and what the integration into EA

The EA involvement changes during a project's life cycle

governance boards (see Chapter 4) might look like. Other approaches to project control are, of course, also possible. Agile methodologies specifically allow for a similar control level when properly applied, and are also more lightweight [4], [5].

Table 6.1: Generic approach for assessing projects from an EAM perspective

EA review	What is the goal of the review?	What is reviewed?
1. Project charter review *Does the project align with the EA strategy?*	• Preventing projects that generally violate the EA strategy.	The project charter created when a project is conceived or proposed.
2. Feasibility study *Is the project feasible in terms of architecture?*	• Identifying hidden conflicts that compromise feasibility.	The project charter and the content of a feasibility study or proof of concept conducted by a temporary team before approval; particularly relevant to large, strategic projects.
3. Review of the initial concept *Does the initial solution architecture fit with the EA strategy?*	• Ensuring that EA goals and EA strategy are considered when approving the project proposal.	The initial solution concept, and specifically its architectural aspects, prepared for final approval in the project portfolio management process.
4. Design review(s) *Does the (detailed) design fit with the EA strategy, EA standards and EA principles?*	• Designing the best solution *within the boundaries* of the EA specifications. • Accelerating the project in the long term through fewer corrections in the implementation phase.	The *conceptual* solution during a project's design phase; the choice from solution alternatives should receive special attention.
5. Implementation review(s) *Is the solution evolving as planned and in conformance with the EA strategy?*	• Ensuring that decisions during implementation do not change the emerging solution in ways that violate the design review agreements. • Ensuring sufficient EA documentation during the project.	The evolving solution during a project's implementation phase; the project documents should receive attention, particularly changes to initial specifications.
6. Review of the final solution and roll-out plans *Are there any concerns about the final solution from an EA perspective?*	• Ensuring *final approval* by the overall solution's architect; ensuring that there is no conflict with integration into the EA.	The final solution and the roll-out plans.

Table 6.1: *continues*

7. Project review *What can we learn from this project for our EAM programme?*	• Reviewing the project ex post to determine the EA methodology's acceptance, as well as the EAM-related processes and communication's shortcomings.	The project, 3 to 6 months after the roll-out as documented in the project plans and related material, including meeting and process protocols.
8. Benefits review *Have the EA goals been met?*	• Reviewing the solution ex post to evaluate the impact from an architectural perspective.	The project's impact, following a pre-defined benefit realisation plan. Particularly relevant to large strategic projects; the EA review may be undertaken as part of the general business case review, focusing on the successful integration and adaptation of the solution in the EA.

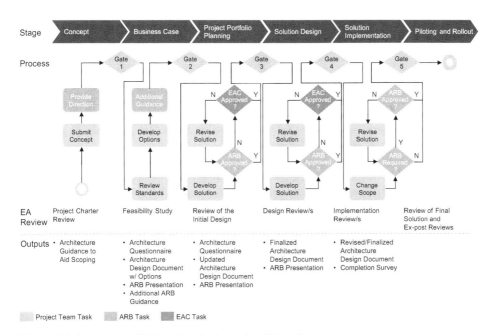

Figure 6.4: Integration of EA reviews in the project life cycle

How a logistics company applies an EA review methodology to control its implementation projects

This company uses domain-specific project boards to conduct reviews at defined quality gates throughout a project's life cycle. Projects are assigned to a domain-specific review board, depending on the domain in which the solution's primary usage unfolds. The following stakeholders usually participate in meetings: the business (i.e. the project sponsor), the development team, IT operations and the architecture team.

(1) At the start of each project, the team develops the detailed design concept, which includes the business case and an implementation concept, as well as the migration, integration, and architectural information. During the concept's review from an architectural perspective, business and data architects analyse the interfaces, data storage aspects and data consistency.

(2) After approval of the detailed design, the project stakeholders identify, evaluate and select different technical solution alternatives. The designers and architects discuss the solution alternatives with the project team. The architects provide the project team with architecture information. Later, the designers and architects review the resulting architecture descriptions in order to ensure architecture consistency. In this phase, the architects and project members discuss whether the architecture standards can be kept, or whether there are good reasons for making exceptions. If necessary, the review boards resolve these conflicts. At a second gate, the selected solution alternative is then reviewed from an architectural perspective. Unresolved architectural conflicts may lead to the project's termination.

(3) While there are no EA reviews during the implementation, the architects attend the testing phase prior to a solution's roll-out. They assess the implemented solution and the roll-out time plan. The architects ensure that the project's migration plan fits in with other projects.

(4) The architects further support the project review for three months after the roll-out. They help to compare the actual operating costs to the planned costs, and use this as feedback to further improve the architectural practices.

Escalation handling

Escalation mechanisms should solve conflicts, not intensify them

What happens if, during a review, an enterprise architect is of the opinion that a solution design decision conflicts with the EA standards or EA principles? Usually, the architect seeks to successfully explain the problem and to convince the project manager of an alternative design. However, if the project manager insists on the chosen design, an escalation may be necessary. The escalation procedure (as presented in Figure 6.4) should first appeal to the architecture review board (ARB) and then, if a final decision cannot be reached, to the enterprise architecture council (EAC). Chapter 4 provides more information on these organisational components.

Escalation does not necessarily mean that enterprise architects will succeed in having their solution design accepted. In many cases, project sponsors favour the project team because project results are needed swiftly, or because the cost pressure is high.

Exceptions are acceptable if they are well justified

In such cases, project managers can also be tasked with developing a plan for transforming an exceptional solution into an architecture-compliant solution within a given timeframe.

EA implementation progress reporting

While project reporting is important for project management and to steer the project portfolio, EAM should extend the reporting processes to document the EA implementation progress. Based on the EA models and documentation, enterprise architects can define the metrics that capture the solution design's quality and progress, as well as the implementation from an EAM perspective. For more information on EA reporting and EA key performance indicators (KPI), please refer to Chapter 7.

EAM can extend the existing project reporting

6.4 Piloting and roll-out: Closing the implementation

How EA documentation can help

In the piloting and roll-out phase, the solution is tested in practice for the first time (piloting). Subsequently, it is made available to the entire organisation (roll-out). Depending on the EA archetype (see Chapter 4), EA information can be an important input for the different piloting and roll-out approaches:

- *Model-driven EAM.* Architects use the EA repository to obtain an overview of the affected business processes, their applications systems' usage, the involved persons, follow-up processes, and so on. They can thus identify organisational units that have an immediate need for the solution, or have particularly good knowledge of the process or system being changed. Such units should conduct pilot tests. *Select the best suitable units for pilot tests*
- *Strategic applications and vendors EAM.* The centralised governance structure (which can be introduced with EAM) controls the piloting and the roll-out (see example below).
- *Architecture paradigm EAM.* The roll-out should fit the chosen paradigm. A SOA approach, for example, implicitly supports the provision of reusable services with its middleware-oriented concept. Instead of physical or technical distribution, the difficulty often lies in sufficient communication to ensure that the new solution is used.
- *Governance EAM.* In organisations characterised by this archetype, EA repositories provide important information for roll-outs, similar to the model-driven approach. However, organisations that choose the governance-oriented approach usually have a more complex EA and political situation within their company or corporate group. The focus therefore should be on clearly defined rules and decision rights for pilot tests and roll-outs.

How a food and health company organises piloting and roll-out

In a food and health firm, the architectural group identifies the most suitable or best-in-class markets for the new solution. In these markets, the firm conducts pilot tests within each of the three major geographical regions in which it operates. Business experts usually test the solution and proofread the documentation; with regard to process advancements, these experts improve the mapping of existing processes to the new best practices. The goal is to provide a solution package that is easy to apply. In major projects, there is a sign-off workshop during which all participating markets sign off the new solution on behalf of the rest of the company. Key participants in these workshops are the three pilot organisations, the business domain heads, architects and project members.

The roll-out usually happens as part of an integrated plan that shows all of the domain's deployment projects and helps coordinate the roll-out; it plans all resources needed within a one-year scope. The roll-out is then tracked on the regional level and reported to the central architectural organisation.

Updating the EA information – A "must" in the closing phase

Implementation projects are a step towards the target architecture. As such, they alter the as-is architecture - often in many layers and in various domains. These changes need to be recorded so that the organisation can continue working with up-to-date EA information.

It is unlikely that the project team will do all its modelling and designing solely with EA tools

The best way to keep EA information current is by letting the project team work with the EA repository so that any project-related modelling and design activities automatically lead to updated EA models. However, in many cases project teams operate on a different level of abstraction and have very specific tool requirements that make it hard, or even impossible, to apply the EA toolset. For example, as part of a software project, requirements engineering requires far more detailed models and information about a solution than enterprise architects usually need. It is therefore not surprising that many organisations face the challenge of persuading project teams to update EA information after the solution has been developed and deployed. From our case research, we have learned the following:

- It is advisable to connect EA documentation duties to milestone or gate approval processes so that the project team is forced to update the EA repository before it can proceed with the project.
- The burden of updating the EA repository can be reduced if the information required is collected and captured step by step

throughout the project life cycle. Very basic information on the solution can already be entered right at the beginning of a project, whereas information that relates to the operation of a solution may only be available after the final roll-out.

• Organisations with a low EAM maturity may support project teams by providing assistance when it comes to working with the EA repository. EA tools are often not very intuitive or user-friendly, and if support is provided, this can overcome resistance.

6.5 Management implications

In organisations with a low degree of *EAM awareness and maturity*, it will be difficult to simultaneously implement all the EAM practices described in this chapter. In such cases, it is more promising to follow a step-by-step approach in order to make the project life cycle architecture-aware. A second contextual factor is the *organisational power of an EAM programme*, which determines the extent to which you can implement EA realisation practices (in terms of their reach). Depending on these two factors, we distinguish three basic modes of incorporating EAM into project processes (Figure 6.5):

Organisations require a certain EAM maturity and a powerful EAM team to make their project lifecycle architecture-aware

- *Advising* – a more passive role for architects, due to their relatively low decision power in projects,
- *participating* – a more active role for architects, due to strong management support, and
- *managing* – the alignment of the project portfolio (management) with the EA (management).

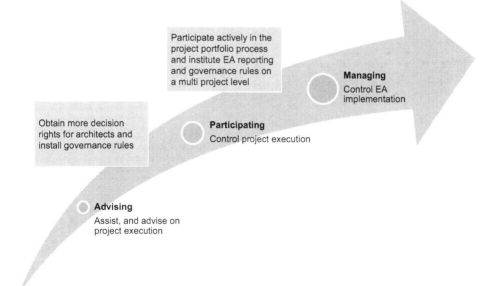

Figure 6.5: How to increase architecture awareness in project practices

Table 6.2 describes these three modes of incorporating EAM into the project lifecycle. Each of these three modes has specific advantages and shortcomings, which makes it suitable for specific situations. Although 'managing' seems the most mature stage, some organisations may choose to refrain from implementing this stage for cultural reasons, as this mode might impose many constraints on project teams.

Table 6.2: Three modes of EA realisation in the project lifecycle

Mode	Common EA practices	Benefits / Shortcomings	Recommended focus of EAM programme
Advising: assist with, and advise on project execution	• Single projects are accompanied and monitored by architects. • Architects advise project members, but have no right to suspend project execution. • Architects provide projects with information by means of EA documentation.	• Projects recognise and consider EA standards and documentation. • Deviations from EA standards and specifications become visible. • Project managers can push through non-EA-conformant solutions.	• Provide consistent, up-to-date EA information. • Advise on projects regarding architectural decisions. • Initiate a cultural change. • Communicate success stories and the advantages of using EA documentation and EA specifications.
Participating: control project execution	• Architects can influence project execution. • Enterprise architects have veto rights regarding violation of EA standards and principles. • Escalation routines for EA conflicts are in place. • Project reporting processes include EA information.	• Projects follow EA standards and specifications. • Higher management is aware of problematic issues that can be incorporated into the next EA strategy definition. • No EA implementation monitoring across projects. • No transparency about the EA progress and development.	• Strive for constructive results and minimise natural resistances. • Implement and communicate governance rules that define the architects' work on projects, for example, how architects use their veto rights to activate the ARB (see Figure 6.4).

Table 6.2: *continues*

| **Managing**: control EA implementation | • Architecture as a whole is monitored regarding the transition process and the planned architecture.
 • EA-related project goals are defined.
 • The KPI system is in place.
 • EA reporting processes are in place. | • Transparency regarding a project's contribution to the EA strategy.
 • Transparency and control regarding the EA realisation progress.
 • Automated reporting of aggregated KPIs.

 • Reduced local flexibility to implement adequate solutions.
 • Increased administrative and governance efforts. | • Implement clear routines that help to achieve the planned EA.
 • Compare the present EA with the planned EA and track the progress.
 • Facilitate domain-specific exchange between architects.
 • Launch dedicated architecture initiative and projects. |

References

[1] Project Management Institute, *A guide to the project management body of knowledge*. Philadelphia, Pennsylvania, USA: Project Management Institute, 2004.

[2] G. Caupin, H. Knöpfel, P. Morris, E. Motzel, and O. Pannenbäcker, *ICB-IPMA Competence Baseline*. Nijkerk, Netherlands: International Project Management Association, 1999.

[3] A. Murray, *Managing Successful Projects with PRINCE2™*, Norwich, UK: Office of Government Commerce, 2009.

[4] Agile Alliance, *"Manifesto for agile software development"*, 2001. [Online]. Available: http://agilemanifesto.org/.

[5] J. Highsmith, *Agile software development ecosystems*. Boston et al., MA, USA: Addison-Wesley, 2002.

Chapter 7

Embedding EAM into operation and monitoring

Christine Legner, Jan Löhe

Table of contents

Management summary

Strategic initiatives and projects are carefully planned and systematically develop an enterprise architecture (EA), but many smaller changes occur daily. If not properly managed, these operational changes might cause an organisation to lose control of and deviate from its target enterprise architecture roadmap. However, given the number of changes and their urgency, making changes requires efficient and lean EAM practices that do not delay business operations.

In this chapter, we outline three fields of action related to EA operations and monitoring. Firstly, pragmatic procedures must be established to manage operational changes and their architecture impact. Here, EAM practices help identify and keep track of operational changes that cause critical changes in the enterprise architecture. Secondly, monitoring systems and KPI (key performance indicator) reporting are a prerequisite for assessing the EA's current status and ascertain whether its development is in line with the architecture vision and roadmaps. Ideally, EAM teams define metrics and put procedures in place to track them effectively from the beginning. A comprehensive EAM cockpit covers three complementary aspects: EA impact in business terms, EA's current status and EAM adoption in the organisation. Thirdly, we bring to light additional beneficial uses of enterprise architecture documentation that support the organisation to understand and track complex organisational dependencies. This particularly applies to the areas of compliance, risks and business continuity management.

7.1 How to run the EA: The challenges in daily business

The myth of the stable EA target state

Among an enterprise architect's (EA's) most frustrating experiences is that the architecture constantly changes, even once a desired target state has been reached. Usually unforeseen by EA strategy planning and implementation, individual architecture components change slightly every day. These changes tend to happen almost unnoticed. For example, sudden organisational responsibility reassignments or small business process adaptations might occur, or a bug might need to be fixed urgently in a core information system. Such changes are mostly driven by operational requirements and can be neither suppressed – due to their urgency –, nor become fully aligned with the enterprise architecture strategy – due to the effort required to align them, their perceived lack of strategic importance, or because the architects simply do not notice them.

Small changes continually transform the current enterprise architecture

In total, these permanent changes might significantly affect the EA as a whole. In fact, companies often report a strong correlation between such changes' realisation and support incidents, due to the lack of coordination between and changes' unintended side effects. Therefore, if these changes are not managed properly, organisations do not only face operational problems. They also risk the current architecture's gradual divergence from its proposed trajectory towards the target architecture. At the same time, the frequency and focus areas of these changes may call for a strategic reflection on systematic problems with the as-is EA. They may also question the defined enterprise architecture principles.

As enterprise architecture management (EAM) is intended to be more than a once-off effort, it is vital to prepare for EA operation and monitoring. This chapter deals with how you run the enterprise architecture in a typical business setting. It focuses on operation and monitoring, which complement strategic planning (see Chapter 5) and the project life cycle (see Chapter 6). The main steps in operations and monitoring are (also see Figure 7.1):

Organisations need to prepare for EA operation and monitoring

1. Collecting demands and requests for change,
2. assessing the changes,
3. implementing the changes, and
4. monitoring the EA.

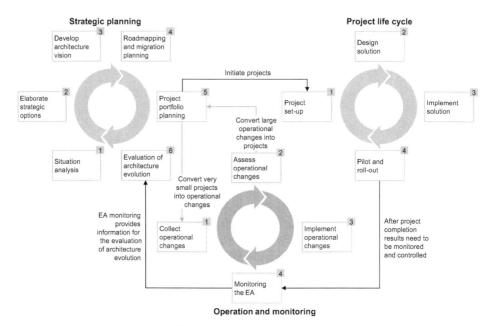

Figure 7.1: EAM process cycles

The operational control cycle and how it differs from strategic planning and the project life cycle

Contrary to strategic changes, operational changes occur in large numbers

Whereas strategic changes are carefully planned and have a long-term to mid-term horizon, the operational control cycle comprises the frequent (planned and unplanned) changes, which typically have a shorter time horizon and a local scope. Table 7.1 compares strategic and operational changes with regard to their size and impact on the EA. Many EA practices, such as comprehensive EA analysis and the design of a target state, migration planning and project reviews, which are applied during strategy development and realisation, are resource-intensive. They are not well suited for managing operational changes. The operational cycle needs pragmatic and 'slim' EA practices to cope with the daily changes triggered by problems, incidents, change and service requests, as well as to solve them within a short time frame.

Table 7.1: Differences between strategic and operational changes

Change dimensions	Strategic changes	Operational changes
EAM process cycle	Strategy planning and project life cycle (Chapters 5 and 6)	Operational control cycle (Chapter 7)
Time horizon	Long term or mid term	Short term
Focus	Realisation of business benefits and performance improvements	(Operational) excellence, stability, risk management
Size of changes and EA relevance	Major (strategic) changes with high EA relevance (global scope)	Many small changes, triggered by problems, change or service requests, with relatively little or no EA relevance (local scope)
Organisational set-up	Projects or programmes	Defined processes to monitor operations and respond to incidents, problems, change and service requests
Realisation effort	Medium to high	Low to medium
Duration of realisation	Months to years	Days to months
Frequency	Tens to hundreds of projects per year	Thousands to tens of thousands of changes per year
Monitoring and control	Integrated with existing budget, portfolio, programme or project reporting	Part of existing KPI systems, such as business process or SLA monitoring and incident reporting.
Risk	Size and impact of changes on the organisation	Number of changes and unintended side-effects, management of interdependencies

The questions that we address in this chapter include:

- *How should operational changes be managed?* If the organisation doesn't track tactical and operational changes systematically and consider their impact on architecture, it will deviate from the EA roadmap.
- *How should the enterprise architecture be monitored?* If monitoring is not undertaken, little can be said about the EA's development or current state, and whether these (still) fit the architecture vision and principles. Furthermore, monitoring also provides an important feedback loop to identify systematic EA-related issues and to initiate architecture initiatives.

- *Which further beneficial purposes can EA documentation be used for?* Once EA documentation is available, there are many ways to leverage this information base in order to facilitate decision-making and to support the business and IT functions.

7.2 Managing operational changes

Why even small changes are relevant in EAM

Organisations must constantly respond to unanticipated incidents, and requirements that change their existing EA. Such changes help maintain operational excellence, for example, where business processes are adapted, or system functionality is extended to create management reports or grant new user group's access rights. Operational changes are also required to minimise business risks, for example, when implementing security patches or upgrades. Most of the changes have a defined, relatively local scope. However, the major challenge is that these changes occur in locations all over the organisation, in relatively large numbers and cannot be anticipated.

Each operational change alters the EA slightly. But are all the changes relevant for the architecture?

Why should EAM processes take these operational changes into consideration? Although each operational change changes the EA slightly, its side-effects and implications are often underestimated. In addition, employees who decide on and implement changes are often unaware of potential conflicts with EA targets and their implications. They are not up to date on EAM in general, nor are they trained to analyse how changes affect the EA. In the following examples, we further outline the relevance and consequences for EAM.

Changes to a bill of material data base at a large automotive manufacturer

This large automotive manufacturer is reliant on the information stored in a central bill of materials data base. Over time, many applications interfaced with the bill of material system. The interfaces were usually implemented as hardwired data base requests in the application's source code. At a maintenance life cycle's end, the IT organisation decided to migrate the bill of material system to the latest data base technology. During migration, the data base was reorganised without taking the interfacing applications into consideration. The change resulted in several applications' malfunction. These had to be fixed in time-consuming and costly follow-up initiatives. Finally, an architecture team collected the dependencies between the data base and the interfacing applications in the form of context diagrams and information exchange models. The application staff and project managers improved this EA documentation during a long reconciliation phase. Today, information about the interfaces between applications is stored in a central EA repository and is always consulted before changes are made.

Assessment of local changes to a global IS platform at a large nutrition company

This large nutrition company decided to use SAP as its global IS platform, with the goal of establishing standardised best practices across the different local organisations. A standardised SAP template allowed the company to leverage centralised procurement. It could also conduct aggregated negotiations that improved large-scale deals with suppliers. However, local markets' requirements, such as their tax rates and tariffs, which had previously led to individual IS/IT developments, were a source of problems for the global platform. When implementing business-driven change requests that the local market organisations required (e.g., for financial reports), it was difficult to align the local adaptations and determine their side-effects on the other organisations. In addition, no governance process or EA assessment criteria were in place, which threatened the global template's consistency due to the local adaptations.

Currently, when a local business requirement or change request emerges, a local business excellence (BE) group assesses the requests on the basis of EA guidelines. Such requests are then directly mapped with the EA roadmap for the corporate SAP template. Simultaneously, the different local BE groups collaborate closely with the technical template team, which transfers and implements the local requirements that a BE group has defined to a usable global solution. The nutrition company can therefore be sure that its local organisations simultaneously improve the best practices implemented in the system and adhere to the current global template.

Managing operational changes to the enterprise architecture

Changes should be atomic, consistent, isolated and durable

As these examples illustrate, operational changes must be coordinated and controlled to avoid unforeseen side-effects or a complete deviation from the EA roadmap. This implies that changes fulfil the so-called ACID (atomic, consistent, isolated and durable) requirements [4]:

- *Atomic* means either the change is successfully conducted or rolled back completely.
- *Consistent* implies that the suggested solution for implementing the change integrates seamlessly – and without unexpected effects – with the environment.
- *Isolated* means that the change does not affect other EA changes or components besides those that form part of the suggested solution.
- *Durable* indicates that the change implementation is complete, stable, permanent and documented.

EAM practices support the ACID characteristics in several ways: Ideally, EA analysis techniques help check and approve the consistency and isolation requirements. If the EA documentation is updated after implementation, it contributes to atomic and durable changes.

Most companies have established standardized procedures which facilitate efficient and prompt handling of changes and minimize the impact of change-related issues. Typically, these procedures build on data from a configuration database. To identify the small number of changes that conflict with EA targets or have a major impact on them, these procedures need to integrate specific EAM practices. The goal is to establish pragmatic processes to assess changes that have a significant architecture impact, without slowing down the organisation. Given that most employees outside the architecture teams do not grasp the EA implications of operational changes, a key prerequisite is to create EA awareness and improve EA thinking in the IT operations teams.

In Figure 7.2, we depict an extended change management process, based on the process suggested by the IT Infrastructure Library (ITIL) [3]. This process complements the change process with additional tasks to analyse the architectural relevance and EA impact of

Pragmatic procedures should identify the changes that affect the EA

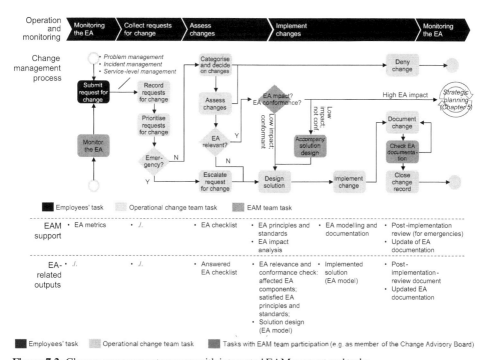

Figure 7.2: Change management process with integrated EAM support and tasks

the requested changes, to verify conformance with EA principles and standards, as well as to complement EA documentation after implementation. Some of these tasks need direct participation of the EAM function. For this purpose, enterprise architects should be member of the Change Advisory Board (CAB) which assists in the assessment, prioritization and scheduling of high-impact changes.

Collect changes

Systematically collect and record requests for change from different sources

Following the IT service management literature [4, 5, 6], different parties, including users and IT operations staff, request changes with different granularity levels and scopes. Firstly, to properly collect and identify such requests, organisations should identify and group the requesting parties, and identify their concerns. Next, organisations should determine the recipients (e.g., service desk) for each

Table 7.2: Typology of requested operational changes

Type	Service request	Incident	Problem	Other change requests
Scope	A regular request comprising predefined modification requirements of an existing (IT) service or functionality	An irregular (regarding occurrence) request to recover an existing (IT) service or functionality, due to an unplanned interruption or quality reduction	A request to recover an existing (IT) service or functionality, due to recurring incidents	A request to alter or enhance an existing EA component or functionality that goes beyond a predefined configuration scope
Example	A new user account, a change in the times support is available, installation of new software on new desktop PC	Recovery of an application or of an existing IT service, for example, due to network outages or application errors	Correcting persistent information processing failures of a single EA component	A user interface changes, new functionality, more load capacity
Requestor	Users	User	Operations or EAM team	Business units or functional management
Recipient	Service desk, those responsible for application	Service desk or those responsible for application	Operations or EAM team, those responsible for application	Business analyst or key user
EA relevance	No EA relevance in general, due to predefined modification scope	Must be evaluated ex post due to time criticality	Must be evaluated ex ante	Must be evaluated ex ante

group and the procedures for handling such requests. In Table 7.2, we distinguish between different request types for operational changes on the basis of their requestors, recipients and scope. Experience shows that defining request types and focusing on interfaces between the requestors and recipients help to produce a shared understanding in organisations and to implement a distributed but mutual change management process.

Some requests for change, such as incidents, are business-critical and require immediate recovery. In these cases, the follow-up process always focuses on recovery first, without any further prior EA assessment, whereas all other change types are categorised and assessed by means of standardised and formal procedures. However, organisations must take care to evaluate and document an incident, as well as any escalated change,– ex post to guarantee architecture consistency.

Assess changes

We estimate that only about 1-10% of all operational changes ever affect the EA and should therefore be considered architecturally relevant. An EA-relevant change either has a significant impact on an EA component by modifying its characteristics, or entails significant side-effects in other EA components. In order to ensure the efficient and prompt handling of changes, organisations need a set of decision criteria to determine whether or not a change is architecturally relevant. The check-list in Table 7.3 contains decision criteria that identify EA-relevant changes.

Assess changes to identify the small number of changes that are architecturally relevant

Table 7.3: Check-list to identify architectural relevance of operational changes

Changes are architecturally relevant if they...
• *alter business-critical EA components* (e.g., a product or service offering, key customers, distribution channels, core business processes or applications),
• *impact (existing) interfaces* (e.g., logically or technologically) between different EA components (e.g., two applications),
• *bear high risks* (e.g., high costs, volatile requirements or doubtful investments) and *impact the business continuity,*
• *change the main IS/IT security features* (e.g., communication with external parties),
• *impact external factors* or *resources* (e.g., supplier structure changes), and
• *violate regulatory guidelines* (e.g., Basel II, SOX, KonTraG, compulsory archiving or FDA), *company standards*, and *working models* (e.g., violation of or non-conformance with architecture principles and standards)

The example in Table 7.4 applies the criteria to potential master data changes. As shown in example 1, a new master data attribute for an instant messaging address is not considered architecturally relevant by five of six criteria, with the exception of '*interface dependence*', which must be checked further. This implies that, with support of EA documentation, the organisation must evaluate whether other applications besides the CRM system will use the new master data attribute and whether interfaces need to be adapted. If so, the change is classified as EA-relevant. Otherwise, implementation can proceed according to existing change management processes.

Table 7.4: Examples of EA relevance of different master data changes

Change example	Business criticality	Interface dependence	Business continuity	Security	External factors	Compliance
1. Introduction of a new master data attribute: In a customer data base, the client's data set should be enhanced with an instant messaging address attribute that can be used in the CRM system.	✗	?	✗	✗	✗	✗
2. Change in an existing master data attribute: The account numbers are changed from five numeric digits to seven alphanumeric digits.	✗	✔	?	✗	✗	?
3. Technology upgrade of a master data base: The customer data base is upgraded from Oracle Version 9i to Version 10g.	✗	✗	✗	✔	✗	✗

Check the impact on EA and all the side-effects of architecturally relevant changes

To change an existing master data attribute (as shown in example 2 above) and to upgrade the technology platform (as shown in example 3 above), there is at least one EA relevance category labelled '*yes*'. This implies that the change passes through an extended change management process of additional EA checking and analysis. In this case, enterprise architects (1) ensure that the change conforms to the organisation's EA principles and standards, and (2) assess the suggested solution's impact on other EA components. For this purpose, the affected EA components are listed in the change description. Ideally, the recipient (e.g., a service desk employee) has already identified the affected business processes, organisational entities, applications, master data and interfaces when recording the change request in the service desk tool.

To estimate the effect of a change, organisations can apply different EA analysis techniques, notably impact, coverage and dependency analysis. Figure 7.3 contains an example in which we assess the impact of a J2EE platform upgrade on the application, task, process and organisation levels. By means of such EA assessments, organisations can ensure that changes meet the consistency criterion, and are seamlessly integrated without having any unexpected side-effects on the environment. Additionally, these types of EA analyses are the basis for coordinating the planned change with other changes to the same EA components (e.g., configuration items, applications and projects). EAM thereby supports configuration and release management to ensure that the isolation criterion resolves dependencies and to avoid conflicts with other changes and redundancies.

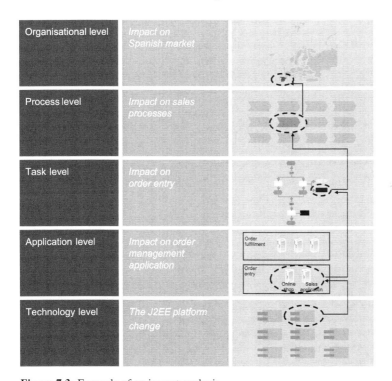

Figure 7.3: Example of an impact analysis

The outcomes of the EA conformance check and the impact assessment determine the subsequent procedure for implementing the change (as depicted in Table 7.5). If the suggested solution is in accordance with existing EA principles and standards and has little impact on other EA components, it can be implemented as planned.

Table 7.5: Outcomes of EA conformance check and consequences

Outcomes of EA conformance check	Outcomes of impact analysis	Consequence	Action
Yes, fulfils existing EA principles and standards	Little impact on other EA components	Solution is EA-conformant; EA will be changed in a controlled and planned scope	Implement suggested solution as planned and update EA documentation
Not in accordance with EA principles and standards	Little impact on other EA components	An alternative solution that fulfils existing EA standards and principles is preferable	Reject change and rework solution
Not in accordance with EA principles and standards	Significant impact on other EA components	Solution significantly alters the EA. It needs further requirements definition and solution design	Integrate change into an initiative or project planned in the strategic EA cycle
Not in accordance with EA principles and standards, but change is imperative or business-critical	Little impact on other EA components	Management decides to escalate change process	Implement escalated solution and update EA documentation

Implement change

Keep the EA consistent and up to date after implementing a change

The planned changes are swiftly implemented as a durable, high-quality solution. However, a successful change process involves both a working solution and up-to-date documentation. Hence, in respect of all the changes made, organisations must have defined and documented responsibilities and tasks:

- Firstly, they must define who will document the changes in the EA repository, where this will be done and in how much detail. Management can react with role descriptions that encompass or enforce documentation tasks, can monitor the documentation quality, and make successful task accomplishment part of employees' compensation schemes.
- Secondly, the EAM team must be assigned responsibility to check that the EA documentation in the EA repository is updated before the change is closed.

7.3 Monitoring the EA

Although the adage 'that which cannot be measured cannot be man-aged' also refers to EAM, organisations still struggle to define suita-ble key performance indicators (KPIs) for EA monitoring.

EA KPI monitoring is still in its infancy

Despite KPI reporting's popularity in the fact-based management approach, our case studies reveal that even EAM forerunners are still at an early stage, either defining EA-related KPIs or running simple EA reports. Simultaneously, many senior managers complain that, notwithstanding their efforts to create EA models, the existing EA documentation does not satisfy information requirements. Accord-ingly, analysts' studies [1] report that, while many enterprise archi-tects work hard to set up EAM in their organisation, they have a poor record for identifying metrics and tracking them effectively from the beginning. According to the Enterprise Architecture Executive Council [2], of the groups that report on EA:

- 44% report on the EA environment and activities,
- 31% report on EA compliance and adoption,
- 16% report on IT cost savings, but
- only 9% report on business value creation.

This underlines that even EA forerunners still fail to demonstrate EA's impact in business terms. Companies face two major EA moni-toring challenges: Firstly, they struggle to define appropriate EA metrics, and, secondly, they realise that their information base is not sufficient for the ongoing monitoring of EA-related KPIs.

Currently, IS and IT infrastructure layer monitoring are among the most advanced EA monitoring areas, but are often undertaken by means of fairly simple KPIs. Monitoring is often limited to the number of instances (e.g., applications or hardware components), the incurred costs per instance, or other instance features (e.g., its availa-bility or number of incidents). On the business side, business process owners often capture KPIs for business process efficiency and effec-tiveness, such as cycle time, customer service level or process costs. However, it is still difficult to display the existing KPIs according to the primary EA components and dimensions, since KPI reporting on the business and IT sides is not linked to the EA documentation. Consequently, creating EA-related KPI reports is a time-consuming manual effort.

In short, the necessary information base is lacking to analyse the multi-level dependencies between EA components, as well as to assess EA's impact on the business or IT performance, as existing KPIs are not tied to the primary EA layers and dimensions.

The EAM cockpit

The EAM cockpit should monitor three complementary aspects: EA impact in business terms, EA status and adoption of EAM

If EA monitoring is taken seriously, companies must create an EAM cockpit that helps track the KPIs related to the most important aspects, as well as the different EA perspectives. As in any KPI system, this cockpit should be multi-dimensional to support the informational requirements of the EA stakeholders, notably the senior management and enterprise architects. We suggest that every EAM cockpit cover three complementary aspects (see Table 7.6):

- Firstly, the EAM cockpit must monitor the *EA impact in business terms*, which is the *EA's efficiency and effectiveness at achieving business and IT goals*. As the EA's main purpose is to support the organisation's strategic targets, the cockpit should start by displaying the existing KPI set – as defined by a balanced scorecard or other management reporting system – according to the EA dimensions and layers. For example, business-related KPIs (e.g., customer satisfaction, financial performance or new products' time to market) can be refined and related to EA elements (e.g., key business processes or supporting IT applications). By drilling down these KPIs to the relevant EA components, strengths and weaknesses become visible.
- Secondly, the EAM cockpit should track the EA's *current status*, with a specific focus on *EA conformance with defined targets and the enforcement of architecture principles and guidelines.* This provides the basis for measuring progress towards the planned state, but also for escalating non-conformance. For example, the number of instances of a certain EA component (e.g., the number of applications or the number of business process variants) is often a good measure of EA complexity. Architecture principle and guideline enforcement can be measured concurrently by dividing the number of conforming instances by the total number of instances.
- Thirdly, the EAM cockpit should also capture *EAM adoption in the organisation* by measuring EAM-related activities and skills. These KPIs provide a backwards glance at the different activities related to EAM implementation, such as the number of projects that used and updated the organisation-wide EA models, the

number of employees in EA trainings and the number of applications documented in the EA repository.

As a rule of thumb, EA-related information stored in the EAM tool should link to existing KPI reporting to facilitate the set-up of the EAM cockpit. As a multi-dimensional KPI system, the EAM cockpit complements the firm's existing monitoring systems by providing a holistic and inter-divisional perspective on the EA components.

Table 7.6: Multi-dimensional EAM cockpit

Dimension	KPIs	Stakeholders
EA quality and impact in business terms (efficiency and effectiveness at achieving business and IT goals)	Business KPIs, as defined by the balanced scorecard or other management reporting systems, linked to EA components and layers: • **Financial perspective** (e.g., costs, revenues, operating margin). • **Customer perspective** (e.g., customer retention rate). • **Learning and growth** (e.g., time to market or time to launch new products). • **Internal business processes** (e.g., cycle time and service level).	**Senior management** (business units and IT)
EA status (conformance with target architecture and architecture principles)	KPIs that illustrate the EA's purposeful development and its conformance with architecture targets and principles: • **Total instances** in respect of the different **EA components.** • **Percentage instances** that **conform to the defined architecture standards** (e.g., percentage of data bases using the harmonised customer master data definition; percentage of interfaces that conform to specifications). • **Percentage of customisations** and local exceptions (e.g., percentage of local process variants). • **The EA component** *point costing* (see EA status example).	**Enterprise architects**
EAM adoption (EAM activities in the organisation)	KPIs that describe the adoption of EA: • **Organisational diffusion** of EA knowledge (e.g., number of employees in EA trainings). • **Quality of architecture documentation** (e.g., percentage of applications with documentation, age of architecture documentation and documentation filing level per architecture component). • **Use of architecture documentation** (e.g., percentage of projects using process models and number of users per model)	**Enterprise architects**

Practical examples

In the next sections, we will describe three practical EA monitoring examples for the three EAM cockpit dimensions. These examples illustrate that EA monitoring improves transparency and generates inter-divisional and multi-level responsibility, whereas responsibilities for traditional KPIs often lie with individual line managers. Thus, EA monitoring links individual management systems to a more comprehensive, multi-dimensional and multi-level enterprise management system.

EA quality and impact: Measuring the application landscape's effectiveness

An application landscape's effectiveness can be assessed with measures of functional and operational readiness

The following example illustrates how a global application landscape's effectiveness can be assessed from both business and IT perspectives. It uses KPIs that characterise this landscape's functional and operational readiness. In Figure 7.4, each row represents an application, and each column a region where the application is used. Functional readiness describes whether the functions required to support a business process are available in the required quality. As a subjective measurement of user satisfaction, functional readiness is captured by means of surveys. In Figure 7.4, we use an ordinal ranking scheme for functional readiness with six entries ranging from (1) very good to (6) not satisfactory. A systematic assessment of all the relevant stakeholders (e.g., business managers and users) and an aggregation of the global and overall average ratings are all taken into account to contribute to a comprehensive picture and to cover different aspects of application quality. The functional assessment is complemented by an operational assessment – in our example, the number of incidents per 1,000 transactions. The assessment uses metrics related to incidents or service requests created automatically from existing information sources, such as the incident management system.

In our practical example, application managers or architects regularly analyse these reports and seek optimisation potentials. Since the report covers the entire application landscape, similar incidents (e.g., problems with Web frontends, which are used by different applications) and common issues in the OEM's order management process can be detected. This demonstrates the advantages of using a consistent EA model to link incident reporting not only to single item in the configuration data base, but also to EA components.

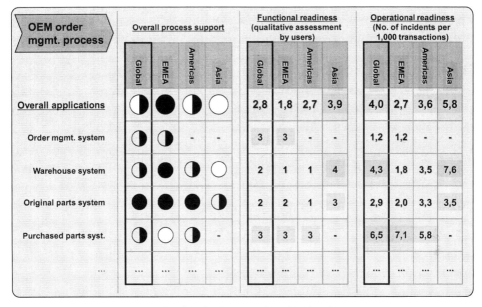

OEM order mgmt. process	Overall process support				Functional readiness (qualitative assessment by users)				Operational readiness (No. of incidents per 1,000 transactions)			
	Global	EMEA	Americas	Asia	Global	EMEA	Americas	Asia	Global	EMEA	Americas	Asia
Overall applications	◑	●	◑	○	2,8	1,8	2,7	3,9	4,0	2,7	3,6	5,8
Order mgmt. system	◑	◑	-	-	3	3	-	-	1,2	1,2	-	-
Warehouse system	◑	●	◑	○	2	1	1	4	4,3	1,8	3,5	7,6
Original parts system	●	●	●	◑	2	2	1	3	2,9	2,0	3,3	3,5
Purchased parts syst.	◑	○	◑	-	3	3	3	-	6,5	7,1	5,8	-
...	...	...	...	...	...	...	...	...	...	...	...	...

Figure 7.4: Measuring the application landscape's functional and operational readiness

EA status: Measuring EA complexity by means of the point costing concept

Since complexity is an important cost driver, we recommend tracking KPIs that measure EA complexity. Analogous to function point analysis, which is used in software development, organisations can apply the EA component *point costing* to assess their EA's complexity [4]. This concept assesses complexity on the basis of ratings for EA components and characteristics considered to be complexity drivers. For an application, such complexity drivers are an EA component's compliance and security requirements, its business criticality, or multiple dependencies between and interfaces to other EA components. The overall objective is to minimise ratings and, thus, reduce the EA's overall complexity. Table 7.7 shows examples with specific EA component characteristics' weightings. For example, organisations can evaluate their interface's complexity by means of the EA component *point costing* concept, or reduce the number of interfaces based on proprietary technology. If an application's interface rating exceeds 50 points, replacing the direct application-to-application linkages with a service-oriented architecture (SOA), based on an enterprise service bus, might be recommendable. By

The EA component point costing measures complexity

means of EA component *point costing*, organisations can quantitatively justify this SOA initiative as a complexity reduction improvement and track its impact on the EA.

The EA component *point costing* requires the definition of EA component characteristics that drive complexity and the estimation of weightings, as suggested in our example. The relevant characteristics and their weightings need to be selected based on the organisation's specific needs and experiences. In addition, EA repositories, or a configuration management data base that encompasses as many EA components and attributes as possible, are further prerequisites to derive reasonable characteristics.

Table 7.7: The EA component *point costing* concept

EA component characteristic	Weighting
Application characteristics	
Core business application (business-critical, extended SLA)	20 points
Supporting business application (not business-critical, standard SLA)	10 points
SOX compliance significance	10 points
Modification of a function (non-upgradeable)	5 points
Interface characteristics	
Point-to-point interface to or from other application (proprietary technology)	10 points
Hub-and-spoke interface to or from other application (proprietary technology)	5 points
Bus interface to or from other application (web service standard)	2 points
…	

EAM adoption: Monitoring architecture documentation

The third example measures EAM adoption in an organisation by assessing architecture documentation. Documented EA models are a prerequisite for applying EA analysis techniques (e.g., impact and dependency analysis) at a later stage. Consequently, organisations should systematically determine EA documentation requirements and assign those responsible for creating it in the different phases of the software development lifecycle (SDLC). Table 7.8 depicts a reporting system that evaluates EA documentation's existence and quality at defined quality gates in the SDLC.

Table 7.8: Monitoring the EA documentation in the software development lifecycle (SDLC)

SDLC phase	Concept		Development		Testing
Quality gate	1	2	3	4	5
Attributes to be documented	Names of those responsible for application	Business support functional description	Beginning and end of operations	Technical architecture	Operations concept
EA models to be prepared	-	IS land use plan	-	Interface diagram	Deployment model
Those responsible for documentation	Functional application responsible	Functional architect	IT operations	IT architecture	IT operations
Number of applications	644	613	589	445	599
% documented attributes	100%	95,19%	91,46%	69,1%	93,01%
% EA models	Not applicable	85,89%	Not applicable	17,58%	29,29%
Average document age	4,5 years	6,7 months	2,3 years	10,4 months	1,2 years

In our example, KPIs include different applications' EA documentation existence, measured as the proportion (%) of documented EA attributes and the proportion (%) of available EA models. These KPIs are complemented by the architecture documentation's average age. Accordingly, architects can draw the following conclusions from the proposed KPI reporting: Firstly, how to improve the overall EA documentation for a specific quality gate, (e.g., level 4: technical architecture). Secondly, check and revise outdated EA documents (e.g., level 1: due to changed responsibilities).

Determine the EA documentation to be filed in the different phases of the software development lifecycle

7.4 Using EA documentation

Although EA initiatives often begin by modelling and documenting the organisation's architectures, most EA documents are only used during such initiatives, and only by the enterprise architects. However, EA documentation has many benefits outside the EAM function and may even become a critical information source for business.

EA documentation has many benefits outside the EAM function

Litigation risks force an automotive manufacturer to document data usage and storage

To address the risk of potential litigations in the US, one large automotive manufacturer uses EA documentation to protect its intellectual property. In the case of a legal dispute, lawyers are allowed access to information within different IS systems. Owing to the interdependencies between the different applications (car development, production planning and financial IS), the challenge is to protect car construction and development plans or production and quality knowledge that are not part of the inquiry. The manufacturer's architects started documenting these system dependencies, as well as knowledge in the company's data bases, in an abstract but comprehensible way. Business lines use this information to implement measures to protect their intellectual property in case of litigation.

In Table 7.9, we provide a short overview of how EA documentation can be used outside the EA initiative's narrow scope. In the following section, we delve into two examples and illustrate how EA documentation supports business continuity and risk, as well as compliance management.

EA documentation can be a valuable information source for continuity, risk and compliance management

Table 7.9: Use of EA documentation

Scenario	Stakeholders	Goals	Relevant EA documentation
Benchmarking (e.g., for business processes)	Functional management, process management and organisational development	Assess performance and compare to that of competitors, other best practice companies, or industry reference models (e.g., SCOR [7]) Identify best practices and measures for improvement	Documentation about EA components and related KPIs (e.g., costs, processing or waiting time and service levels)
Organisational knowledge management	All employees	Transparent and efficient information provision about all aspects of the EA: Where to find information (e.g., product documentation, process descriptions and application documentation), and who to contact (e.g., roles and responsibilities)	Documentation about EA components with related meta-data, such as responsibilities (e.g., RACI matrix), and attached information (e.g., links to intranet resources or files) EA models can be made available on the company intranet or on wikis
Procurement or sourcing	Purchasing department and logistics	Monitor relationships with external suppliers on the basis of EA information Provide EA standards and guidelines (e.g., development guidelines) with which external contractors must comply	Documentation of EA components and related meta-data (e.g., contracts, outsourced responsibilities for applications) EA monitoring of supervising standard violations (e.g., vendor evaluation per application)
Business continuity management	IT operations and auditors	Manage business risks by identifying the root causes of emerging problems and determining investments in fail-proof resources that support business-critical tasks and processes	EA dependency and impact analysis of different EA layers and components (e.g., applications, processes and customer groups)
Compliance management	Compliance manager, auditors	Document legal compliance and conformance with external or internal standards (e.g., data protection and security standards)	Compliance information linked to attributes of EA components (e.g., SAP FI is SOX compliant)

Using EA documentation in business continuity and risk management

The purpose of business continuity management (BCM) is to completely recover operations in case of a disaster or an emergency [8, 9]. Executive management and shareholders care about effective BCM. Their key concerns are to identify the organisation's key vulnerabilities, weaknesses and risks, as well as to circumvent single points of failure. Business continuity management consists of three main phases: Firstly, to analyse and develop a comprehensive contingency plan; secondly, to provide procedures to ensure continuous operations; and thirdly, to conduct ongoing analyses to improve business continuity management.

EA models help companies understand risks and resource dependencies

To provide the required procedures to ensure continuous operations, it is imperative for BCM planners to understand the priorities, risks and dependencies of their organisation's resources. Given that multi-level dependencies and the mass of available information related to corporate resources are the main challenges, BCM can benefit from systematic and well-structured EA documentation, which displays the different EA components and their relationships. Since EA documentation builds on predefined models, it can also be used for automated analysis. Compared to flat documentation (e.g., reports or interview transcripts), EA documentation restricts the scope for interpretation [9]. Analysis results can either be presented in a cross-reference report or in a visual representation, for example, as a dependency graph. Such a dependency graph makes the complex web of interrelationships visible and answers questions such as [10]: How are the applications distributed across server clusters? or which business processes are affected if we switch off a certain network node? If EA components' documentation is complemented by additional attributes for risk, priority or benefits, reports can be generated to display critical organisational or IS resources. EA documentation therefore reduces guesswork. Simulation or 'what if' scenarios that use different EA planning scenarios allow emergencies' impacts to be assessed. Informed choices can be made and BCM procedures can be improved by comparing different variants, for example, with or without redundancy of critical or non-critical EA resources. Furthermore, formalised EA models of all architecture layers can ensure continuous operations during emergencies by documenting the responsibilities (who) and emergency solutions (what, how and when) in few words but with great clarity and accuracy.

*Assign
responsibilities and
document whether
EA components
comply with
regulatory
guidelines and
principles*

Using EA documentation in compliance management

Compliance management's purpose is to document adherence to regulatory guidelines and principles (e.g., Solvency II, Basel II or SOX), as well as internal data protection and security standards. Internal and external auditors, government agencies and executive management are concerned with and monitor whether process documentation requirements, resource responsibilities and obligations to preserve records are met and are available on demand [11]. In order to leverage EA documentation for compliance management, organisations must complement their EA models by assigning employees to take ownership and by adding compliance classifications to EA components (e.g., to processes, applications or data). Based on this information base, they can apply coverage analysis to show conformance with certain regulations or assignment to a responsible person [10]. Furthermore, EA models and compliance analysis can be used to assess whether certain authorisation or recovery mechanisms, access rights or ownership policies have been implemented, and whether the user actions and changes are traceable. Depending on its focus and granularity, EA documentation can also be used to support certain certification procedures, such as ISO-9001 or BS-7799.

7.5 Management implications

When EAM activities are launched, much effort goes into developing EA models, documenting the current EA architecture and designing the planned architecture. However, the operational changes that continuously alter the EA are often overlooked. If not properly managed, the sum of the changes can cause the organisation to lose control and the EA to deviate from its path towards the target EA. In order to establish EAM practice, three key issues must be highlighted:

- *Managing the high number of operational changes and their impact on the EA*
  Firstly, changes' EA relevance must be evaluated. To identify the small number of changes that conflict with EA targets or have a major impact on them, employees need to be EA aware, but also trained and motivated to identify EA-relevant changes. Smart and efficient rules should be defined to assess the changes' EA relevance without slowing down the organisation. We recommend the use of pragmatic processes with simple check-lists and quality gates with (enterprise) architects doing the assessing and decision-making.
- *What gets measured gets managed – establishing EAM-related KPI reporting*
  To create the first KPI set, the existing KPIs must be displayed according to EA components and layers. Initially, this can be done manually and will generate interesting insights into and discussion about the organisation's strengths and weaknesses. It will also help to create awareness of EAM activities among the employees. As EAM matures, the metrics should be complemented and a comprehensive EAM cockpit should be built. Ensure that KPI reporting covers three key dimensions: Firstly, the EA's status as described by statistics on EA instances and their conformance to architecture principles; secondly, how well the EA supports the company in meeting business objectives, which can be assessed by linking the business KPIs to EA models and instances; and, thirdly, EAM adoption as measured by the availability and quality of the EA documentation, as well as the training and skills in the organisation.

• *Getting the most from your EA documentation*
Finally, the many benefits of using EA documentation outside the
EAM function should be explored, most importantly in the areas
of compliance, risks and business continuity management. This
can be achieved by talking to the stakeholders who need to understand and maintain information on complex organisational
dependencies.

References

[1] Vollmer, K., *EA and Metrics: For Maximum Impact Measure The Business Value*, Cambridge, MA, USA: Forrester Research, 2007

[2] Enterprise Architecture Executive Council, State of the EA Function – EA Priorities, Activities, Metrics, and Organizational Models, Corporate Executive Board, 2005

[3] Andenmatten, M., *ITIL IT Infrastructure Library-Foundation – Die Grundlagen Ausbildung*, 2006-L01-01, Glenfis AG, Bösch, Switzerland, 2006

[4] Betz, C., *Architecture and Patterns for IT Service Management, Resource Planning, and Governance. Making Shoes for the Cobbler's Children*, Waltham, Massachusetts, USA: Morgan Kaufman Publ Inc., 2006

[5] OGC, *Service Design, ITIL, TSO (The Stationery Office)*, London, 2007

[6] Zarnekow, R.; Brenner, W.; Pilgram, U., *Integrated Information Management*, Berlin: Springer, 2006

[7] SCOR, *Supply-Chain Operations Reference-model (SCOR), Version 6*, Supply-Chain Council, Inc., Pittsburgh, PA, 2003

[8] The Business Continuity Institute, *Good Practice Guidelines 2008 A Management Guide to Implementing Global good Practice in Business Continuity Management*, Caversham, UK: The Business Continuity Institute, 2007

[9] Clarke, G., *How Enterprise Modelling can help Business Continuity Managers to understand complexity*, Welwyn Garden City, UK: VEGA Consulting Services Ltd, 2009

[10] Bucher, T.; Fischer, R.; Kurpjuweit, S.; Winter, R., *Enterprise Architecture Analysis and Application – An Exploratory Study, to appear in: Proceedings of the EDOC Workshop on Trends in Enterprise Architecture Research*, Hongkong, 2006

[11] Keller, W., *IT-Unternehmensarchitektur, 1*, dpunkt.verlag, Heidelberg, 2007

[12] Chief Information Officers Council, *Clinger-Cohen Act, February 10, 1996*, Chief Information Officers Council, 1996

Chapter 8

EA frameworks, modelling and tools

David Basten, Dorothea Brons

Table of contents

Management summary

As enterprises can be large and complex, their architecture (EA) also tends to be large and complex. Frameworks, models and tools have been developed to address this complexity and to support enterprise architecture management (EAM) endeavours.

EA frameworks use different approaches, each with its particular strengths and weaknesses. Primarily, an EA framework is a practical starting point for EAM. It is not easy to know which EA framework, or which combination of EA frameworks, is best for your organisation. For many organisations, a 'blended' approach might be best; this means creating an EA methodology out of parts of existing methodologies that provide the highest value in specific areas of concern.

Regardless of whether you use an EA framework or not, it is essential that the EA is documented. EA models help with this task, as they are far more comprehensive than pure business process models: Beside the key factors that position an enterprise (or domain) in the market and in terms of its value generation, they describe the organisation and processes, the information systems and technology used, the people and the corporate competencies on a conceptual or logical level, as they are today, or how they should be in the future.

This richness of objects, levels and views is the reason why EA tools are widely used to support EAM. Furthermore, a sound EA tool always meets different stakeholders' needs. It is essential that this tool provides a user-friendly model development interface, as well as support for workflows and automation. Product extendibility and customisation could also be crucial. EA tools should provide analytical and reporting capabilities that help to manage and improve the EA; therefore, a robust but flexible repository is key. Last but not least, while you might favour one EA tool over another for reasons such as good value for money and sufficient vendor support, we recommend that you follow a structured process when selecting an EA tool.

8.1 Frameworks, modelling, and tools: How they are intertwined

Enterprise architecture management (EAM) builds on multifaceted EA models that comprise multiple views, layers and domains. 'While the architecture for a new building is captured in blueprints, enterprise architecture is often represented in principles, policies and technology choices. Thus, the concept can be difficult for managers to get their arms around' [1]. The basis of architecture analysis is the description of the existing architectures. This provides relevant information; for example, it allows the enterprise to identify organisational bottlenecks or redundancies, as well as gaps in the business processes' IT support. The impact of adaptation and design activities on other components then also becomes visible and can be taken into account when taking decisions.

Frameworks, models and tools have been developed to cope with architecture's complexity

Enterprise architecture frameworks organise and systemise the complexity by including reference architectures, methodologies, checklists, best practice processes and so on (see Chapter 8.2). An EA framework therefore provides a practical starting point for enterprise architecture management. Furthermore, it avoids the initial panic when the task scale becomes apparent. To create an integrated perspective of an enterprise, techniques are needed to describe architectures coherently; enterprise architecture modelling offers the solution (see Chapter 8.3). Tools are also needed to manage enterprise architecture (see Chapter 8.4). In this chapter, we will moreover consider the management implications of applying enterprise architectures, models and tools (see Chapter 8.5).

The number of EA frameworks, models and tools has risen sharply in the past few years. Owing to the many different approaches, confusion, and questions such as the following abound:

- What is the right and adequate EA framework for my organisation?
- What must be taken into account when selecting or creating a framework?
- Why should I use EA tools and how can I find the right EA tool?
- How can an architecture be considered target group oriented?
- What are the benefits of frameworks, tools and methods?

This chapter seeks to provide an overview of the available frameworks, models and tools. Best practices are described, as well as the benefits and limits of existing frameworks, models and tools.

8.2 Main facts about EA frameworks

An EA framework is a skeletal structure that defines suggested architectural artefacts, describes how these artefacts relate to each other, and provides generic suggestions regarding these artefacts [2]. Enterprise architecture frameworks typically embrace the following components [3]:

EA frameworks offer a standard approach to architecture

- a reference enterprise architecture,
- a methodology for planning and implementation,
- instruments and guidance for conceptualising and documenting enterprise architecture, as well as
- a common vocabulary or glossary.

EA frameworks capture tried and tested solutions. Each EA framework focuses on different aspects.

A brief history of EA framework development

The development of EA frameworks, as shown in Figure 8.1, dates back to J.A. Zachman's publication in 1987 [4].

The development of EA frameworks started in 1980s

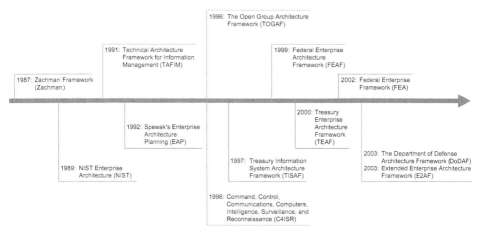

Figure 8.1: Development of EA frameworks

The Zachman framework had a major influence on one of the earliest attempts by a branch of the US Government – the Department of Defence – to create an EA. This attempt, known as the Technical Architecture Framework for Information Management (TAFIM), was introduced in 1994. Influenced by the benefits promised by the TAFIM, the US Congress passed a bill known as the Clinger-Cohen Act in 1996. This Act mandated that all federal agencies take steps to improve their IT investments' effectiveness. The Federal Enterprise Architecture Framework (FEAF), which was released in 1999, is a result of the Clinger-Cohen Act. FEAF was developed by the Office of Management and Budget (OMB) and renamed the Federal Enterprise Architecture (FEA) in 2002. The work done on TAFIM was turned over to The Open Group. They morphed it into The Open Group Architecture Framework (TOGAF™). Many enterprise architectural methodologies have come and gone over the past 23 years. Table 8.1 provides an overview of the most established EA frameworks.

EA frameworks have developed from various sources

Table 8.1: The most established EA frameworks[1]

Enterprise-developed Frameworks	• The Open Group Architecture Framework (TOGAFTM) • Generalised Enterprise Reference Architecture and Methodology (GERAM) • Reference Model of Open Distributed Processing (RM-ODP) • Guide to the Enterprise Architecture Body of Knowledge (EABOK)
Commercial Frameworks	• Integrated Architecture Framework (IAF) • Zachman Framework • Architecture of Integrated Information Systems (ARIS) • OBASHI Business & IT methodology and framework (OBASHI)
Defence Industry Frameworks	• Command, Control, Communications, Computers, Intelligence, Surveillance, and Reconnaissance (C4ISR) • Department of Defence Architecture Framework (DoDAF) and Technical Reference Model (TRM) • NATO Architecture Framework (NATO) • Technical Architecture Framework for Information Management (TAFIM) • Joint Technical Architecture (JTA) • UK Ministry of Defence Architecture Framework (MODAF) • Department of National Defence and the Canadian Forces Architecture Framework (DNDAF) • France DGA Architecture Framework (AGATE) • International Defence Enterprise Architecture Specification (IDEAS)
Government Frameworks	• Federal Enterprise Architecture Framework (FEAF) • Government Enterprise Architecture (GEA) • Treasury Enterprise Architecture Framework (TEAF) • European Interoperability Framework (EIF) • NIST Enterprise Architecture (NIST) • Treasury Information System Architecture Framework (TISAF) • Standards and Architectures for eGovernment Applications (SAGA)
Other Frameworks	• Extended Enterprise Architecture Framework (E2AF) • Spewak's Enterprise Architecture Planning (EAP)

---

[1] For more information on EA frameworks please refer to the appendix.

At present, the vast majority of organisations apply one of three EA frameworks, namely:

- the Zachman Framework,
- the Open Group Architectural Framework (TOGAF™), or
- Federal Enterprise Architecture (FEA).

These frameworks are popular because of their maturity (all three), their age (Zachman being the oldest), free access to resources and information (TOGAF, FEA), as well the obligation to comply with them (FEA in respect of the US government).

The vast majority of the field uses either the Zachman framework, TOGAF™, or FEA

The Zachman Framework:

The Zachman Framework [5], although self-described as a framework, is more accurately defined as a taxonomy for organising architectural artefacts. Zachman recognised two dimensions: specific target audiences' perspectives and the architectural description types. He proposed six descriptive foci (data, function, network, people, time and motivation) and six player perspectives (planner, owner, designer, builder, subcontractor and enterprise). These two dimensions can be arranged in a grid. According to Zachman, an architecture can only be considered complete when every cell in this grid has been populated. He does not provide a methodology for creating a new architecture.

The Zachman Framework is more accurately defined as a taxonomy for organising architectural artefacts

The Open Group Architecture Framework (TOGAF™):

TOGAF™ [5] divides an EA into four categories:

- Business architecture: Describes the processes that the business uses to meet its goals.
- Application architecture: Describes how specific applications are designed and how they interact with each other.
- Data architecture: Describes how the enterprise data stores are organised and accessed.
- Technology architecture: Describes the hardware and software infrastructure that supports applications and their interactions.

The main parts of TOGAF™ are the *Architecture Development Method* (ADM), the *Enterprise Continuum*, and the *Resource Base*. The ADM is a process for creating architecture. It consists of an initialisation phase, followed by an eight-phase cycle (Figure 8.2).

TOGAF™ is a process-oriented framework that divides an EA into business, application, data- and technology architecture

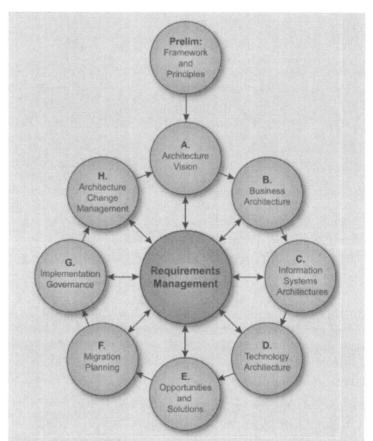

Figure 8.2: TOGAF™ Architecture Development Method (ADM) Cycle

TOGAF™ allows phases to be done incompletely, skipped, combined, reordered, or reshaped to fit any organisation's needs. TOGAF™ views the world of enterprise architecture as a continuum of architectures (enterprise continuum), ranging from highly generic to highly specific. The most generic architectures are called *foundation architectures*. In theory, these can be used by any organisation. The next, more specific, level is called *common systems architecture*. These are principles that one would expect to see in many types of enterprises. The next level is called *industry architectures*, which are specific principles across many enterprises in one industry. The most specific level is called *organisational architectures*, which apply to a given organisation.

TOGAF™ defines various knowledge bases. The *Technical Reference Model* (TRM) is a suggested description of a generic IT architecture. The *Standards Information Base* (SIB) is a collection of standard and pseudo-standards that The Open Group recommend for consideration during enterprise architecture development.

Federal Enterprise Architecture (FEA):

FEA is the most complete of the three methodologies. It has both a comprehensive taxonomy (like Zachman) and an architectural process (like TOGAF^{TM}). FEA consists of:

- A set of *reference models* for describing different EA perspectives: Business Reference Model (BRM), Components Reference Model (CRM), Technical Reference Model (TRM), Data Reference Model (DRM), and Performance Reference Model (PRM). These reference models provide standard terms and definitions.
- A *perspective* on how EAs should be viewed.
- A four-step *process for creating an EA*:
  Step 1: architecture analysis (definition of a simple and concise vision);
  Step 2: architectural definition (definition of the desired architectural state: document the performance goals, consider design alternatives and develop an enterprise architecture, including business, data, services and technology architectures); Step 3: investment and funding strategy (considering how the project will be funded); and Step 4: programme management plan and project execution (creation of a plan for managing and conducting projects, including the milestones and performance measures to assess the project success).
- A *transitional process* for migrating from a pre-EA to a post-EA paradigm.
- A *taxonomy* for cataloguing assets that fall within the EA's scope.
- An *approach* for measuring the EA's success in enhancing business value.

Comprehensive taxonomy, like Zachman, and an architectural process, like TOGAF^{TM}

Framework usage of study participants

Clearly, the leading EA frameworks have very different approaches. This makes it hard for organisations to choose one EA framework and we find it reflected in the study participants' usage of EA frameworks. Some participants in our study do not use an EA framework at all, while certain organisations use and adapt well-known EA frameworks (e.g., Zachman and TOGAF^{TM}). Others have developed their own EA framework, 'cherry-picking' from a variety of frameworks (Table 8.2).

The usage of EA frameworks differs vastly among the study participants

Table 8.2: Framework usage by study participants

Study Participant	Framework Usage
Government department	Developed own framework based on Zachman
Cargo carrier	Little usage of frameworks, TOGAF™ oriented
Bank	Developed own framework, no standardised framework in use
Consumer products manufacturer	No frameworks in use
Insurance	Zachman framework, TOGAF™
Construction industry products manufacturer	No frameworks in use
Retailer	ARIS used for BPM, no pure EAM framework
Automotive manufacturer	Developed own framework based on available frameworks but not used consistently within the company

How to find the right EA framework

Which EA framework is best for your organisation? Since none of the approaches have been complete as yet, a 'blended' approach might be a good starting point for many organisations. These organisations can create their own EA methodology from the methodologies that provide the highest value in specific areas of concern. The government department that developed its own EA framework based on the Zachman Framework serves as an example.

A blended approach, through which they create their own EA methodology, might be the best for many organisations

How the government department adapted the Zachman Framework

The government department considered the complete Zachman Framework too complex; therefore, they developed their own EA framework. The first version of this framework was published in 2005. Its purpose was to raise awareness of EAM, as well as to provide guidelines for EAM and to illustrate how these should be applied in other government departments. These guidelines included the architecture standards, architecture governance and architectural processes. The framework has been found helpful and is frequently used, for instance, when determining the point at which the IT must take over. The current version lacks procedures and methodologies that specifically describe how to conduct EAM in detail. The plan is to include these in a future version, along with methodologies for establishing service-oriented architectures. TOGAF™ will be included in the framework's further development.

The following example shows how an organisation developed its own EA framework without using much from any established EA frameworks.

How a cargo carrier developed its own EA framework

The cargo carrier's EAM team established certain basic EA principles that, for instance, determine how legacy systems should be integrated and domain-spanning communication should be established. These are motivated by strategic objectives, such as achieving cost-optimised up-to-date systems and using open standards for interfaces. The goal is to match business requirements with EA principles. However, the principles are not precisely recorded in a fixed catalogue. A common EA meta-model is being developed. The technical standards are updated once per year by the technical architect, who coordinates this task with the infrastructure operations unit. The review boards discuss and approve the changes suggested for the following year. Although the EAM team refers to TOGAF™ from time to time to obtain input for methodologies, EAM frameworks are rarely used.

A framework comparison is a good starting point for selecting or defining your specific EA framework. The following dimensions can be used to understand and compare existing frameworks, or to create a new framework [7-9]:

- **Taxonomy completeness**. How well does the framework classify the various architectural artefacts (information, business process, organisation, technical, others)?
- **Process completeness**. Is there a methodology that guides you in a step-by-step process to create an EA?
- **Scope**. What is the breadth and level of detail covered by the framework (such as the industry sector, organisation or domain)?
- **Level of detail**. How much detail does the framework support (high, medium or low)?
- **Addressed stakeholders**. Who is the target audience (such as client, end user, architect or developer)?
- **Reference model guidance**. How useful is the methodology in helping you to build upon a relevant set of reference models?
- **Practice guidance**. How helpful is the methodology in assimilating the EA mindset into your organisation and developing a culture in which it is valued and used?
- **Maturity model**. How much guidance does the methodology provide for assessing the effectiveness and maturity of different organisations within your enterprise?

- **Business focus**. Does the methodology use technology to drive the business value (specifically defined as either reducing costs or increasing income)?
- **Governance guidance**. How helpful will the methodology be in creating understanding and an effective governance model?
- **Partitioning guidance**. How well will the methodology guide you in an effective autonomous partitioning of the enterprise, which is an important approach for managing complexity?
- **Prescriptive catalogue**. How well will the methodology guide you in setting up a catalogue of architectural assets and capabilities that can be reused in future activities?
- **Representation**. How is representation organised (formal, semi-formal or informal)?
- **Vendor neutrality**. How neutral is the framework?
- **Information availability**. How much free or inexpensive information is available on this framework and what is the quality thereof?
- **Time to value**. What length of time will you need to engage with this methodology before you start building solutions that deliver strong business value?
- **Transformation**. Which architectural phases does the framework cover (such as the current situation, the short-term and long term)?

The long list of criteria implies that each organisation should thoroughly define its individual EAM focus and analyse what framework would best serve it, if any.

8.3 Notes on EA modelling

Whether an EA framework is applied or not, it is essential that the EA is documented. Enterprise architects use various methods, analytical techniques and conceptual tools to understand and document an enterprise's structure and dynamics. In doing so, they produce catalogues, drawings, documents and models that are collectively called artefacts. These artefacts describe the logical organisation of business functions, the business capabilities, business processes, people, information resources, business systems, software applications, computing capabilities, information exchange and the communications infrastructure within the enterprise. EA practitioners consider a collection of artefacts sufficiently complete to describe an enterprise in useful ways as constituting an EA model. EA models illustrate architecture descriptions. In a simple way, they represent different views of the architecture (Figure 8.3).

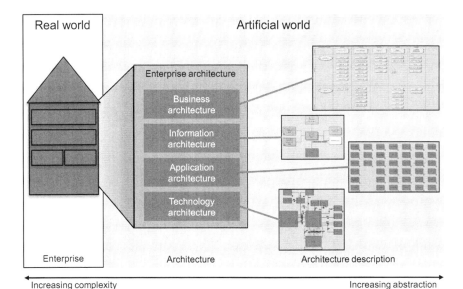

Figure 8.3: Architecture descriptions as representations of the real world

Practitioners and researchers have developed a large number of different modelling techniques that vary in terms of abstraction, layers considered, graphical representation, richness, and so on. Enterprise architects either have to select one of the existing modelling techniques or develop their own.

Architecture models are more comprehensive than pure business process models, as they holistically describe related enterprise capabilities and different layers' assets (see Figure 8.4).

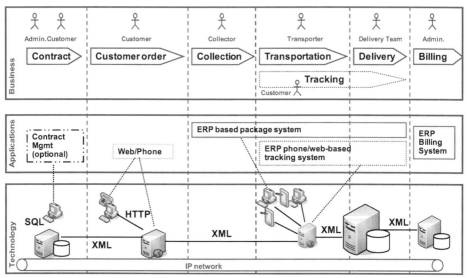

Figure 8.4: Simple EA modelling example

Contrary to pure business process modeling, architecture descriptions are more comprehensive

The government department case below shows how different modelling techniques can be used in the context of an EAM initiative to improve cross functional alignment and governance.

The organisation started off with a data and process modelling initiative

How a government department started EA modelling

The government department started by creating a process glossary as a reference inventory of all its processes. Thereafter, the organisation's EAM mainly focused on data and process modelling, and used the outcomes to guide new development projects. Process improvement and optimisation were not within the initial initiative's scope. However, the organisation considered the existing models a starting point for future process improvement endeavours.

Process and data mapping, a business rule directory, conceptual data models, and a data and process matrix were the deliverables of the organisation's initial modelling initiative. The process and data modelling was seen as a means for the business and IT to communicate in a shared language, and to enable the IT to better understand the business needs. The government department's new information system developments are expected to use the process models to take the business perspective into account.

After the initial set-up, EA models and artefacts' maintenance process is still a challenging task. Developers are often confronted with a broad scope and a lack of appropriate governance. The models' scope and level of detail, as well as the number of people and departments involved in the maintenance process affect the resulting artefacts' quality. The following cargo carrier case shows how domains, sub-domains and cross-domains can be used to structure and manage a broad modelling scope.

How a cargo carrier structured and managed a broad modelling scope

The cargo carrier's EA comprises business, information and technical models. It has developed common modelling conventions and standards that guide central and domain designers during modelling of the as-is and to-be architecture. The central EAM team generally provides EA models at a high level; these are then refined and detailed by the domain architects.

Architects are also closely involved in normal project work. This helps them to understand the project issues, while ensuring the relevance of the architectural guidelines. Overall, the communication between the central and domain teams is well facilitated.

Low-level application architecture changes are incorporated during the project implementation phase. The documented landscape includes description of the interfaces between the applications and communication services. The documented business and system information is also frequently reviewed and maintained.

Besides the IT master plan, which describes the strategic application landscape (with a horizon of about five years), the EAM team documents application landscapes with a shorter horizon, showing changes caused by current projects.

The cargo carrier has achieved advanced transparency of the current organisational situation by modelling the business, information, application and technical layers. This helps, for instance, with analysing projects' effects on the organisational structure and with identifying interdependencies between projects.

Practitioners have sought to identify the critical success factors for EA modelling, namely:

- **Vision and mission.** Define the initiative's objectives. Identify relevant stakeholders and target groups. Name and communicate benefits, and define how they can be measured.
- **Scope.** Based on the objectives, define the scope of the modelling activities.
- **Modelling conventions.** Create a convention manual to ensure consistency and uniform modelling within the organisation.

- **Level of detail and quality.** Precisely define the level of abstraction and the level of detail to ensure high-quality documentation that can deliver benefits for the business. The different levels can be defined by a process hierarchy.
- **Processes for authoring, quality assurance, approval, publication and rights management.** Define all the processes connected with the EA model's creation, review, publishing and maintenance.
- **Interfaces to other processes.** Define how the modelling processes are integrated into other processes (e.g., demand management and project portfolio management).
- **Governance concept.** Define all the roles and responsibilities for the modelling processes, including a description of all the relevant tasks.
- **Change management.** Incorporate the stakeholders into the modelling activities to ensure commitment and a shared understanding of the EA modelling initiative.
- **Documentation repository.** Define how documentation should be structured, stored and published. A search functionality integrated into an intranet allows for swift and efficient documentation retrieval.
- **Workflows.** Consider workflow support for the EA modelling processes to control the current state of documentation and ensure high process quality.
- **Compliance.** Consider compliance features (e.g., audit trail and version control) to ensure that all changes are documented and traceable.
- **Cycle management.** Consider tool-supported cycle management to ensure continuous modelling in a development environment, while already finalised models await approval in a validation environment. As soon as models are approved, they can be published in a production environment. If modelling activities are performed locally, a distribution concept should be considered to complete the cycle management.
- **Tool support.** Define which tools should be used for supporting the EA modelling activities.

With a sound EA modelling in place, organisations will be empowered to gauge the company's state in various dimensions and at any time.

8.4 EA tools: How to find adequate software support

Why you should use an appropriate EA tool

Many enterprises start off using simple drawing tools, spreadsheets, and content management tools to document and share their EA models. Although this might fulfil their initial requirements, it becomes extremely difficult to ensure these documents' consistency once multiple teams view and change the artefacts. Thus, users of drawing tools recognise the limitations of an overly basic approach when they enter larger implementation projects' or programmes' design phase.

Simple drawing tools often reach their limits when EA models become more complex

---

How a government department is working on finding the optimal EA tool

The first EA framework version attempted to illustrate everything by using standard office tools. However, the architects were aware that, when seeking to optimise processes and to achieve a global view on EA, dedicated EA tools were relevant.

The EAM team is currently evaluating EA tools that support the entire cycle, from modelling to execution. The EAM team employs a Governance Information Systems (GIS) tool, which is used to store all ongoing and planned projects, along with the respective information systems under development. The GIS is also used to maintain a global list of processes identified in a recent initiative. Advanced EA analysis is hindered by the absence of a specific government-wide EA tool. By maintaining a list of business processes and associated information systems, the organisation is capturing only a small part of the overall architecture at a rather abstract level. The EAM team is aware that it is limited in conducting in-depth impact analysis within an acceptable time and effort. The team members realise that they need to use a common modelling tool and the same modelling conventions across all government departments in order to compare processes and identify shared services. A tool that provides different stakeholders with role-based access to the initiative's results is also considered necessary.

At the cargo carrier, described in the example that follows, several tools are used to create architecture descriptions, leading to a tool integration issue.

How the cargo carrier uses a variety of EA tools

The cargo carrier's business functions use ARIS Business Designer and Business Architect tools to model all management, core and support processes and store them in a central database. The IT department also models present and planned processes within an EA tool from its perspective. These processes include data models in the form of entity relationship diagrams. The domain models and application landscape are mainly documented using MS Visio and PowerPoint. Information concerning processes and applications is stored in different tools, such as wikis. The tools employed are not well integrated and the EAM team is currently evaluating how to address this situation. Integrating the information will allow for more effective information use, for instance, by representing all relationships and keeping the data consistent. The cargo carrier has installed a process of monitoring, documenting and approving the technical standards. The company is working on specific EA tools and reports that will help it keep track of projects and analyse the captured EA information.

What are the lessons learnt? At the beginning of EA initiatives, the use of standard office tools or intuitive drawing tools might be a good starting point when investments (such as in new tools or training) are low and users are familiar with these applications in their everyday work environment. This way, experience with EA can be built up, thereby maintaining the focus of those involved on the EA concept rather than on new software. However, once EAM becomes a vital part of the organisation's strategy and operations, the introduction of a dedicated EA tool is beneficial for several reasons: The information stored in an EA tool allows for multiple architectural viewpoints, including business, information, application and technology. EA tools with multiple models, tracking links and dependencies offer impact and risk analysis, as well as summary dashboards and also help prioritise different initiatives. These tools are more management oriented, in contrast to the modelling-oriented drawing tools.

Important qualities of an EA tool

Regardless of the EA paradigm that an organisation follows, there are common criteria with which EA tools should comply [6]:

Meeting different stakeholder needs

An EA tool should support the creation, collection, analysis and presentation of information related to EA to meet different stakeholder needs. Furthermore, all relevant stakeholders should be able to document their EA perspective using the tool. The tool should also provide the ability to change the way the models and artefacts are represented and viewed, possibly including viewing models from particular perspectives (e.g., IT perspective vs. business perspective).

Providing a user-friendly model development interface
EA tools must facilitate the designing, building and maintaining of the models comprising the architecture. Generally, models are built and maintained graphically by selecting graphical elements and connecting them. The tool's model development interface may also use textual interfaces to allow additional information to be appended to the graphical models. Features include automated drawing functions to lay out models, or to provide lists of alternative values at the appropriate places during modelling. Some tools also provide integrated publishing capabilities (e.g., provide information via web browsers).

Providing support for automation
By providing support for automating parts of the EA development processes, a tool can help speed up the overall development. A tool may support the creation of macros or scripts to automate common functions or actions, or to group several functions into one action. The tool may automatically generate EA models based on the data within its repository. Some tools also have the ability to provide information in executable forms.

Supporting extendibility and customisation
EA tools may support customisation by allowing users to add new modelling approaches, or to modify the modelling approaches already in use by the tool to meet an organisation's unique EA requirements. A tool may also support modification by providing a programming interface, allowing the tool's functions to be modified, or allowing the tool to be integrated with other software products (modifying or adding meta-models). Integration might also be supported by importing information from relevant sources, such as various design tools, IT management tools, packaged IT applications, and exporting information from the tool to facilitate stakeholder use.

Providing support for analysis and reporting
EA tools may also provide support for analysing the developed models. Analytical capabilities related to EA may include gap analysis, impact analysis and KPI analysis of repository information. This

way, key performance indicators (KPIs) can be tracked within the EA tool. The type of analysis support that the tool provides is often tied to its particular modelling approaches. EA tools may enable the comparison of different model versions or the delta between present and planned EAs.

Providing a robust yet flexible repository

Most EA tools use some kind of data repository to store the developed models. A repository may include support for collaboration by allowing multiple, concurrent users on one repository, or by combining models developed by different modellers into one model. The repository may also provide many different data management functions, including model versioning, rolling back to previous versions, locking parts of the model against change, and controlling access to parts of the model, or to the model as a whole.

Offer good value for money and sufficient vendor support

The costs of EA tool licences can range from open source to more than 7,000 EUR per licence. Optional extras are often available at an additional cost. The licence agreements vary from desktop licences to floating licences, allowing shared usage in a user group. Some vendors offer discounts for bulk purchases or site licences. Maintenance, support, training and technical support are usually available at additional costs. Some vendors offer free or discounted software upgrades.

EA tool market and trends

The trend is toward adoption of dedicated management-oriented EA tools

A vast variety of EA tools exist on the market. Most sophisticated EA tools are based on business modelling tools or enhance these by offering functionalities for EA management. The tool capabilities' richness continues to increase, especially concerning EA management and the exchange of information with other tools. EA tool features are converging. Most vendors have added some governance and collaborative features to their products, and the lines between them are beginning to blur. Import and export functions still remain weak points. Most products offer meta-model customisation. The most flexible products currently include both a complete web-based architecture and a stand-alone modelling environment.

How to find the right EA tool

When searching for adequate tool support, many questions arise, for example:

- Which functionalities do we need?
- What standard software packages are available and how do they differ?
- What are the licence, maintenance and operations costs?
- How many people do we need and which skills do they need?
- How does the new tool fit into the existing software environment?

A structured software selection can help identify the right EA tool

Structured software selection can help answer these questions (see Figure 8.5).

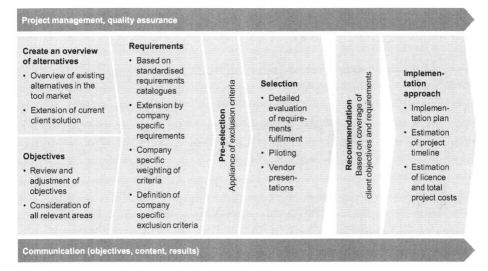

Figure 8.5: Structured software selection for EA tools

At the start, the EA tool support objectives should be clearly defined. Without this activity, there is a high risk that an EA tool will be selected that does not fit the organisation's practical needs. An overview of existing alternatives (long list) should then be created. Existing EA tool evaluations, as well as published surveys and studies, can help to reduce the number of candidates [7-9]. The next step is to determine the functional and non-functional requirements. These should be documented and reviewed, including the weightings and exclusion criteria. The models, languages and visualisations expected from the tool should also be considered. Both high-level conceptual and detailed domain-level architecture principles should be included as screening criteria. The following evaluation areas can serve as a starting point for defining your specific requirements before comparing the tools (see Table 8.3).

Table 8.3: Candidate tool evaluation criteria

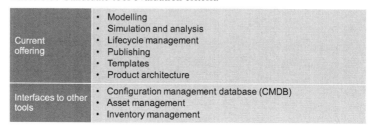

Current offering	<ul><li>Modelling</li><li>Simulation and analysis</li><li>Lifecycle management</li><li>Publishing</li><li>Templates</li><li>Product architecture</li></ul>
Interfaces to other tools	<ul><li>Configuration management database (CMDB)</li><li>Asset management</li><li>Inventory management</li></ul>

Besides tool selection, the right vendor is vital. The following criteria can be applied when analysing EA tool vendors (Table 8.4):

Table 8.4: Candidate vendor evaluation criteria

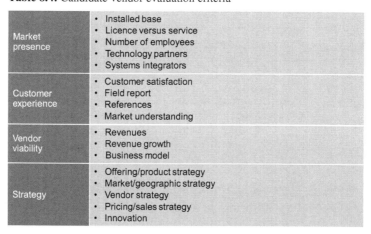

Market presence	<ul><li>Installed base</li><li>Licence versus service</li><li>Number of employees</li><li>Technology partners</li><li>Systems integrators</li></ul>
Customer experience	<ul><li>Customer satisfaction</li><li>Field report</li><li>References</li><li>Market understanding</li></ul>
Vendor viability	<ul><li>Revenues</li><li>Revenue growth</li><li>Business model</li></ul>
Strategy	<ul><li>Offering/product strategy</li><li>Market/geographic strategy</li><li>Vendor strategy</li><li>Pricing/sales strategy</li><li>Innovation</li></ul>

In the next step, exclusion criteria should be applied to the tools and vendors to shortlist them. Thereafter a detailed requirements fulfilment evaluation should be conducted, including usability testing against a prototype installation. The degree of coverage of the predefined objectives and requirements determines the best tool. The tool selection should also include an implementation strategy covering an implementation plan and project timelines, as well as the estimation of licences and total implementation and operations costs. Finally a business case that mirrors the financial resources needed and the anticipated EA tool's benefits should be compiled.

8.5 Management implications

Relevance of frameworks for EAM

Contrary to the intuitive presumption, EAM success does not depend on following an EA framework. Standard frameworks can provide guidance for an EAM implementation, but they are often not complete enough to meet an organisation's specific requirements. On the other hand, standard frameworks are often very large and are seldom used all-over and continuously; the content is the major constraint. Furthermore, frameworks do not show how existing processes have to be changed in the EAM context. This must then be done outside the framework. For this reason, many organisations either do not use a framework, or build their own. After analysing our study data, we conclude that every organisation should thoroughly consider which EAM framework to follow. In some cases, developing your own procedures and artefacts may be the optimal solution.

An EA framework is not crucial for EAM success

EA modelling best practices

EA modelling activities should always focus on benefits. Practically, this means considering the benefits of all the artefacts and models that will be modelled. Therefore, we strongly recommend clearly defining the modelling objectives and benefit measures at the outset of the project, and reviewing them regularly. Furthermore, the scope of EA modelling activities should not be too large, and the level of detail should not be too granular, especially with regard to maintenance effort, to keep the models up to date. The focus should be firmly fixed on value-added documentation and a pragmatic 80/20 approach should be chosen. Including all the relevant stakeholders, especially middle and senior management, in the scope definition allows for the necessary commitment and support. It is also essential to communicate modelling activity benefits and added value. Modelling activities should be integrated into the EAM processes, including project handling, strategic planning and committees. Therefore, swift and easy authoring and retrieval processes should be ensured. All relevant stakeholders need access to the models. In order to safeguard uniform modelling, one should set up a modelling conventions guide. The manual should be as concise as possible and as detailed as

Focus on value added documentation and choose a pragmatic 80/20 approach

needed. Crucial aspects should be published target oriented by means of quick reference guides.

Typical pitfalls of EA tool selection and implementation

Use a structured software selection process to select the right EA tool or combination of tools

EA tool selection projects frequently do not achieve the desired results if the selection process begins before the EA approach, methodology and EAM processes have been agreed upon. This way, organisations might implement a tool that does not serve their needs. Furthermore, in some cases, EA tool objectives are not clearly defined. In the process, vital requirements (e.g., functionality and technical restrictions) are neglected. The assumption that the market-leading EA tool will fit any organisation is a false one, and can lead to EA tools being selected that do not match (e.g., oversized or wrong priorities) the organisation's EAM activities. EA tools are seldom 'ready to use', as each organisation must define its own EAM path. In fact, users must be trained. Also, as with any software introduction, change management activities are required to increase user acceptance (see Chapter 9). Finally, tool selection activities, as well as tool implementation projects often lack resources. In our experience, such activities cannot be done parallel to day-to-day operations. Where this does happen, one of the two suffers.

Success criteria for EA tool selection

The following success criteria should be considered when selecting and implementing an EA tool: The EA tools' objectives should be thoroughly defined. It is important to include all stakeholders' views in this definition to achieve user acceptance from the outset. Objectives should be translated into measurable requirements, including exclusion criteria for EA tool selection. It might be helpful to use an existing tool evaluation as an input or starting point. It is crucial to pilot a tool before purchasing it. Thus, representatives of all stakeholders should be introduced to the shortlisted EA tools for demos, test usage, and so on. Technically, the EA tool's integration into the existing system landscape should be considered. This may lead to the selection of a combination of tools, rather than selecting one tool (e.g., for capturing data, modelling, repository, reporting and analysis). A business case should be written that documents the objectives, costs and benefits. This business case should be tracked alongside the EA tool implementation and initial operations to ensure that the initiative stays on track.

References

[1] J. Ross, P. Weill, D.C. Robertson, *"Enterprise Architecture as Strategy, "* Boston: Harvard Business School, 2006, p. 50.

[2] Sessions R., *"A Comparison of the Top Four Enterprise-Architecture Methodologies,"* 2007. [Online]. Available: http://msdn.microsoft.com/en-us/library/bb466232.aspx. [Accessed: 17-Dec-2010].

[3] P. Bernus, L. Nemes, G. J. Schmidt, *"Handbook on Enterprise Architecture, "* Berlin: Springer, 2003.

[4] J.A. Zachman, "A framework for information systems architecture," *IBM Systems Journal*, vol. 26, Sep. 1987, pp. 276–292.

[5] The Open Group, *TOGAF™ Version 9*. USA: The Open Group, 2009.

[6] J. Schekkerman: *Enterprise Architecture Tool Selection Guide, Version 5.0*, Institute for Enterprise Architecture Developments, 2009.

[7] S. Leist and G. Zellner, "Evaluation of current architecture frameworks," in *Symposium on Applied Computing*, 2006.

[8] R. A. Handler and C. Wilson, *"Magic Quadrant for Enterprise Architecture Tools 2009, "* Gartner Inc.

[9] F. Matthes, S. Buckl, J. Leitel, Schweda, and C. M., *Enterprise Architecture Management Tool Survey 2008*. sebis, 2008.

Chapter 9

People, adoption and introduction of EAM

Frederik Ahlemann, Kunal Mohan, Daniel Schäfczuk

Table of contents

Management summary

Enterprise architecture management (EAM) has emerged from a fairly technical perspective on enterprises, and did not initially fully realise the importance of 'soft' human factors. Consequently, EAM practices were developed and implemented without significant atten- tion to the needs and perspectives of EAM practitioners and the rele- vant stakeholders. Neglecting these individuals' requirements sometimes leads to the implementation of EAM practices considered unsuitable, which are then rejected by their stakeholders. In short, because key users and important EAM stakeholders are the ones who eventually decide a new management approach's success or failure, aligning EAM practices with stakeholders' needs is a critical success factor. We find that, among other things, we need to ensure that EAM practices are perceived to be useful to and by the actual stakeholder. Furthermore, EAM practices should be recommended by influential colleagues and managers to generate positive word of mouth. We also find that the use of EAM practices can be increased through organisational support in the form of training and technical assistance. Such training and assistance will reduce people's doubt that they are capable of using such practices properly. Providing incentives and making the techniques fun to use are further ways to encourage individuals to apply EAM practices. Based on these insights, organisations can develop specific change strategies to foster the organisational adoption of EAM and to integrate these strategies into a cyclic process of introducing EAM. Such an intro- duction process consists of ten steps from identifying the project sponsors to the final roll-out and continuous improvement of EAM practices. Each process cycle should not take longer than three to nine months, allowing for the quick realisation of benefits and an on- going improvement of EAM practices. In order to avoid working in an ivory tower, management should adopt a pragmatic 80/20 approach, combined with a strong stakeholder orientation. This strategy also ensures a lasting impact.

9.1 The relevance of the human dimension of EAM

How EAM practices can produce resistance

The introduction of enterprise architecture management (EAM) is often seen as a mere engineering initiative, one that focuses primarily on methodologies and models. While such practices are definitely important, this one-sided approach is not sufficient to ensure that EAM benefits are fully realised. 'Soft' factors, such as professionals' and stakeholders' needs are rarely explicitly taken into consideration. Failure to incorporate these people's needs and intentions into EAM practice development and implementation might lead to resistance. A number of surveys and empirical studies support this view [1], [2], [3].

Soft factors are important for EAM success

Organisational experts have long recognised that individuals' behavioural resistance to the use of new practices is partly due to employees not sharing their employer's goals or values. The roots of the non-acceptance of EAM practices lie – among other factors – in the failure to understand individuals' attitudes to the use of specific practices. This lack of understanding ultimately leads to the development and implementation of EAM practices that might be considered unsuitable, and are consequently rejected [4-7]. The changes associated with the EAM introduction influence:

Introducing EAM means change, which can produce resistance

- new joint planning and decision-making processes,
- avoidance of local improvements to favour global optimisation,
- budget allocations, as well as matters of authority, and
- the people responsible for different EA layers and who have to coordinate these layers' activities.

As noted in the preceding chapters, these changes are a functioning EAM initiative's goals, but may not be very popular with everyone. Nevertheless, the above-mentioned changes are often more acceptable than the most incisive change associated with EAM: A modification of the organisation's power structure. Therefore, it is not surprising that the adjustment of an enterprise's decision-making and steering structure will elicit stakeholder resistance. Employees' responses to change can manifest themselves in the following two ways: Firstly, people can demonstrate passive resistance by disobeying the introduced rules and guidelines. Such resistance is difficult to uncover, because people will seldom honestly confess that they are not willing to change and accept new practices. Secondly, employees can be antagonistic towards EAM, which means that they openly resist EAM and the associated power structure change, and also seek to convince their colleagues to participate in this protest.

This situation has severe consequences for EAM introduction in any organisation, since EAM success is directly related to people's willingness to follow EAM rules and guidelines. Thus, overall, people are one of the critical success factors of EAM introduction and implementation. If people are convinced, and their buy-in of EAM practices is secured, this is likely to lead to strong EAM performance in terms of proper decision-making, working EAM processes and optimal EA development.

This chapter's objectives

To overcome the above-mentioned problems of resistance, we recommend change management of employee behaviour, which highlights people and their EAM acceptance and includes, for example, persuading stakeholders of EAM's benefits. Another aspect of change management is to reduce people's fear and concerns regarding the new management practice. The iterative adoption of EAM practices also helps to make the changes comprehensible to stakeholders.

While change management is not new, a number of specific questions are usually raised concerning EAM implementation, including:

• *Why* do people adopt or reject EAM practices?
• *What* can you do to excite people about EAM?
• *How* can you introduce EAM into your organisation?

This chapter seeks to answer these three fundamental questions. It is structured as follows: Section 2 introduces the psychological mechanisms that may prevent people from engaging in EAM initiatives (i.e. we concentrate on the *why*). In Section 3, we derive recommendations to reduce resistance (we concentrate on the *what*). Section 4 presents a process model for structured EAM introduction, as well as a step-by-step solution to the *how* question. Section 5 shows how the proposed methodology can affect the organisational culture. Finally, Section 6 summarises the findings.

9.2 Why do stakeholders cooperate? – A psychological perspective on EAM adoption

The usefulness of the psychological lens

The question regarding whether or not EAM methodologies are accepted and applied by an organisation's employees can be traced back to individual employee decisions. In other words, individual acceptance leads to organisational EAM acceptance. This means that, ultimately, EAM adoption cannot be achieved by management decision, but is dependent on individual decisions influenced by diverse internal and external psychological factors. A thorough analysis of these factors prior to EAM development and introduction increases the likelihood of adoption, which is what executives and enterprise architects seek to achieve.

EAM organisational acceptance depends on acceptance by individual employees

The advantages of individual EAM acceptance include:

- Quicker implementation,
- reduced conflict and less need for escalation,
- limited or no negative impact on the company culture,
- stable employee satisfaction, and
- potentially lower costs.

These points are reason enough to take a closer look at the psychological mechanisms underlying adoption decisions.

What are the reasons for applying EAM practices?

Individuals are unique. When confronted with a situation, they respond differently, depending on their individual beliefs and perceptions. For example, while some people readily embrace new ideas and methods, others might be sceptical and hesitant, while yet others might be totally opposed to them and do everything in their power to prevent implementation. Understanding how individuals make their decisions to accept, embrace, commit, oppose, reject and hinder innovations is crucial to predict future behaviour.

Individuals' characteristics influence their attitude towards EAM practices

We focus on examining the behaviour of *individual users* of EAM practices, because, although a particular EAM practice is developed and implemented by an organisation, the extent and nature of its use are usually determined by the method's actual users [8], [9]. Furthermore, individual users play a critical role in an EAM concept's success, because without proper use, it might be difficult – if not impossible – to realise planned EAM benefits. In the following, we derive and discuss a model to identify and understand the various factors that motivate people to adopt EAM practices (Figure 9.1) [10].

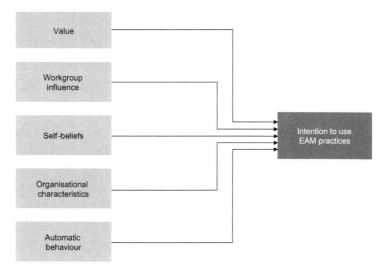

Figure 9.1: Reasons for EAM adoption

Reason 1: I apply EAM practices because they *have value* for me

The usefulness of management practices is reflected in the value that their goal-oriented use could generate for an individual and is generally the most important EAM practice acceptance motivator [11-13]. We can distinguish several types of value.

Users apply EAM because they expect it to produce benefits

Utilitarian value. The term utilitarian value or usage value denotes any form of instrumental value that a management methodology might have for the user, such as increasing task performance, efficiency and productivity [14].

Hedonic value. Hedonic value is generated as a result of pleasurable experiences encountered while using EAM practices [14]. Hedonic value might therefore be defined as the extent to which using EAM practices is perceived as being enjoyable in its own right, besides any performance anticipated consequences [15]. For example, some people invest hours in creating appealing graphics in presentations, even though this might not be the most productive use of time, because they find the act enjoyable and it helps them express themselves artistically.

Materialistic value. Materialistic value is based on an orientation that considers material goods and money important for personal happiness and social progress. Accordingly, people will find a management practice desirable and will be inclined to use it if it generates materialistic value for them.

In a recent study of management methodologies [16], the majority of the interviewees mentioned that a key determinant of their decision to use a methodology is its usefulness in achieving set goals.

One project manager gave an example of a methodology that the organisation had developed over a period of two years and with the input of considerable resources. He mentioned that the methodology was never used as it was supposed to be used because it was so complex, comprehensive and 'over-engineered'. He maintained that most managers considered it counterproductive.

The interviewees occasionally mentioned experiencing 'pride', 'accomplishment' and 'self-actualisation' when using a methodology, because they had mastered its use. One person felt 'loyal' to the organisation when using the methodology strictly as requested. Some IT managers mentioned experiencing 'excitement' at the thought of being able to experiment with various methods and practices.

One interviewee mentioned that he used a methodology as insurance in case projects fail. By adhering strictly to the methodology, he can deny responsibility for a failed project and simply 'blame the methodology'. In such a scenario, a methodology is used because its use allows the user to avoid negative career or monetary consequences.

Users apply EAM practices because important people are applying and endorsing them

Reason 2: I apply EAM practices because *people who are important to me* say it's the right thing to do

Extensive research on human behaviour shows that a person's perceptions and behaviour are generally influenced by individuals around him or her who he or she considers important [17]. In an organisational setting, this implies that all the employees' intentions to use EAM practices will be influenced by their seniors, colleagues and team or unit members whose opinions they consider important [18], [19].

This view is supported by the transformational leadership concept [20], [21], which describes leaders who are able to inspire followers to transcend their self-interests and who are capable of having a profound and extraordinary effect on their followers. Such leaders will probably be more successful in establishing EAM than transactional leaders. The latter usually motivate by concentrating on role and task requirements that will definitely be important at the beginning of an EAM initiative but will not establish the required cultural change.

In general, we can distinguish between two types of influence by other people:

Normative influence refers to an individual's tendency to meet the group members' expectations. It implies that a person uses EAM practice to obtain certain benefits from his or her workgroup (e.g., if I use an EAM practice because my superior wants me to or because he will be impressed by this), or due to professional respect or admiration for those he or she wants to emulate (e.g., if my superior uses certain EAM practices, then I would be inclined to imitate him and to use the same practices, as I want to emulate him).

Informational influence refers to people's tendency to perceive information received from others as correct [19], and implies that a person's decision to use EAM practices is influenced by the information provided by 'mediums of knowledge', such as experts or subject publications.

In a recent study of management methodologies [16], some participants were influenced by the opinions of external consultants who were methodology engineering experts. Workshop participants reacted positively to solutions and explanations provided by these experts and actively sought their advice by asking questions.

Reason 3: I apply EAM practices because *I believe I can do it*

Although EAM practices might be perceived as useful and employees might want to use them, they will be less motivated to do so if they cannot use them easily. EAM practice use can be perceived as difficult if a person thinks that he or she does not possess the necessary skills and knowledge to master the correct usage. Such self-perceptions – namely belief in one's capabilities and skills – therefore play an important role in motivating people to use new EAM practices. The more positive a person's self-beliefs, the stronger his or her intention to use EAM practices, the greater the effort invested in using them, and the stronger his or her persistence and resilience will be.

Users apply EAM practices because they think they are able to use the EAM techniques

In methodology workshops conducted as part of a recent study of management methodologies [16], we observed that inexperienced professionals often doubted their skills and knowledge regarding a methodology's correct use. We also noticed that professionals with more than five years' experience were more actively involved in the interactive workshops and provided suggestions on how to improve the methodology. In interviews and workshops, people with less than two years' experience with methodologies repeatedly mentioned that they needed better training in the use of complicated methodologies. Some raised a number of questions regarding the effort involved in learning the new methodology, as well as about organisational support.

Reason 4: I apply EAM practices because my *organisation supports me* in doing so

Another important factor is the degree to which a person believes that organisational resources are available to help him or her use the EAM practices. These sought-after organisational resources include support, consulting services and training offered by organisational units (such as the enterprise architecture team) in the form of guidance to correctly use the practices, or even political backing. The more a person believes that he or she can access such external resources when he or she needs them, the more confidence he or she will have in successful usage, and the more inclined the person will be to use the EAM practices.

People use EAM due to the organisational support

In a recent study of management methodologies [16], demands for more support and political backing were reported in the interviews. One manager noted that "we don't get help from the organisation when we run into conflicting situations regarding methodology usage. The only way we resolve the problem is by using our social networks and getting help from experienced colleagues. A person who doesn't have a good social network because he is new in the organisation finds it extremely hard to use the methodology correctly".

Reason 5: I apply EAM practices because *I am used to doing so*

Users apply EAM because they are used to doing so

If organisations already have management concepts in place for their enterprise architecture, and if employees have been using these methods for some time, then they might have become accustomed to using them. They use these old methods out of habit and they might be reluctant to change their habits. Introducing new EAM practices in such a scenario means that people would have to change their old ways of doing things. In response to such changes, people may resist the new practices, thereby causing delays in the development and implementation. The stronger a person's habitual use of previous methods, the less likely he or she will be to change and adopt the new EAM practices.

About the weight of these factors

All the presented factors affect individual behaviour to different extents

In reality, individual behaviour is influenced by many factors. Each individual is unique, has a specific attitude towards EAM practices, and will make an individual decision either supporting or resisting EAM adoption. Although it might not be possible to address each stakeholder individually, change management activities might take the above-mentioned factors into account and plan an EAM initiative accordingly. This would significantly increase the likelihood of EAM adoption.

9.3 How can stakeholders be convinced to cooperate? – A methodological perspective

In the previous section, we stated that understanding the psychological determinants of readiness to apply EAM practices makes it possible to develop change management guidelines for increased EAM adoption [22-24]. In the following section, we use the insights outlined in the previous section to make recommendations for an EAM introduction with closer stakeholder involvement.

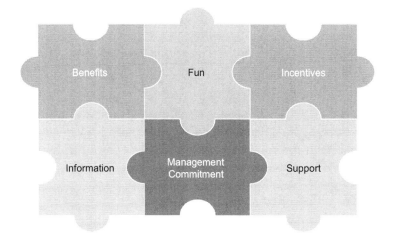

Figure 9.2: How to convince stakeholders to cooperate

Benefits – make EAM useful to people

As noted in Section 2, the probability of adopting EAM is higher when people feel that EAM practices will help them speed up their work or enhance their work quality. However, EAM will almost never satisfy *all* practitioners in terms of efficiency gains. EAM requires some effort in terms of data collection and data maintenance, which will not have a direct and immediate return; consequently, there will always be a group of people who invest more than they get in return. However, a carefully designed EAM methodology will offer a greater amount of benefits to more stakeholders than a

EAM should be made useful to users

poorly designed methodology demanding much but giving little. The benefits of a well-designed EAM include a goal-oriented analysis of information needs and the generation of reports and visualizations for different user groups. The key to making an EAM methodology valuable to those who apply it is simple and straightforward: Talk to them, try to understand their needs, involve them and design the methodology accordingly. Our proposed measures are therefore perhaps neither surprising nor revolutionary:

- **Stakeholder analysis.** One of the first steps to addressing stakeholder needs and concerns is doing a thorough stakeholder analysis. In addition to the standard stakeholder analysis requirements, we especially encourage you to find out how the EAM methodology can generate value for stakeholders and how these benefits can be prioritised for later implementation. For example, the value for a team leader can be the optimisation of his or her application portfolio, whereas a service manager may receive insights into his or her service's technical implementation.
- **Participatory development.** Implementing participatory development of parts of the methodology, or even the methodology as a whole, may be the next step. Select a number of stakeholders who can leverage the EAM introduction, and invite them to a workshop series on the joint development of the methodology's cornerstones. Make the key stakeholders part of the methodology development initiative; allow them to provide input. This will not only improve the methodology's usage value, but also its acceptance by the stakeholders.
- **Quick wins.** Stakeholder analysis and the participatory development will help you identify potential quick wins. Quick wins are tangible benefits that can be realised with limited effort and within a short period of time (e.g., three months). Quick wins may help you to convince the stakeholders and can also be exploited as success stories. You should try to engineer the EAM methodology in a way that realises quick wins for as many stakeholder groups as possible.
- **Persuasive business case.** As long as you target people who will actually apply the EAM methodology, you can focus on individual usage benefits. However, perspectives change when you talk to management, who may seek to assess an EAM initiative from an organisational and financial perspective. It is therefore also advisable to analyse the EAM's impact on the organisation as a whole and to develop a sound business case, for example, in terms of a process harmonisation initiative, or the clearing of the application portfolio. As is often the case, forecasting costs is easily done,

while identifying, structuring and assessing benefits are more chal-lenging. The latter can be facilitated by means of a *benefit depend-ency network* (BDN) [25] (see Figure 9.3). The business case and the underlying BDN may be used to achieve final approval for the EAM initiative. Nonetheless, it can also serve as a tool for commu-nication and controlling purposes.

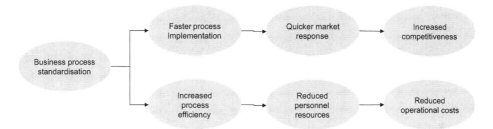

Figure 9.3: Exemplary Benefits Dependency Network (BDN) for harmonis-ing the business process layer

Make EAM fun to apply

EAM methodologies that involve fun – in the sense of exploration, challenges and learning – are more likely to achieve adoption, prima-rily because highly skilled professionals are motivated if they have an opportunity to learn, grow and improve their competencies. A good EAM methodology should be designed to support this:

- **Experimentation and piloting.** Give key users the opportunity to participate in the methodology design. Furthermore, it may be advisable to test the methodology in a pilot environment (e.g., a business domain) to allow people to experiment with it. Needless to say, employees must have the chance to modify whatever doesn't work in the methodology. This increases motivation and improves your EAM.
- **Lean and flexible methodology.** Methodology engineers tend to plan for every eventuality. This produces heavyweight methodolo-gies with only a few degrees of freedom, which inhibit profession-als from acting on the basis of their experience and expertise. In order to stimulate individual commitment to and identification with the methodology, we recommend making it as lean or light-weight as possible. Avoid patronising professionals; give them the freedom to act and decide with reasonable latitude. When design-ing the methodology, we recommend a focus on crucial practices, emphasising employees' expertise and making the methodology

EAM use should be fun and not irritating

easy to understand. Address all the key aspects, and provide professionals with the freedom to decide how to do things.

- **Continuous improvement.** People's motivation to use a methodology will also depend on whether or not professionals perceive their input as appreciated. Loss of motivation may result if people think that their suggestions are not considered or their advice is not taken seriously. A continuous improvement process with feedback to those making suggestions has a twofold advantage: It motivates professionals and it strengthens the methodology.

- **Adequate software support.** For many people, EAM will manifest itself in the form of an intranet website or specific EA tools. EAM practices are fun if they have a modern, intuitive and compelling user interface that allows for efficient work with EA-related information. Data analysis capabilities are of particular importance for non-architects and cannot be underestimated. Attractive reports with useful information for decision-makers can help professionals do their job better or obtain positive feedback from superiors. Those who model or document the EA will benefit from intuitive and powerful data input, modelling and planning features (see Chapter 8).

- **Training and certifications.** Most professionals enjoy training sessions. They can escape the stressful everyday business for a few hours and concentrate on new and interesting topics. For many, learning involves fun and self-fulfilment. Providing EAM-related training may therefore have a dual effect, as it aids the company's EAM capabilities and motivates people to apply these capabilities. External trainers and official certificates (preferably from professional associations or renowned institutions; see Appendix) can further stimulate motivation, as these training sessions and the respective certificates may improve employees' CVs.

Incentives – Reward people who apply EAM

People using EAM should be rewarded

There are two ways of responding to staff EAM performance: You can either reward successful people, or punish those who underperform. Studies show that a positive attitude towards employees yield more results (than the opposite), thus making rewards the preferable solution. When employees don't receive rewards, they consider this a form of 'positive punishment'. Punishment in the sense of financial disadvantages or disciplinary measures should be a last resort when all other means to motivate and convince people have failed. Positive incentives to apply EAM practices include:

- **Management by (EAM) objectives.** Directing people by setting objectives is a common management practice, at least for higher management levels, but increasingly also for professionals on all levels. If you want to accelerate EAM introduction in your organisation by increasing individual support for this initiative, it is helpful to agree upon individual EAM-related targets and to couple these targets to financial compensation, such as bonuses. If you do not want to add financial incentives, you can use other forms of compensation, such as the attendance of EAM training, EAM certification or EAM conferences.

- **EAM awards.** Once your EAM is under way, you can award ground-breaking EA-related projects or departments. Awards may be delivered during a company social event, preferably a celebratory event such as Christmas or annual meetings. These not only have a motivating effect, they may also be exploited for marketing purposes. Properly communicated, such awards may popularise EAM to a broader audience in your company and may help increase the enterprise architects' esteem. You should also consider attaching small indulgences to the award to underline its importance and relevance.

Information – Convince people that EAM is great

Informing people about an EAM methodology is perhaps the most intuitive approach to increase adoption. However, despite its intuitiveness, a proper information strategy is not trivial – it needs to be balanced and tailored to professionals' needs and expectations. As noted in the previous section, people react differently to different kinds of informational offerings; a strategy should therefore be both multi-channel and multi-content.

People should be convinced of the utility of EAM

- **Multi-channel communication.** Different people tend to choose different strategies to seek and process information. Some prefer internet and intranet sources accessed via a notebook or desktop PC, while others prefer printed text, and yet others mobile devices.

- **Multi-content communication.** There are many different formats in which EAM-related information can be distributed; examples include newsletters, brochures, professional articles, glossaries and EAM frameworks.

- **Let external experts provide EAM information.** In terms of content, it is advisable to provide your own material, as well as external sources that address EAM to describe how it works and what results it yields. Expert opinions and scientific sources frequently have more credibility than internal sources produced by those 'selling' EAM. Useful sources include research reports, scientific articles, professional magazines and books. Consider setting up a small EAM library for the EAM professionals and interested stakeholders in your organisation.

- **Success stories:** As soon as you have realised a first major EAM success, consider communicating it as a success story. Success stories are perhaps the most convincing and compelling way to win over stakeholders. Beyond abstract arguments in favour of EAM, success stories provide you with proven cases of EAM's ability to improve performance. By sharing these stories, you can show that EAM can actually pay off in your organisation.

Success stories to promote EAM at a large bank

The effects of EAM within the organisation can often only be analysed with approximate values. One domain architect notes that there 'is no detailed and sharp controlling of performance indicators at our bank'. The bank mostly applies qualitative indicators and measures. It successfully uses examples, best practices, anecdotes and communication patterns as measures. These examples function as success stories and help transfer knowledge of EAM and its achievements in the organisation. According to the head of architecture, the most important success factor was the appointment of domain architects, who exchange information throughout the business fields and support the above-mentioned ways of communicating.

Demonstrate authority through management commitment

Top management support for the EAM application is important

Up to this point, the strategies we have discussed for convincing stakeholders imply a positive perception of employees characterised by a will to learn, improve and help the organisation. Unfortunately, this is not always the case. In some cases, people jeopardise the introduction of EAM by not following the defined guidelines, recommendations and principles. For this reason, we recommend that you demonstrate the necessary authority to enforce EAM-compliant behaviour. Top management support is vital here:

- **Let top executives talk about EAM.** It is often enough to let top executives talk about EAM. This underlines that the management understands the relevance and importance of the EAM philosophy (see Chapter 3). It also demonstrates that the management is willing to invest a significant amount of time in the topic. Top managers can talk about EAM in, for example, external and internal conferences, workshops and meetings. Consider the value of recording such talks and making the video or audio files available. Besides speaking about EAM, the top management should also elaborate why EAM is important for the specific enterprise, how it generates value and why they support it.

- **Use top executives to break resistance.** In very rare cases, it might also be necessary for top managers to directly influence people in the organisation. If resistance is high and cannot be overcome by conventional means, it is sensible to let top management intervene. Direct orders or penalties (e.g., staff transfer) may be necessary in the case of persistent counterproductive or destructive behaviour.

Provide all the support that is needed to apply EAM

Even if people are well disposed towards EAM and want to apply EAM practices, there may still be adoption inhibitors. As pointed out in the previous section, the ultimate decision to practice EAM depends largely on the perceived organisational support, which needs to be designed carefully. To demonstrate full organisational commitment to EAM and to encourage people to take the first steps towards EAM, we recommend that you institute the following support processes. Medium-sized organisations may not be able to implement these measures on their own, but may want to opt for support from professional associations and external training companies.

EAM support should be effective

- **Help desk.** To answer technical and methodological questions related to correct EAM practice usage, setting up a fully equipped call centre for EAM support is probably not feasible. However, many architecture teams are able to organise accessibility for eight hours per day. A special help desk phone number and flexible routing to mobile phones are all you need to this end. A help desk function can provide EAM-related tool support, methodology support, and answer general EAM questions.
- **Training.** As noted, training is a reasonable means to support EAM initiatives. Besides general EAM training, we recommend developing company-specific training sessions in which people can become familiar with the EAM methodology. It is advisable to have a set of mandatory and voluntary training sessions and to tailor them to the stakeholder groups' individual needs. You may want, for instance, to have a training session for enterprise architects, one for line managers and one for project managers. In sec-

tion 4, we show how to identify relevant roles and stakeholders in the proposed introduction process as Step 4.

• **User groups and user conferences.** Professionals may receive support from peer groups. Exchange with peer group members offers an opportunity to learn from colleagues and to exchange experiences, thoughts and ideas. User group and user conference meetings may convey a sense of being part of a group of like-minded people, which may increase one's identification with EAM practices (for further details, see Chapter 4).

9.4 How can EAM be introduced? – A process perspective

Overview

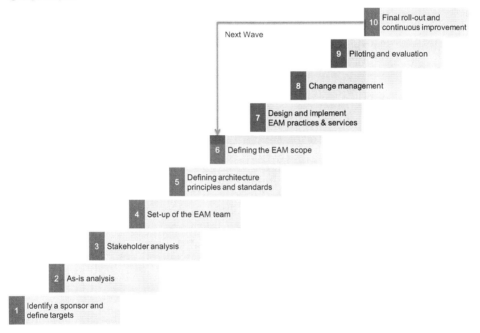

Figure 9.4: Ten steps for a successful EAM initiative

We will now propose a process model for structured EAM introduction and will answer frequently asked questions about EAM introduction. The process model consists of 10 steps, with a cyclic reiteration after step 10. The EAM scope should iteratively expand in defined waves (see Figure 9.4), which should lead to sustainable EAM initiative success. Please be aware that the process model is only a framework for introducing EAM. As seen in the previous chapters, EAM is highly company-specific; formulating an overly detailed step-by-step procedure for its introduction is thus neither feasible nor reasonable.

Top management
support can make it
easier

Step 1: Identify a project sponsor and define EAM targets

Before you can begin to define the ways in which EAM changes the ways people plan, develop and monitor your company's architecture, you need to obtain top management support and to ensure that EAM-related targets are clear (see Section 3).

Having the EAM introduction initiative driven by senior executives is winning the first prize. You can then directly proceed to discussing the EAM targets. If top management sponsorship is not present from the outset, you will need to find and convince a supportive manager, as well as secure a budget (for more information on an EAM agenda for CxOs, see Chapter 3). Sponsors generally derive from three levels:

- **Board members.** This is the best-case scenario. Board members have enough authority and visibility to thoroughly support EAM. Board members can also help you to optimally anchor the EAM team in the organisation (see Step 4). Unfortunately, board members are often unavailable.
- **Business department or division heads.** Business department or business division heads are good sponsors of EAM initiatives. However, their influence is usually limited, which might impede implementation in other departments.
- **Chief information officers (CIOs).** Owing to EAM's roots in software engineering, CIOs are most often EAM initiative sponsors. They tend to have a very good understanding of the subject matter. However, in many organisations, CIOs have limited influence on the business side, unless they are also responsible for business process management, which is an excellent starting point for establishing EAM practices.

Once you have identified and convinced your sponsor, define a clear and realistic set of EAM-related targets. These targets are crucial because they help you to prioritise your work, as well as measure and prove your success. When discussing and setting (and later adjusting) these targets, keep the following in mind:

- Targets should be derived from *top management needs*. This makes it easier to convince stakeholders.
- Think about potential *quick wins* (see Section 3).
- Negotiate the *EA layers and domains* you want to start from and focus on.

- Define the *metrics and KPIs* for measuring the fulfilment of targets.
- Agree on specific targets and document them as a *business case* (see Section 3).
- Define *reporting standards* for communicating the degree of fulfilment.

As the one responsible for EAM introduction, you might consider this a little too binding. What if you don't succeed? This should not be as serious a concern as not understanding what management really wants. What would happen if you were suddenly confronted with new targets? Also bear in mind that clear targets will help you steer and control the EAM initiative.

Step 2: As-is analysis

Familiarise yourself with the current EA, as well as with the previous EAM approaches in your organisation. An EA analysis allows you to identify the most important fields of action in terms of problems and decision needs. You can also verify if the targets negotiated in the previous step are actually feasible. When assessing the current situation, we recommend asking the following questions about the EA and EAM:

The current status of the organisation should be analysed

- Enterprise architecture
  - What does the EA in the domain and layers of interest look like?
  - What are the current problems in terms of risks, costs, quality and time?
  - Who is responsible for which parts of the EAM?
- Enterprise architecture management
  - What EAM practices were applied in the past?
  - What is the organisation's maturity in terms of EAM philosophy?
  - How are decisions made?
  - What is the existing EAM skills set?

This information is usually collected by means of interviews with relevant people (e.g., application owners or process managers) and the analysis of documents (e.g., EA models and EAM manuals).

Step 3: Stakeholder analysis

Stakeholders and team members are crucial factors for the introduction

It will be difficult to introduce EAM without knowledge of the stakeholders. Any form of change management will require an in-depth understanding of those involved. The stakeholder analysis described here can be performed concurrently with, or shortly after, the previous step. In fact, the as-is analysis may reveal potential stakeholders, and interviews conducted in the previous step may have already been used to collect information required for the stakeholder analysis.

In general, the stakeholder analysis, as proposed here, consists of three steps:

1. **Identify stakeholders.** Stakeholders are all those responsible for EA-related decisions, as well as those who must apply EAM practices and are involved in EAM initiatives. Potential stakeholders include architects, project managers, solution architects, line mangers, IT managers, service managers and general managers. In many cases, it makes sense to identify stakeholder groups rather than individual stakeholders.
2. **Evaluate stakeholders.** During the evaluation phase, you assess the positive and negative attitudes and emotions, including the hopes, fears and concerns of each stakeholder (Figure 9.5). You also may want to identify explicit promoters and inhibitors of EAM.
3. **Define stakeholder strategies.** Finally, you can develop strategies for involving and convincing key stakeholders. You can apply the above-mentioned strategies where necessary (see Section 2). At any rate, consider every strategy's cost-benefit ratio.

The stakeholder analysis usually applies interviews and documents analysis as data collection methods. Potential documents include organisational charts and job descriptions, if available.

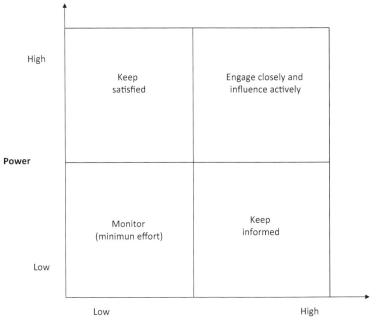

Figure 9.5: Stakeholder matrix

Step 4: Set up an organisational anchoring of the EAM team

The organisational anchoring and the EAM team's composition are critical EAM success factors. Our case studies show that successful enterprise architects often have stronger business skills than IT skills. However, they are good analysts with the ability to structure problems. They should also be proactive, strong communicators and negotiators, and smart at office politics. If not, they are likely to struggle to balance the diverse stakeholders' interests during the EA development. Filling such staffing positions with internal people is a good idea but, unfortunately, not always possible. In this case, you will need to look to the market. We recommend taking people from the same industry, as this will increase the likelihood of familiarity with your business processes.

The organisational anchoring of your EAM team is another important issue. As a rule, the higher the anchoring, the better. Anchoring on organisational units close to board members increases the EAM group's visibility and provides access to the organisation's most important decision-makers. In many cases, EAM teams are positioned as support functions for CxOs, preferably the CEO, which leverages an EAM team's work. Based on the organisational anchoring, you should also think about an EA governance that defines the decision rights and accountabilities of all the parties involved. More information on this topic can be found in Chapter 4.

Apart from the architectural team and its anchorage, you also have to put in place boards and committees that accompany architectural processes and represent the most important stakeholders. You should especially consider establishing an Enterprise Architecture Council (EAC) and an Architecture Review Board (ARB). The former serves as the principal overseeing body for enterprise architecture. It implements and governs the EAM within the enterprise. The latter assesses initiatives' compliance with architecture standards, guiding principles, reference architectures and blueprints. More information on these organisational components can be found in Chapter 4.

Step 5: Defining architecture principles and standards

Defining architecture principles means structurally describing what kind of conventions the EAM initiative intends to satisfy. If the EAM is more technologically driven, architecture principles often describe a proposed shared understanding of the provided IT applications and underlying infrastructure. Standardisation is often a major task in respect of the application portfolio and IT services. Architecture principles often define standards for these matters. A business approach to EAM would focus more on the business aspects, processes and demands that IT needs to satisfy.

EAM principles as a cultural aspect at a large service sector company

One of our case studies showed that EAM principles are a good way of approaching a vital EAM culture. The architecture principles within this organisation determine how IT services and applications are allocated. By providing standardised and formalised services and applications, the company can support these principles' goals – consistency, cost control, efficiency, governance mechanisms and risk management.

Step 6: Defining the EAM scope

It is particularly good to have a clear understanding of the services that the EA team provides to customers when it has an advisory role in an organisation (see Chapter 6 and 8). The team can clarify this understanding by clearly stating and documenting what the EAM services are. Even if the role is more proactive and the architecture team can actively drive and moderate management processes, such a service portfolio may help clarify the EAM team's role and prioritise EAM-related activities. Defining what the EAM should provide requires taking contextual factors into account. These factors include:

Standards, architecture principles and the defined scope facilitate a goal-oriented introduction process

- **Overall EAM objectives.** The EAM objectives negotiated with your primary sponsor will limit the spectrum of potential services. The EAM team's objectives can be deduced from the overall EAM objectives.
- **Results of the as-is analysis.** The as-is analysis may provide hints about the services that are required. Your current architecture may render certain actions necessary. For example, an overly complex application landscape may lead you to concentrate on this layer first.
- **Stakeholder analysis.** The stakeholder analysis may reveal quick wins and urgent stakeholder needs that can be translated into services.
- **Standards and literature on EAM.** Take a look at EA frameworks (see Chapter 8) and EAM literature, which may contain information about EAM-related fields of action and allow for the derivation of EAM services. In addition, study Chapters 5 to 7 as their process descriptions may prove helpful.

After this process step, decide on one of the EAM archetypes, as outlined in Chapter 4.

Step 7: Design and implement EAM practices and services

Once you have defined the service portfolio, think about the design and implementation of such services. This may involve a number of different conceptual activities, which are either organisational or methodological. Organisational activities include:

- defining processes and procedures, and
- defining role and organisational models.

Methodological activities include:

- defining meta models, modelling techniques, analysis procedures and reports,
- defining document templates, and
- selecting and configuring software tools.

What you do, how, and in what order depends on many different aspects, as discussed in the previous chapters. Your priorities and approach will primarily depend on the EAM archetype you choose for your organisation (see Chapter 4). Successful organisations implement EAM step-by-step, defining work packages of several months, releasing the results, and moving on to the next work packages. This way, the EAM initiative stays visible, realises benefits steadily and is easy to control.

Step 8: Change management

Convince people throughout all phases, and start the roll-out in pilot mode

As seen in Section 3, change management is crucial for successful EAM introduction. Parallel to your project plan, you should also develop a change management plan, comprising all the activities and measures necessary to convince people of EAM, to overcome resistance, and to familiarise people with your firm's EAM approach. We recommend that you engage in change management activities from the outset, not only after the start of roll-out. Sometimes a group's opinion may contradict your objectives. Furthermore, change management activities need to accompany all subsequent phases and address the perspective of the individual employees (see Section 3).

Step 9: Piloting and evaluation

Most organisations that apply EAM must deal with large enterprise architectures that comprise numerous organisational units, business processes, applications and infrastructure components. In such cases, EAM often affects hundreds of people in their daily work. Therefore, prior to introducing EAM, you want to be sure that your EAM approach works and will not fail or yield unintended side effects. Piloting is a way of testing your EAM approach in a relatively controlled environment. You can limit the complexity and impact when problems occur. We recommend piloting EAM practices, unless your organisation is very small, in which case piloting would affect the entire EA. When selecting an organisational domain for your pilot, consider the following criteria:

- Will potential problems have a limited impact on the organisation?
- Are you able to respond when problems occur?
- Are the stakeholders of the pilot domain in favour of EAM?
- Do you have powerful promoters in the pilot domain?

If you can answer all these questions in the affirmative, you have found an adequate candidate for a pilot domain. After piloting, we recommend that you carry out a thorough analysis of what went wrong and what went well. Derive a list of the improvements needed to be made to your EAM approach and prioritise them. Encourage the stakeholders to participate in the evaluation. Implement the most important and urgent improvements immediately. Now you are prepared for Step 10.

Step 10: Roll-out and continuous improvement

A successful pilot indicates a high probability that the subsequent roll-out will be successful. This roll-out should comprise the same set of activities as the pilot, except on a broader scale. After completing your final roll-out, you should be prepared for a continuous improvement process. The work on your EAM approach will be ongoing, at least for a few years, until the necessary cultural shift has been achieved and people have fully adopted the EAM practices.

9.5 From methodologies to culture

This chapter has specifically focused on systematic and structured strategies, based on change management activities, with which an EAM methodology can be established in an organisation. However, we know that EAM works best when it is based on a specific culture of EA awareness, as well as holistic thinking and decision-making, which have little to do with the enforced compliance of a standardised methodology. How can we resolve this obvious contradiction?

When the EAM methodology is internalised in the organisation, success is near

From our studies and related research, we know that methodologies (together with change management measures, as outlined above) can combine very well to foster culture change. By introducing a methodology, an organisation establishes certain work routines, which in turn change the way actors in the organisation perceive their work environment, which is – in this case – the EA. For example, through regular architectural reviews during project execution, project team members learn how their project impacts the overall EA and they realise why EAM is important. We expect an organisation to internalise the methodology and the underlying philosophy if the EAM introduction is done well. An organisation will learn how to deal with architectural challenges, and the architectural awareness will increase. Throughout this process, the organisation will gradually develop EAM competencies and capabilities that will help it to become more successful on a broader scale. After some time, it will even excel at the expertise embodied in the methodology, and professionals will strive to further improve this expertise by, for example:

- breaking the rules of the methodology,
- establishing knowledge and experience sharing, and
- looking for additional external expertise.

This is why the role of strict methodologies diminishes over time. They are often only needed at the start of an organisational learning process. In the end, you are likely to have a lightweight methodology that only includes the most important governance rules.

9.6 Final recommendations for management

As noted in this chapter, EAM methodology development is by no means the only challenge. EAM is a management discipline that affects people by changing the way they think, decide and act. You must be prepared for social, psychological and other problems when you introduce EAM. This chapter provides some starting points for addressing these challenges. We conclude by providing additional basic principles for developing EAM in your organisation:

1. **Develop your EAM incrementally**. This is a fundamental pre-condition for realising quick wins and involving stakeholders.
2. **Try to develop your EAM in short cycles** of no more than 6 to 9 months, as short cycles allow you to correct your actions when necessary.
3. **Design your cycles as learning experiences** by running through a step-by-step sequence: Define a target, design a solution, discuss it with stakeholders, implement it, deploy it, evaluate it, learn and improve.
4. **Be pragmatic and follow an 80/20 approach**. Experience shows that with 20% to 50% effort, you can already gain 80% of the potential quality. The remaining 20% quality will require an additional 50% to 80% effort.
5. **Do not implement everything at once**. Streamline your architecture down to architectural layers or domains of interest. Concentrate on the parts with which you can realise the most impact.

We trust that these recommendations will help you move forward in developing, introducing and improving EAM in your organisation.

References

[1]   R. L. Glass, "A Snapshot of Systems Development Practice," *IEEE Softw.*, vol. 16, no. 3, pp. 112-111, 1999.

[2]   N. L. Russo, R. Hightower, and J. M. Pearson, "The Failure of Methodologies to Meet the Needs of Current Development Environments," *Proceedings of the British Computer Society's Annual Conference on Information System Methodologies*, pp. 387-393, 1996.

[3]   M. Eva and S. Guilford, "Committed to a Radical approach?" A Survey of Systems Development Methods in Practice. *Proceedings of the Fourth Conference of the British Computer Society Information Systems Methodologies Specialist Group*, pp. 87-96, 1996.

[4]   J. de Bony, "Project management and national culture: A Dutch-French case study," *International Journal of Project Management*, vol. 28, no. 2, pp. 173-182, Feb. 2010.

[5]   H. Kerzner, *Project Management: A Systems Approach to Planning, Scheduling, and Controlling*, 8th ed. Wiley, 2003.

[6]   A. Munns and B. Bjeirmi, "Role of Project Management in Achieving Project Success," *International Journal of Project Management*, vol. 14, no. 2, pp. 81-87, Apr. 1996.

[7]   M. Winter, C. Smith, P. Morris, and S. Cicmil, "Directions for future research in project management: The main findings of a UK government-funded research network," *International Journal of Project Management*, vol. 24, no. 8, pp. 638-649, Nov. 2006.

[8]   C. K. Riemenschneider, B. C. Hardgrave, and F. D. Davis, "Explaining Software Developer Acceptance of Methodologies: A Comparison of Five Theoretical Models," *IEEE Transactions on Software Engineering*, vol. 28, no. 12, pp. 1135-1145, 2002.

[9]   M. Khalifa and J. M. Verner, "Drivers for Software Development Method Usage.," *IEEE Transactions on Engineering Management*, vol. 47, no. 3, p. 360, 2000.

[10] K. Mohan and F. Ahlemann, "Understanding the Acceptance and Usage of IT Project Management Methodologies: Towards a Conceptual Model supported by Case Studies," *AMCIS 2010 Proceedings*, 2010.

[11] V. Venkatesh, M. G. Morris, G. B. Davis, and F. D. Davis, "User Acceptance of Information Technology: Toward a Unified View," *MIS Quarterly*, vol. 27, no. 3, pp. 425-478, 2003.

[12] V. Venkatesh, "Determinants of Perceived Ease of Use: Integrating Control, Intrinsic Motivation, and Emotion into the Technology Acceptance Model.," *Information Systems Research*, vol. 11, no. 4, p. 342, 2000.

[13] F. D. Davis, "Perceived Usefulness, Perceived Ease of Use, and User Acceptance of Information Technology.," *MIS Quarterly*, vol. 13, no. 3, pp. 319-340, 1989.

[14] H. van der Heijden, "User Acceptance of Hedonic Information Systems," *MIS Quarterly*, vol. 28, no. 4, pp. 695-704, 2004.

[15] F. D. Davis, R. P. Bagozzi, and P. R. Warshaw, "Extrinsic and Intrinsic Motivation to Use Computers in the Workplace.," *Journal of Applied Social Psychology*, vol. 22, no. 14, pp. 1111-1132, 1992.

[16] K. Mohan and F. Ahlemann, "A Theory of User Acceptance of IS Project Management Methodologies: Understanding the Influence of Psychological Determinism and Experience," in *Proceedings of the 10. Internationale Tagung Wirtschaftsinformatik*, Zürich, 2011.

[17] I. Ajzen, "The theory of planned behavior," *Organizational Behavior and Human Decision Processes*, vol. 50, no. 2, pp. 179-211, 1991.

[18] V. Venkatesh and F. D. Davis, "A Theoretical Extension of the Technology Acceptance Model: Four Longitudinal Field Studies.," *Management Science*, vol. 46, no. 2, p. 186, 2000.

[19] M. Deutsch and G. B. Harold, "A Study of Normative and Informational Social Influences on Individual Judgment," *Journal of Abnormal and Social Psychology*, vol. 51, no. 3, p. 629–636, 1955.

[20] B. M. Bass, B. J. Avolio, D. I. Jung, and Y. Berson, "Predicting Unit Performance by Assessing Transformational and Transactional Leadership," *Journal of Applied Psychology*, vol. 88, no. 2, pp. 207-218, Apr. 2003.

[21] R. T. Keller, "Transformational Leadership, Initiating Structure, and Substitutes for Leadership: A Longitudinal Study of Research and Development Project Team Performance," *Journal of Applied Psychology*, vol. 91, no. 1, pp. 202-210, Jan. 2006.

[22] A. M. Aladwani, "Implications of Some of the Recent Improvement Philosophies for the Management of the Information Systems Organization," *Industrial Management & Data Systems*, vol. 99, no. 1, p. 33–39, 1999.

[23] K. E. Hultman, "The Path of Least Resistance. Preparing Employees for Change.," 1979. Learning Concepts, Austin, Texas, USA.

[24] J. N. Sheth and W. H. Stellner, *Psychology of Innovation Resistance: The Less Developed Concept (LDC) in Diffusion Research.* College of Commerce and Business Administration, University of Illinois at Urbana-Champaign, 1979.

[25] J. Ward, S. De Hertogh, and S. Viaene, *"Managing Benefits from IS/IT Investments: an Empirical Investigation into Current Practise,"* presented at the Hawaii International Conference on System Science, Hawaii, 2007.

Chapter 10

EAM 2020 – the future of the discipline

Eric Stettiner, Markus Fienhold

Table of contents

Management summary

In this chapter, we briefly assess the current status of enterprise architecture management (EAM) and describe the gap that needs to be closed if it is to meet organisations' requirements. We introduce a method that allows for valuable qualitative forecasting, and then discuss relevant trends and developments, which help us to describe the challenges in tomorrow's business environment. Applying these findings, we use different viewpoints to explore alternatives for developing EAM. Finally, we make predictions that seek to summarise the key EAM developments anticipated in the next decade:

1. EAM will be represented at the board level.
2. Federated and combined teams from business and technology will shape the enterprise.
3. The process of strategy development, tactical planning and operations will be more intertwined.
4. EA tools will be an integrated part of the enterprise application portfolio.
5. EAM monitoring will be established.
6. Best practice EAM operations will be defined.
7. EAM will have a new name.

In this chapter, we intend to help you relate our views to your personal expectation of future developments, which may help you to amend or adjust your strategic positioning.

10.1 Introduction

People say that it is difficult to make predictions, especially about the future. Frankly, when we started working on this chapter, we discovered that we held many views of the future. Predicting the future did not prove our greatest obstacle. We spent most of our time validating and reducing the different views to reasonable statements that would allow you to follow or challenge our thinking. There are simply too many variables, beliefs and possible events for any one forecast to be completely convincing. While the art of developing credible views of the future remains difficult, it is our vision of tomorrow that informs and drives our decisions today. This is why we felt it important to work on an outlook of EAM.

EAM 2011: Mind the gap!

As noted in previous chapters, we understand EAM as a management philosophy that approaches corporate change holistically. While many of our interview partners would agree with this view, enterprises often concentrate their efforts on the information system and technology layers. Today, the primary EAM focus is to make IT landscapes transparent by modelling the as-is indifferent degrees of detail, and to secure or optimise IT-business alignment using to-be landscapes and roadmaps. This leaves room for improved strategic integration, the definition of the business architecture, and its alignment with established IS and infrastructure models, as shown in the SWOT diagram below (Table 10.1):

EAM was successful in the companies that we observed. However, further advancements are needed to unfold EAM's full potential. We believe companies will move towards this stage in the next few years. John A. Zachman, the great enterprise architecture mastermind, wrote '(...) we are on the verge of seeing architecture 'come into its own' and in the 21st century it will be the determining factor, the factor that separates the winners from the losers, the successful and the failures, the acquiring from the acquired, the survivors from the others.'[1] If this is true, then it is worth thinking about how enterprise architecture management could develop in this relatively young century.

Table 10.1: Assessment of EAM 2011

Strengths	Weaknesses
• EAM represents a proven IT-business-alignment approach. • EAM increases transparency in complex IT, data and process landscapes.	• EAM's benefits outside the IT function are currently not sufficiently understood. • EAM is often implemented in IT-oriented and tool-driven ways.
Opportunities	**Threats**
• EAM concepts can provide the required transparency to master organisational complexity in a volatile environment. • An EAM philosophy can integrate proven management practices into a consistent corporate change approach.	• It might be difficult to attribute resulting benefits to EAM decisions or concepts. • Lack of relevant skilled staff. • Large-scale, centralised and overly detailed EAM initiatives increase the risk of building an ivory tower.

How we can predict the future

Strategic decisions are usually taken with incomplete knowledge and in situations with considerable uncertainty. Before making a significant decision, reasonable businesspeople seek to collect all relevant available information. Today, much of this information is based on forecasts, and the quality and value of the derived predictions will be judged by criteria like data quality and quantity, as well as by the analysis's transparency and logic. While quantitative forecasting methods have reached an acceptable maturity level, the same cannot be said for qualitative predictions, which play an important role in strategic business decisions.

The value of qualitative forecasts increases when based on different viewpoints

Following an approach suggested by John H. Vanston [2], we can improve the results and value of qualitative forecasts by considering two or more viewpoints when predicting future developments. A viewpoint is a method successfully used in the past to make valuable predictions:

• We predict the future based on trends that can be extrapolated from historic developments. We can call this a deterministic viewpoint.

- We analyse the past for repeating cycles and events, as nature and human beings react consistently when exposed to similar situations. This can be called a pattern-based viewpoint.
- We analyse the past to identify overarching and lasting changes that will have a more significant impact in the future. This is a megatrend viewpoint.
- We think that ideas and technologies that are currently being conceptualised or implemented will have a greater influence in the future than established ideas and technologies. We consider this a current developments viewpoint.
- We believe that organisations and people will shape the future and we need to study their values, objectives and influence to derive good predictions. We can refer to this viewpoint as goal-driven.
- Finally, we predict the future based on personal beliefs, experiences and subconscious processes. This is a visionary viewpoint.

We will use these viewpoints to derive an outline of a possible EAM future.

10.2 The shaping factors

The enterprise architecture management discipline will look quite different in the future. In our view, two factors will drive this change:

- A fundamentally changing business environment and the need to orchestrate a complex delivery organisation of external and internal service providers to render an effective and efficient operation.
- A further developing technology basis, which brings new opportunities to mature EAM operations.

Both factors will change the current EAM context, as well as the expected EAM objectives and outcomes. It is therefore reasonable to explore relevant businesses and technology changes in the years to come and to subsequently discuss the future requirements in the context of a holistic corporate change approach.

Three ways of doing business

As we have laid out in Chapter 3, we can observe today strategic management directions that will change the way we do business tomorrow. Outsourcers and insourcers are already using the web to offer and consume an ever-increasing number of business and infrastructure services. If this trend continues for some time, we can expect three basic business patterns to appear in the near future [3][4]:

Three business patterns will appear: CRM, Product Champions and Infrastructure Providers

- **Customer Relationship Managers (CRMs)** – These organisations currently outsource non-strategic business activities, while the number of perceived core business processes is decreasing. CRMs progressively focus on building relationships and managing the information flow – from generating customer demand to delivering orders and creating differentiating and value-adding services. The management of technology and commodity processes is left to specialised service partners. In the process, they become customer relationship managers.
- **Product champions** – These companies dominate the product development process and are or will be well known or even synonymous with their product(s). As flexibility and innovation are key differentiators for them, they tend to remain small in (corporate or unit) size and will prefer to remain largely self-sufficient.

As a result, they will seek to maintain most of their necessary corporate skills and assets in-house.

- **Providers of global business services and infrastructure** – These businesses are currently insourcing and enhancing their capabilities and assets in order to extend their business model, offering an increasing number of business services and infrastructure to new business partners and end users.

While in real life we may find companies that represent two or even all the patterns in different parts of their structure, these diverse ways of doing business will affect and alter organisations' focus, capabilities and assets (as indicated in Table 10.2).

Table 10.2: Three basic business patterns

Type:	Customer Relationship Manager	Product Champion	Infrastructure Services
Process Strength	Good at adopting and orchestrating best practice processes and solutions	Good at R&D, packaged offerings and local customer service	Good at developing and deploying best practices
Structure	*Management:* Virtual *Operations:* Locally orchestrate global services *Support:* Regional, orchestrate global services	*Management:* Strong regional centre(s) *Operations:* Depend on business or industry *Support:* In the regional centre, supported by external services	*Management:* One global HQ *Operations:* Global centres of excellence *Support:* Regional, supported by other external services
People and Talent Focus	Marketing, sales, product bundling / customisation, product life cycle management and service management	R&D, customer service and all corporate skills required	Service management, service development and service delivery
Technology: Key area of expertise	Communications, mobile tools, versatility tools and integration of services	Special (product or regional) tools, versatility tools and basic corporate platform	Infrastructure, communication, service management and reporting

EAM relevance: The projects required to transform the current operating model to align with one of the business patterns are of a fundamental nature. They extend across many architectural layers and demand consistent corporate change in order to be successful. The requirement for an integrated, end-to-end back-office process that ensures the execution of strategic decisions will increase.

Business challenges in 2020

Independent of their strategy and structure, we expect businesses to face common future challenges with markets and customers, volume and profit, statutory requirements and compliance, ability to implement change, and resource efficiency in a globalised world. We address each in turn.

Market and customers

Today, customisations of consumer products such as cars or holidays are common services. In the coming years, we expect the individualisation trend, as we observe it today in the telecom and media industry, to inflate available goods and services. A demanding digital generation is meeting a globalising market, which is enabled by technologies, standards and the use of external partners. This set-up will allow enterprises to offer extremely customised solutions to their customers, who will differ from person to person, as well as today and tomorrow.

EAM relevance: To increase the transparency of resources and capabilities available to support orchestration and convergence of services, goods and suppliers, so as to meet, maintain and grow customer demands.

Volume and profit

Shareholder interests, global resource limits and new product combinations will lead to an increase in M&A and carve out activities [5]. We can also expect more frequent occurrences correcting exaggerated asset allocations. Executives will put much effort into supporting the transformation to new or changed business models, as well as into the successful integration and de-integration of people, processes and technologies into or out of the organisation.

EAM relevance: To promote and support management practices that consider and manage change holistically and that inform the business about assets' value.

Statutory requirements and compliance

Acting more globally will require enterprises to comply with diverse financial and tax standards. Companies will have to implement financial accounting and transfer-pricing systems that adhere to changing local statutory and tax regulations. Further, ever-stricter regulations will result in significant changes to the underlying software solution(s) and will drive the demand for event and pattern-based real-time monitoring of business process performance and results.

EAM relevance: To offer insight into data structures and flows, and to show how they relate to business information requirements, process design and execution.

Ability to implement change
A common challenge for companies will be the time-to-market available to maintain a superior customer experience, while responding to new or changing market conditions. The use and orchestration of multiple business service and infrastructure providers will require different skills and knowledge to ensure stable business operations. The overall complexity of the management tasks will increase but will be supported by dedicated technology and management practices.

EAM relevance: To provide a basis for the identification of the implications of change activities and the planning and management of the necessary actions.

Resource efficiency in a globalised world
Reuse of assets and components, virtual teaming and shifting effort to suppliers and customers are strategies that many companies already use. Declining communication costs and improved technologies have reduced the need to physically co-locate staff. But this effect does not stop at the enterprises boundary and is the driver behind today's shared service centre and outsourcing projects. We expect this trend to continue. As a result:

- Companies or units will rebundle their capabilities and assets to become a CRM, product champion or service provider (see the three business patterns mentioned earlier on),
- the importance and number of virtual teams working on solutions across enterprises and country borders will increase.

Successful enterprises will seek to establish superior support and tools to integrate and manage end-to-end processes' transactional and versatile tasks:

- A collaboration platform will significantly increase the integration of co-workers, customers and suppliers in front and back office processes.
- Web 2.0, or later functionality, crowdsourcing and swarm intelligence principles will be used to exploit the talents and views of unknown user communities for design decisions, product development and implementation or after-sales problem solving.

EAM relevance: To supply a complete catalogue of available resources and capabilities, to link them to usage cases and to define and manage integration architecture requirements.

The platform of the future

By responding to the business challenges and available technologies, successful enterprises will build a specific ecosystem of networked resources and capabilities that will best support their way of doing business. As indicated in Figure 10.1, they will use an interconnected business platform in which customers, vendors and business partners can drive mutual growth and satisfaction.

The 2020 business ecosystem

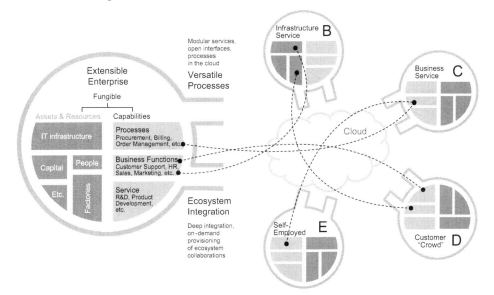

Figure 10.1: Interconnected enterprise service ecosystems[6]

Enterprises will be able to plug suppliers in or out within a fraction of the time required today. This, however, will not apply to customers and partners. Their opinion, reputation, resources and capabilities will have a higher impact on the market and profit margin than today; therefore, enterprises will spend more attention, care and support on managing the relationship.

10.3 The future of the EAM discipline

A new role: The chief change officer (CCO)

Based on our view of the current capabilities and future business requirements, we will now detail possible viewpoints and expectations and then predict key future EAM developments.

Developing viewpoints

Deterministic viewpoint. We observe that EAM started as a detailed and technology-related approach and is developing both horizontally and vertically, covering all layers and domains of the enterprise. As a result, we predict that EAM will extend its use into business and strategy. We expect that joint teams from business and IT will work together on solution architectures and we believe that the EA tool market will continue to mature, resulting in fewer vendors, offering greater functionality.

Pattern-based viewpoint. Looking at it from this perspective, we could argue that EAM might be another buzzword that describes concepts that have been around for years. We expect the principal idea and related approaches to stick around and mature, but by 2020 we will be using different terminology for them. In addition, we imagine that EA tools will be included in the portfolio of all major enterprise application software vendors.

Megatrends viewpoint. The following topics fall under this classification: Globalisation, energy supply, risk control, regulations, collaboration, mobility and use simplification. When we think about what these themes could mean for future business, we can extract the requirement for the increased transparency of corporate asset and capability usage, their interaction with human beings, and improved change control and change management. Corporate change will become a key topic for senior management and, as a result, some businesses might make this a top priority, placing it close to the board level. EAM might be the management philosophy that supports them.

Different viewpoints impact our expectation of future developments

Current developments viewpoint. Current developments that are relevant for EAM are multifaceted and include improved features and the integration of mobile technology, greater support and incorporation of versatile people-driven and creative tasks, or different web-based sourcing approaches, such as cloud-based services or crowdsourcing. Overall, the business environment's complexity is increasing. Furthermore, companies and business units will develop their organisations to align with their chosen business pattern. We can predict the need for a higher level of standardisation, which allows organisations in 2020 to orchestrate internal and external service offerings under a seamless user interface. We therefore expect monitoring tools to mature, using software agents to collect architectural meta-data that can help analyse and monitor the current architecture.

Goal-driven viewpoint. While there are too many options available to paint a complete picture, we expect relevant influential players' goals to include growth, efficiency, profit, influence and innovation targets. This could form the basis for continuous change, the need for business transformation and the ongoing integration of enabling technologies.

Visionary viewpoint. We leave this one to your imagination.

Architecting the future of EAM

Using these viewpoints, we make the following predictions:

1. EAM will be represented at board level

In 2020, change will be frequent and often of critical importance for the organisation. Teams involved in managing corporate change will seek to establish:

- a holistic management practice that supports change from strategic planning to benefit realisation, and
- transparency about available capabilities and resources, their inter-dependencies, process and information use cases, and their value contributions.

We expect that a central unit will take care of the general architecture and change principles, translate strategies into initial conceptual solution architectures and standards, and oversee the benefits realisation management while monitoring the change programmes. A chief change officer (CCO) will head up this unit and will be involved and consulted by his or her peers when significant change is considered or underway.

The role of the chief change officer (CCO)

The role of CCO will be new to top management. Possibly on or close to board level, this role will involve taking responsibility for enterprise-wide change management. The CCO will be responsible for implementing and managing the EAM function.

The CCO will co-initiate and monitor EA-design and implementation projects that aim at developing new enterprise capabilities that are required to support the enterprise's strategy. Innovation, regulatory requirements, or the operationalisation of objectives resulting from expansion, growth, daily business, competitor pressure and globalising markets may trigger this demand.

His or her second focus will be to maintain a complete and consistent picture of the enterprise resources and assets by ensuring that other changes comply with the agreed architecture model.

The CCO must understand the current and future enterprise's business and IT issues and strategies, and should seek to enhance its agility and flexibility so as to meet time-to-market and changing customer requirements. He or she should be in charge of tools and methods that will enable the board to decide on major corporate changes.

As the need for dedicated management of processes and technology will be replaced by the demand for more integrated and holistic solutions, we expect the CCO to assume the responsibilities of the current chief information officer (CIO) and the chief process officer (CPO), where the dominant business pattern is CRM or the business is a product champion.

Definition of the enterprise continuum

2. Federated and combined teams from business and technology will shape the enterprise

EAM will be organised in a way that allows the think tanks from different disciplines and geographies to work together without losing their business or technology anchors.

Federated groups will be coordinated by a central team

- Depending on a business's size, spread and prime business pattern, organisations will establish virtual or physical groups, responsible for all layers of a business domain and across all phases of the solution lifecycle. These teams will benefit from an application and communication infrastructure that supports versatile, people-driven processes.
- These groups will be orchestrated by a central team, which will define, set up and maintain the common design and control framework, as well as ensure consistent cross-domain planning, communication and integration. This central team will make use of assigned architects who will rotate back to their anchor function after two to four years. They will translate strategic scenarios into

initial conceptual models, supporting a more intertwined planning approach.

The change portfolio management process will be organised centrally, but will be supported and reviewed by the above-mentioned domain groups. Agreed projects and initiatives will be clustered by the business domains. The domain groups will be responsible for their execution. Members from both teams will participate in architecture reviews that control the solution delivery.

Operations management solutions will be determined by the business pattern in use. CRM companies could establish domain operations led by a business person, while infrastructure companies will organise operations around their services, using a team of technical and service management talents. Product champions are likely to need both business and technology expertise, but should establish good interaction between them. All operations teams will be in direct contact with the domain groups and will discuss the key performance indicators (KPIs), major incidents and EA changes resulting from operations with the central team.

3. The strategy development, tactical planning and operations process will be more intertwined

The documentation of strategies remains a difficult subject and will not follow generally recognised standards. Hence, the interpretation of strategic thinking and its translation into tactical planning will be one of the critical EAM tasks and benefits. We will seek suggestions to ensure a more consistent and complete description of the business goals, which will be used to define alternative target operating models (aTOMs). aTOMs will be simulated by considering the available baseline architecture, as well as alternative components or external service and infrastructure offerings to define the optimal resource allocation and investment portfolio for the required output level. During this planning and simulation process, architects will analyse the EAM layers and will study optional integration levels to maximise the long-term performance (see Figure 10.2).

EAM, innovation management and business development

Different scenarios will be presented to management executives, who will make the decision, considering additional political, ethical and cultural aspects. This target integration level will lead the organisation to search for relevant supporting technologies and innovative solutions as part of the to-be architecture definition. EAM will be in charge of defining, enhancing and controlling these solutions. Architects will base this lifecycle management task on the gap between the current model and the target model, as well as on an evaluation of available technologies and operations-based KPIs, and will evaluate the maturity, re-use, risk and added value of the various components and patterns. This makes EAM an important player in the enterprise's innovation management and business development process.

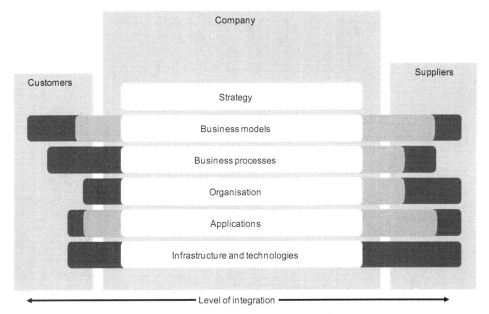

Figure 10.2: Different EAM layers and integration levels

The possible value of such an analysis can be seen when looking at successful contemporary examples of refined integration layers: The Apple App Store, for example, extended the iTunes business model to new suppliers and products; crowdsourcing connects the corporate organisation and business processes with the customer base, using their applications and infrastructure.

The EA tool market will continue to consolidate

4. EA tools will be an integrated part of the enterprise application portfolio

By 2020, enterprise architecture tools will be used to support EAM analysis and monitoring, reducing architecture management efforts and improving communication with the wider business community. In our view, the EA tool market will be consolidated both functionally and in respect of the number of vendors. The driving forces will be the major software vendors of enterprise applications, who will seek to enhance their established implementation and operations toolkits. This scenario will involve continuous acquisitions of tool providers by 'Big ERP'. If no significant M&A activity occurs, leading to a further consolidation of the enterprise application market, businesses will have the choice between offers from the big players like HP, IBM, Microsoft, Oracle, SAP, and – for example – five more EA tool vendors that support all EAM aspects and processes.

Today's tool solutions for process modelling, organisational structure documentation, application portfolios, project portfolios, asset management, configuration management and change request processing will be integrated using one common access layer. A common platform will support the documentation of all layers in an integrated way. This solution will have strong links to end-user documentation, investment management and operations management support.

The platform will provide different EAM views and level of detail, from strategy to detailed documentation. Functionality will be enhanced or added, impacting and changing established EAM processes, including scenario and process simulations, improved business process support and benefit management. Such enhanced modelling and analysis tools will allow organisational change teams to be less technically skilled and to create a demand for more business-focused architects. As a result, the EA job descriptions will change.

5. EAM monitoring will be established

Currently, business and IT operations are only loosely coupled with EAM, leaving significant room for improved integration and information sharing. In our view, this will have changed by 2020. EAM will not only define, but also monitor the defined architecture as part of EAM operations. This enlarged responsibility will be supported by new auto-modelling tools, which will deploy software agents that continuously analyse the enterprise architecture and update its metadata and models. This structured and interrelated enterprise knowledge will form the basis for superior monitoring and KPI reporting, as well as for measuring the maturity, cost, added value and complexity of the architecture components or patterns. Event-driven workflows will compare both architecture pattern and process results to the range of expected outcomes, and may trigger rule-based messages. A dashboard will summarise the relevant information by stakeholder and role.

6. Best practice EAM operations will be defined

To ease the difficult integration, major market players will drive the definition of generally accepted best practices for EAM operations and a higher standardisation level of the relevant methods, models and procedures. Similar to the ITIL evolution into the IT service management framework, EAM will be promoted as a standardised approach for business change management and control. Relevant EAM methods, structures, KPIs and processes will be defined within a framework that is commonly used by many businesses. New types of auditing, benchmarking and certification will measure architecture maturity and compliance with the growing regulatory requirements for enterprise operations. EAM maturity will be assessed using aggregated and weighted results from a standard EAM KPI framework. The management of accelerated change and increased complexity, as well as the enablement of agility and flexibility in response to changing market needs will remain key EAM challenges.

An ITIL-like EAM framework will be defined

7. EAM will have a new name

Given the crucial role we foresee for EAM, and considering the expected business focus, we believe that the technical notion of the term 'architecture' will evolve into a new, process-oriented term that better captures the business community's attention. We would call this process *strategy to execution*, or *S2E*, which guides and supports continuous business change.

References

[1] John A. Zachman, "Enterprise Architecture: The Issue of the Century," *Database Programming and Design Magazine*, Bd., März. 1997.

[2] John H. Vanston, "Better forecasts, better plans, better results," *Research Technology Management*, Nr. 2003, Feb. 2003.

[3] John Hagel, Marc Singer, "Unbundling the Corporation," *Harvard Business Review*, March 1999.

[4] Thomas L. Friedman, *The world is flat: a brief history of the twenty-first century*. New York: Farrar, Straus and Giroux, 2006.

[5] "2011 M&A Forecast « Intelligent Mergers."

[6] David Stuckey andCindy Warner, "Making the extensible enterprise a reality," *PwC Technology Forecast 2010 Issue 4*, 2010. [Online]. Available: http://www.pwc.com/us/en/technology-forecast/2010/issue4/features/enterprise-pg1.jhtml. [Accessed: 22-Oct-2010].

Chapter 11

Appendices

Table of contents

Appendix A: Readings on EAM

S. Aier, C. Riege, and R. Winter, "Unternehmensarchitektur – Literaturüberblick und Stand der Praxis," *Wirtschaftsinformatik*, Vol.. 50, No. 4, S. 292-304, 2008.

S. A. Bernard, *An Introduction to Enterprise Architecture: Second Edition*, 2nd ed. AuthourHouse, 2005.

J. Handley, *Enterprise Architecture Best Practice Handbook: Building, Running and Managing Effective Enterprise Architecture Programs – Ready to Use Supporting Documents. Enterprise Architecture Theory into Practice*. Emereo Pty Ltd London, UK, 2008.

L. A. Kappelman, *The SIM Guide to Enterprise Architecture*. 2009.

M. M. Lankhorst, *Enterprise Architecture at Work*. Springer, 2005.

F. Matthes, S. Buckl, J. Leitel, Schweda, *Enterprise Architecture Management Tool Survey 2008*. sebis, 2008.

J. McGovern, S. Ambler, M. Stevens, J. Linn, V. Sharan, and E. Jo, *The Practical Guide to Enterprise Architecture*. Prentice Hall, 2003.

K. D. Niemann, *Von der Unternehmensarchitektur zur IT-Governance*, Vol. 1. Vieweg, 2005.

H. Österle, *Business in the Information Age. Heading for new Processes*. Springer, 1995.

C. Perks and T. Beveridge, *Guide to Enterprise IT Architecture*. Springer, 2003.

E. Proper, M. Lankhorst, M. Schönherr, J. Barjis, and S. Overbeek, *Trends in Enterprise Architecture Research: 5th Workshop, TEAR 2010, Delft, the Netherlands, November 12, 2010, Proceedings*. Springer, 2010.

J. W. Ross, P. Weill, and D. C. Robertson, *Enterprise Architecture as Strategy. Creating a Foundation for Business Execution*. Harvard Business School Press, 2006.

P. Saha, *Handbook of Enterprise Systems Architecture in Practice*. IGI Global, 2007.

A. Scheer, *ARIS – Business Process Frameworks*, 3rd ed. Springer, 1999.

J. Schekkerman, *How to Survive in the Jungle of Enterprise Architecture Frameworks: Creating or Choosing an Enterprise Architecture Framework*. Trafford, 2003.

J. Schekkerman, *The Economic Benefits of Enterprise Architecture*. 2005.

R. Winter and R. Fischer, "Essential Layers, Artifacts, and Dependencies of Enterprise Architecture," *Journal of Enterprise Architecture*, Vol. 3, No. 2, S. 7-18, 2007.

Appendix B: Useful web resources

Organisation / Title	URL
Association of Open Group Enterprise Architects	www.aogea.org
Center for the Advancement of the Enterprise Architecture Profession	caeap.org/default.aspx
Chief Information Officers Council	www.cio.gov
DAMA International	www.dama.org/i4a/pages/ index.cfm?pageid=3552
Enterprise ArchitectureCenter of Excellence (EACOE)	eacoe.org/index2.shtml
Enterprise Information Management Institute	www.eiminstitute.org
Federated Enterprise Architecture Certification Institute (FEAC™ Institute)	www.feacinstitute.org
Institute for Enterprise Architecture Developments	www.enterprise-architecture.info
InternationalEnterpriseArchitectureCenter	www.ieac.org
Interoperability Clearinghouse	www.ichnet.org
Journal of Enterprise Architecture	www.aogea.org/journal
National Association of State Chief Information Officers (NASCIO)	www.nascio.org
sebis: EAM Pattern Catalog	wwwmatthes.in.tum.de/wikis/ eam-pattern-catalog/home
U.S. General Services Administration Technology Strategy Overview	www.gsa.gov/portal/content/104634

Appendix C: Overview of popular EA tools

Vendor	Tool	URL
alfabet AG	planningIT	www.alfabet.de
BOC Information Technologies Consulting GmbH	ADOit, Adonis	www.boc-eu.com
Casewise Ltd.	Corporate Modeler Suite	www.casewise.com
IBM	WebSphere Business Modeler	www.ibm.com
Software AG	ARIS Platform	www.softwareag.com/corporate/products/aris_platform/default.asp
iGrafx	Enterprise Modeler	www.igrafx.de
MEGA International GmbH	MEGA Modelling Suite	www.mega.com
Metastorm Inc.	Metastorm ProVision	www.proformacorp.com
Sybase	Powerdesigner	www.powerdesigner.de
Troux Technologies Inc.	Troux 7.1	www.troux.com

Appendix D: EA frameworks

Enterprise-developed frameworks	The Open Group Architecture Framework (TOGAF^{TM})	www.opengroup.org/togaf
	Generalised Enterprise Reference Architecture and Methodology (GERAM)	www.ict.griffith.edu.au/~bernus/ taskforce/geram/versions/index.html
	Reference Model of Open Distributed Processing (RM-ODP)	www.rm-odp.net
	Guide to the Enterprise Architecture Body of Knowledge (EABOK)	www.mitre.org/work/tech_papers/ tech_papers_04/04_0104/index.html
Commercial frameworks	Integrated Architecture Framework (IAF)	www.capgemini.com/services-and-solutions/technology/soa/soa-solutions/ ent_architecture/iaf/
	Zachman Framework	www.zachman.com
	Architecture of Integrated Information Systems (ARIS)	en.wikipedia.org/wiki/ Architecture_of_Integrated_Information_ Systems
	OBASHI Business & IT methodology and framework (OBASHI)	www.obashi.co.uk
Defence industry frameworks	Command, Control, Communications, Computers, Intelligence, Surveillance, and Reconnaissance (C4ISR)	en.wikipedia.org/wiki/ Department_of_Defense_Architecture_ Framework (seealso DoDAF)
	Department of Defence Architecture Framework (DoDAF) and Technical Reference Model (DoD TRM)	cio-nii.defense.gov/sites/dodaf20/
	NATO Architecture Framework (NAF)	www.nhqc3s.nato.int/architecture
	Technical Architecture Framework for Information Management (TAFIM)	en.wikipedia.org/wiki/TAFIM (see also DoDAF)
	Joint Technical Architecture (JTA)	www.acq.osd.mil/osjtf/pdf/jta-vol-I.pdf
	UK Ministry of Defence Architecture Framework (MODAF)	www.mod.uk/DefenceInternet/ AboutDefence/WhatWeDo/ InformationManagement/MODAF/
	Department of National Defence and the Canadian Forces Architecture Framework (DNDAF)	www.img.forces.gc.ca/pub/af-ca/ index-eng.asp
	France DGA Architecture Framework (AGATE)	www.achats.defense.gouv.fr/ article33349
	International Defence Enterprise Architecture Specification (IDEAS)	http://www.ideasgroup.org

Government frameworks	Federal Enterprise Architecture (FEA)	www.whitehouse.gov/omb/e-gov/fea/
	Government Enterprise Architecture (GEA)	www.emacao.gov.mo/documents/14/03/ seminar3a.pdf
	Treasury Enterprise Architecture Framework (TEAF)	en.wikipedia.org/wiki/ Treasury_Enterprise_Architecture_ Framework
	European Interoperability Framework (EIF)	ec.europa.eu/idabc/en/document/3473/ 5585.html
	NIST Enterprise Architecture (NIST EA Model)	en.wikipedia.org/wiki/ NIST_Enterprise_Architecture_Model
	Treasury Information System Architecture Framework (TISAF)	en.wikipedia.org/wiki/ Treasury_Information_System_ Architecture_Framework
	Standards and Architectures for eGovernment Applications (SAGA)	www.cio.bund.de/SharedDocs/ Publikationen/DE/ Standards_und_Architekturen/ saga_4_0_englisch_download.pdf?__ blob=publicationFile
Other frameworks	Extended Enterprise Architecture Framework (E2AF)	www.enterprise-architecture.info/ Images/E2AF/E2AF%20A0%20 New%20Poster%2003- 2005%20version%201.4.pdf
	Spewak's Enterprise Architecture Planning (EAP)	en.wikipedia.org/wiki/ Enterprise_architecture_planning

Index

Printed by Publishers' Graphics LLC
MLSI140225.15.16.182